BUILDING A
HOME MOVIE STUDIO
& GETTING YOUR
FILMS ONLINE

D1607261

Kurt Lancaster • Cynthia Conti

BUILDING A HOME MOVIE STUDIO & GETTING YOUR FILMS ONLINE

▼

An indispensible guide to producing your own films & exhibiting them on today's hottest source—the Internet

▲

Billboard Books
an imprint of Watson-Guptill Publications
New York

778.5902 Lancaster c.1
Lancaster, Kurt, 1967-
Building a home movie studio &
getting your films online : an in

Senior Acquisitions Editor: Bob Nirkind
Associate Editor: Elizabeth Wright
Production Manager: Hector Campbell
Cover and interior design: Howard P. Johnson, Communigrafix, Inc.

First published in 2001 by Billboard Books
an imprint of Watson-Guptill Publications
a division of BPI Communications, Inc.
770 Broadway, New York, NY 10003
www.watsonguptill.com

ISBN: 0-8230-7726-8

Library of Congress Cataloging-in-Publication Data is available from the
Library of Congress.

Manufactured in the United States of America.

First printing, 2001

1 2 3 4 5 6 7 8 9/ 09 08 07 06 05 04 03 02 01

To my mother.
—Kurt Lancaster

To Janice.
—Cynthia Conti

Kurt Lancaster is the creator of the video-streaming Web narrative *Letters from Orion*, (www.lettersfromorion.com). His film *A Promised Rain* appears on IFILM.com. He is the author of *Warlocks and Wardrive: Contemporary Fantasy Entertainments with Interactive and Virtual Environments* and *Interacting With Babylon 5: Fan Performances in a Media Universe*. He is a lecturer in both the literature and comparative media studies programs at the Massachusetts Institute of Technology. He lives in Lynn, Massachusetts.

Cynthia Conti teaches television production and media studies at Curry College and at Clark University. She is the former publicity coordinator at Fanlight Productions, a Boston-based independent documentary distributor. She has also helped organize many film festivals, and is currently directing *Out of Bounds,* a documentary about a women's football team. She lives in Somerville, Massachusetts.

ACKNOWLEDGMENTS

We would like to give our deepest thanks to Bob Nirkind at Billboard Books for accepting our project. He is a joy to work with. We would also like to thank the tireless efforts of Elizabeth Wright and everyone else at Watson-Guptill, from the editorial staff to the marketing staff, for putting this book together. They are all part of a team that helped make a couple of authors' ideas available and accessible to the public. We greatly appreciate their work.

We would also like to thank Henry Jenkins and all our colleagues in the Comparative Media Studies program at MIT. Their visions helped shape our vision.

TABLE OF CONTENTS

Introduction: The Rise of the Internet Indies

We are on the cusp of a new film revolution. The convergence of digital video, computers, and the Internet has given rise to the Internet indies: digital filmmaking distributed online. Both amateurs and professionals alike are finding new outlets and a new audience through Internet cineplexes—the online equivalent of a local movie theater. With such Internet cineplexes as IFILM and Atomfilms (among dozens of others), professionals as well as aspiring filmmakers now have a venue for presenting short films to an audience without worrying about the market forces of Hollywood. Thousands of films—a few of which would formerly be found only at select film festivals and for a limited audience—are now garnering large audiences. Additionally, new aspiring filmmakers can build their own digital video movie studio for far cheaper than one year's attendance at a prestigious film school. In many of these we find deeply personal films, daring projects, and experimental works that could not exist without the accessibility of the Internet. But are people watching?

As of January 2001, 170 million people were registered users of RealNetworks' RealPlayer, a tool for viewing streaming video online. According to the RealNetwork's web site there are more than 300,000 hours of programming on the Internet that can be seen with RealPlayer. Whether it's watching CNN online, catching the latest episode of the JenniShow, or viewing a video-feed of the Space Shuttle Atlantis docking to the International Space Station, both professionals and amateurs can reach a potential audience of millions on the Internet. Broadcasting over the Internet does not require any special licenses or fees (as do radio and television), and allows other people to watch shows, movies, and other kinds of programming both on-demand and live.[1] Right now, the Internet provides a viable way to view short films (those under an hour long), but as fiber optic cable becomes standardized (perhaps during this decade), watching feature-length films online will become as normal as watching them on television. In fact, in the early 2000s, we will see a convergence of Internet, film, and television. Television stations are even now broadcasting material found on the Internet and the Internet is broadcasting radio, television, and film. This convergence will increase, and more content will be needed.

At this point in time the aspiring independent filmmaker and the weekend hobbyist, as well as those seeking to break into the Hollywood film industry, have the opportunity to make inexpensive, but professional-looking films more cheaply than ever before in the history of cinema.

---

1 "On-demand" means you can go to an Internet cineplex or other web entertainment site at any time and watch a movie, program, or news story, whereas, to see a live broadcast, you must access a site during a live video streaming transmission at a certain time.

Certainly, film and video are not the same thing. Film requires the emulsion of light to expose an image on celluloid through a chemical process while video uses electrostatic charges to record its image on tape. Film provides a smooth high resolution and high contrast image, while video offers a harder-edged image with lower resolution and contrast. However, with the advent of manufacturer's agreed-upon digital video (DV) standard in 1990s, filmmakers (with today's cameras) can create images that are good enough for television broadcasts for under $1000. (Back in the early to mid 1990s, such a feat that would have cost about $10,000 with professional equipment.) Furthermore, as high definition television becomes affordable, we will receive high-resolution movie-quality images on television and new generations of digital video cameras will be developed to provide images with such quality. This new technology is generating so much excitement that even professional filmmakers are beginning to test its possibilities. George Lucas used high-end digital video cameras to film *Star Wars Episode II* (2002), and even the creators of *The Blair Witch Project* (1999) shot the movie on Hi8mm video (a lower-grade resolution than digital video), then later transferred it to film for distribution after editing.

But we feel that the key to the future of film—especially webfilms—will not be found in the formulas and sequels of Hollywood blockbusters. This approach would be detrimental to the spirit of independent filmmaking we currently find on the Internet. We sincerely believe that there are as many ways to tell a story through film as there are filmmakers.

Speaking as two MIT media scholars, we believe that film and video should not be an elitist medium. Yet, due to high costs and an inward-looking Hollywood system, many people desiring to make films have been shut off from the filmmaking experience. For some people, film school seems to be the only option since these schools own the expensive equipment that students need in order to learn how to make films. However, with the advent of digital video the entire process of filmmaking is beginning to change.

In this book, we address this change and explain the tools you need to produce, exhibit, and distribute your own films. We wrote this book so you can discover a range of equipment available to create a movie and put it online—for a lot cheaper than you might think (certainly far less expensive than attending film school). You can purchase a fairly good computer, a DV camera, a decent microphone, some basic lights, editing software, and a capture card to transfer your video footage to your computer for under $3,000. (As a comparison, it costs about $20,000 in tuition to go to NYU's film school for one year.) But purchasing the equipment is just one step. You will still need to write a story and convey it through a personal vision in order to do something special with the tools. You'll have to gain an artistic eye.

For this reason, whether you go to film school or not, we recommend that you immerse yourself in a liberal arts education. Study art. Read works of literature. Watch good films. Go to plays. Discover who you are and your unique point of view in this world. Then read books on the film writing and filmmaking process. Enroll in some acting and directing classes in theater departments at a local college. Blend your philosophical world-view with your understanding of filmic technique and then you will be able to provide your own unique voice to the world of independent film. What you shouldn't try to do is build on the success of others. If you try to mimic someone else's style or make something to please the desires of others you will become one of hundreds of others who churn out formulaic films resembling works that have been already made. Hollywood and the independent film world already has a Steven Spielberg, an Oliver Stone, a Jim Jamusch—what they don't have is you and your unique perspective on the world: no one else has it. Take what is unique to you and shape it into an art. This is what will make you stand out in the crowd. And with the advent of Internet cineplexes, you have the opportunity to exhibit your own personal films online and reach a large audience.

We do not come from the Hollywood or independent film worlds. We haven't made big-budget features or even modest-budget films. Kurt created *Letters from Orion,* a website that tells a narrative by blending theater, film, and web aesthetics. Cynthia shot a documentary about an amateur women's football team in Boston. We didn't do these projects so we could garner fame and go to Hollywood. We did them because we *had* to do them as a way to express an artistic need. We love movies and we love the web, and we bought our own equipment so we could tell our own personal stories in our own way. But there wasn't a book out there explaining why we needed a camera, software, or lights or how much they cost. This book is the result of doing the research in building our own individual home movie studios.

The filmmakers we interviewed for this book applied their skills to create comedic, touching, beautiful, and honest images that are unique to their own view of the world. From his film *Tatooine or Bust* (1997) to his self-envisioned Internet cineplex, Jason Wishnow has taken new media and envisioned a future for cinema on the Internet with his site, The New Venue (1996). In *George Lucas in Love* (1999), director Joe Nussbaum and producer Joseph Levy were able to tap into their love for *Star Wars* (1977) in order to create a comedic spoof about the nature of creativity and how others around us influence our world-view. Anthony Cerniello, in his short experimental film *Jaunt* (1998), paints the screen with poetically haunting images in order to explore the nature of beauty and paranoia. Jennifer Ringley uses her life as a model for creating reality programming with webcam technology that documents her unedited life in her home (mostly through still digital photographs, but she also hosts a web show). Inspired by a collection of her high school notes she found in her parent's attic, Maya Churi decided to create a web site that would present a personal biography of such note-passing between two fictional high school girls in *Letters from Homeroom.* All of these projects challenge not only how films are viewed, but also challenge the kinds of films we typically find in conventional movie theaters. Many movies found on Internet cineplexes present a unique vision of the world that find an appreciative audience.

What's In The Book

This book has three sections. Part I: "Building a Digital Studio and Getting Your Film Online" comprises the first four chapters and gives you the information you need to create your own home movie studio and how to put your movie projects online. We do not show you how to shoot or edit a movie. We simply provide you with a description of the various equipment you need to shoot a movie and we walk you through the steps you need to take to place a completed film on the Internet and onto a CD-R. The rest of the chapters comprise Part II: "The New Independent Voice of the Internet Indies." In this section, we present several in-depth case studies of how independent filmmakers have gotten their projects online and noticed. It includes interviews with the filmmakers, the steps they took to get their projects online, and how they have received recognition. The final part of the book, the Appendix: "25 Internet Cineplexes and Festivals" provides a detailed description of various online sites that present films and hold festivals.

In Chapter 1 "Building a Home Movie Studio on a Budget," we provide an overview of the equipment you need to create a home movie studio. Breaking the equipment down into budget categories (from $2,500 to over $10,000), we present a brief overview of some of the equipment available that you can purchase in order to build your own studio. Each budget is broken down into the following categories: pre-production, production, and post-production. Pre-production includes a description of books you might want in order to learn about filmmaking. Production includes all the equipment you need to shoot a movie: a digital video camera, tripod, camera stabilization device, microphone, and lights. The post-production section describes various computer systems, software editing packages, special effects software, music soundtrack software, and hard-drive storage. We do not provide an exhaustive list, but we do try to provide several choices within each category. In any case, we recommend that you conduct research in order to get the latest prices and find equipment that best suits your budget. This chapter should be used as a guide, a launching point for your own research into examining and getting the latest equipment and current prices. Due to the lead time to get a book into production, these prices were current for the third quarter of 2001. The profiles will point you in the right direction, but don't take the particular equipment we present as the latest and greatest or cheapest. Computers alone experience price changes monthly, while microphones and lights will pretty much stay the same.

In Chapter 2 "Video Streaming Your Films on the Web," we show you how to place your films online for video streaming, using standard Internet media viewers: Apple's QuickTime Viewer®, Window's Media Player®, and RealNetwork's RealPlayer®. In addition, we explain how to place films online that people can download, as well as how to use existing storage space on the web to place films online. We also explain how to build your own web sites so you can post your own movies online, including ways an audience can give you feedback through bulletin board discussion lists. In all cases, we include screenshot pictures showing these steps with real world examples.

In Chapter 3, "Transferring Your Film onto a CD-ROM and DVD," we explain how you can record your movies onto a CD-ROM recordable disc (CD-R/CD-RW) using a CD rewritable drive (CD-RW), as well as DVD. We walk you through the steps to create a movie in a DVD menu-driven format that can be played in regular CD-ROM drives as well as how to record a movie file onto a disc that others can access using their CD-ROM drives and DVD players.

In Chapter 4, "Submitting Your Films to Internet Cineplexes," we present the process by which one amateur filmmaker, Lowell Northrop, got his movie accepted and hosted by the popular Internet cineplex, IFILM. Through Northrop's experience, we describe the steps involved in sending a movie to an Internet cineplex so you can learn how to do the same thing, allowing you to potentially reach a large audience.

Chapter 5 profiles Jason Wishnow, the founder of the Internet cineplex, The New Venue, and the creator of the documentary, *Tatooine or Bust* (1997). We talk about how he made this film and why he has since shifted his attention from conventional filmmaking to creating a new vision for the Internet cinema movement.

Chapter 6, "Joe Nussbaum & Joseph Levy's *George Lucas in Love:* Presenting Short Films Online and Finding Success," gives an account of how this film received a large recognition and how these filmmakers got their work online.

In Chapter 7, "Anthony Cerniello's *Jaunt:* Non-Narrative Visual Films and the Use of Digital Special Effects," we explore how an experimental "art" film lacking plot can nevertheless be successful by combining a strong realistic visual style, moody music, and rich digital special effects to create an immersive experience for the viewer.

Chapter 8 is an examination of "Jennifer Ringley's *JenniCam:* Live Images from Home," which documents a young woman's everyday life—from working on her computer to sleeping in her bed at night.

In Chapter 9, "Maya Churi's *Letters From Homeroom:* An Interactive Narrative Style in an Age of Media Convergence," we present a project that attempts to create a new kind of a web-based interactive narrative through a convergence of text, audio, and video. The project is inspired by notes that girls write to each other in high school. Audience members can even become a part of the narrative by posting their own letters online. Talking with the site's creator, we examine how she got the inspiration to create the project and why she chose the web as the medium to create her narrative.

In the final part of the book, the Appendix: "25 Internet Cineplexes and Festivals," we provide a detailed description of various online sites that present films and hold festivals, some of which include such sites as IFILM.com, AtomFilms.com, Forceflicks.com, Icebox.com, Filmfilm.com, Screen47.com, TheBitScreen.com, TheSync.com, Mediatrip.com, Newvenue.com, LikeTelevision.com, and UrbanEntertainment.com. We include an overview of the kinds of films found on these sites and how to submit your films to them.

We're convinced that the future of film will thrive as you build your own movie studio. Study the filmmaking process. Direct projects that are meaningful to you.

BUILDING A DIGITAL STUDIO AND GETTING YOUR FILMS ONLINE

Part I covers the tools and the equipment you need to shoot your digital movies. The first part of the book is technologically specific, listing randomly selected microphones, lights, DV cameras, tripods, computers, and software, which—except for lights, microphones, and tripods—may become obsolete in a few years.

However much technology has evolved, the fundamental visual and narrative literacy—storytelling methods and the way of visualizing stories—pretty much have remained the same since Aristotle theorized the dramatic structure of Greek plays over 2300 years ago, and Louis and Auguste Lumière projected their first films at the Grand Cafè in Paris in 1895 with their Cinematographe.

In this section we present samples of the tools you need to create your own projects, tools that the Lumière brothers could not even dream would exist for a consumer market at the end of the Twentieth century. We provide equipment descriptions, as well as steps for building a web site, getting your films online, and onto a CD-ROM or DVD. This equipment is exciting, but however much we may desire the latest new DV camera or a new software update, the films we make will not gather that much attention if they do not tell a compelling story.

For example, just twelve years ago Kurt was shooting a fire at a convenience store in his hometown of Dover-Foxcroft, Maine with his father's then high-tech VHS consumer video camera. The images of the fire were good enough to appear on a local news broadcast that evening, but the camera could not capture the memories of what the now-razed building once contained—years before as children his brothers running down the hill to the store to buy candy bars and comic books after their grandparents gave them each fifty cents. Without the knowledge of storytelling, the fire was just a fire. If he were to shoot the footage today, or take the archived footage and add interviews of people's memories of childhood that revolved around the now non-existent convenience store, perspective gets added. Significance to the destruction gains weight. A story gets told. Technology does not and can not do that. The desire to search for meaning, for artistic truth does. An education in the liberal arts helps us learn to ask the right questions, to seek the truth behind surface appearances.

It may be exciting at first to shoot, edit, and put your projects online, but don't get lost in the technology. Storytelling and depth remain crucial if the Internet is ever going to gain legitimacy as a new place for presenting films. This past year Cynthia has shot a short documentary on an all-women's football team in Boston. Just a preview of the project at MIT's digital film conference last year garnered an invitation from the Internet Cineplex D.FILM.com to submit her project (as yet, unfinished). This past summer Kurt shot a two and a half minute video poem called "A Promised Rain" in Times Square and Washington Square Park in New York City, which has since been accepted and now appears as a premiere at IFILM.com. After shooting the material in one day, he edited and mixed the music on his laptop computer in two hours. Both of our projects were shot on miniDV cameras. The technology made it possible for us to do these projects on zero-budgets (other than the cost of the equipment). But our films attracted the attention of Internet Cineplexes due to the quality of the content—the stories—in addition to their technological quality (shooting, sound, and editing techniques).

As you read over this section and start picking out the parts for your own studio and gain knowledge of how to put your films online, onto a DVD, and submit them to an Internet Cineplex, don't lose sight of your storytelling vision.

1

Building Your Own
Movie Studio on a Budget

Building a home movie studio is no simple task. Just a few years ago, the equipment necessary to shoot and edit a movie was nearly unaffordable unless you attended film school, which could cost as much as $100,000 for a 4-year program. Today, however, you can build a home movie studio for a small fraction of that cost. If you want to make films that can be distributed on the Internet, an inexpensive and increasingly popular vehicle for exhibiting movies, you can do so for as little as $2,500–3,000. For instance, with $2,700 you can purchase a computer, a microphone, lights, a digital video (DV) camera, a capture card (to transfer your movie from your camera to the computer), and editing software, all of which allow you to shoot and edit your movie. Add a modem, and you can distribute your movie online—all for less than the cost of *one course* at a prestigious film school. And, of course, if you want to learn about any aspect of the aesthetics of filmmaking, whether lighting, scriptwriting, or directing, some excellent books are available to show you the basics so you can make your movie look, sound, and feel professional.

The choices that you must make in deciding what equipment you can afford in building your home movie studio require a detailed technical knowledge of everything from DV camcorders and capture cards to editing and music software. The more money you have available, the better the equipment. But even at the low end you can make quality movies and have a good time editing them, mixing in music, and putting them up on the Internet. Please note that the equipment we talk about is for DV movies presented online through video streaming. This book is not about how to make a feature-length film on DV, nor are we suggesting that you shoot on DV and then transfer it to film so you can present them at traditional film festivals.[1] We are talking specifically about getting equipment and making webfilms— films for Internet distribution. With that said, you can certainly make a movie that looks high-quality with a DV camera, and the equipment listed in this book will go a long way in helping you attain that look—from proper stabilization devices to lighting your scenes. However, consumer DV cameras cannot match the quality of film itself, which has richer colors and a wider range of contrast.

Section I: The Equipment Needed For Your Home Movie Studio

We'll begin by identifying the equipment you need and explain why you need it. We describe the equipment in the following three sections: pre-production, production, and postproduction.

DEVELOPMENT AND PREPRODUCTION

BOOKS AND STORYBOARD SOFTWARE

If you don't know much about filmmaking, you need to learn the basics of making narrative films, visually and aurally. You can educate yourself with a few good books. Armed with the knowledge you have gained, you can then write your own film script and shoot it with your own equipment (with a little help from your friends).

Before purchasing any equipment for your home studio, you first need to write your script. This is the beginning of the development phase. After the script is written, then you need to do preproduction, which entails all the up-front planning you need to do to make your movie. It includes the technique of breaking your script down and planning how you will turn it into a story told with pictures and sound. However, due to changing technology, we recommend that you do not purchase any movie studio equipment until you have your script in hand. In this way you will be assured of having the latest equipment when you're ready to shoot. On the other hand, some DV filmmakers may want to experiment with their equipment before shooting in order discover the limits and possibilities of the technology.

If you have a hard time developing a story idea, go to the classics. Shoot scenes from plays written by such late nineteenth and early twentieth century playwrights as Chekhov, Ibsen, Strindberg, or Brecht, or take scenes from Shakespeare—plays that are in the public domain (those not protected by copyright; just be aware that translations of foreign works may be copyright protected). There are books you can purchase that can help you to structure dramatic stories and put them into proper script format.

Once you have a story, you want to visualize it before you start shooting. This way you have a plan of action when you get on the movie set. Storyboards are preproduction drawings that help you visualize the shots you want to take before you start shooting. They become a blueprint of your production. You can draw these storyboards by hand or purchase software that will help you through this process. We don't recommend that you purchase storyboard software—we feel the money is better spent on

---

[1] Most of the consumer DV cameras we talk about in this book will not give you a film "look" when the images are transferred to film. That doesn't mean it can't be done. *The Blair Witch Project* (1999) was shot on Hi8mm—less resolution than consumer DV cameras. If you really want to learn about getting a film look, take a look at Scott Billups *Digital Moviemaking* (Michael Wiese, 2000).

production equipment. But if you're interested, there are software products you can purchase such as StoryBoard Quick™ and Storyboard Artist™ (www.powerproduction.com) and Boardmaster Storyboard™ (www.boardmastersoftware.com). In any case, proper planning will save you many hassles when you start shooting.

PRODUCTION

DV CAMERA

The single most important equipment for your home studio is a digital video (DV) camera. DV cameras provide 520 lines of horizontal resolution and a 480 lines of vertical resolution. Because the images they provide are clear and sharp enough for professional broadcast—unlike VHS and 8mm cameras, which offer lower resolutions not suitable for broadcast—DV cameras offer a breakthrough for the independent and aspiring filmmaker. And DV minidisc offers the recording of digital video on a mini-CD, providing access to stored video without having to fast forward and rewind through a tape.

Also, DV pictures do not noticeably degrade when transferred to the computer, since the data is transferred through the digital computer language. (Analog footage is compressed during recording and during the transfer of tape to computer, resulting in some loss of image quality. When the film is further compressed for Internet viewing, there is a noticeable loss of image quality.) Non-digital cameras lose picture quality when recorded to another tape, but with DV, there is virtually no image loss—the copy is identical to the original. The technology is relatively the same, whether using higher-end camcorders or those priced below a $1000. The more expensive cameras, such as a Sony™ Betacam™, provide less video "noise" (bleeding colors and static) and a higher resolution. But because these cameras are so expensive (up to $20,000 or more), they are used in professional studios and are not practical for the home movie studio.

For their comparatively inexpensive prices, $600–$2,500 digital video cameras provide excellent image quality for creating your movies. You can shoot close to professional-looking video on any DV camera. A professional look is not necessarily determined by camera choice, since the DV format is pretty much the same in most of these cameras. The professional quality of your movie is mainly determined by the aesthetic quality of your shots as well as the quality of lighting and sound recording. For example, if you choose a $2,500 camera, but you cannot afford a good microphone or stabilization equipment, then someone with a $1,000 camera and a better microphone and/or stabilization equipment may be able to achieve a more professional look and feel to their film.

In the end, the choice of camera is determined by your budget as well as by which camera you find more aesthetically pleasing. These cameras all function relatively the same, so your choices will be most likely determined by the camera's size, how it fits in your hand, its weight, and how the zoom lens and focus works (does it have a focus ring on the lens, or is it the focus control button you have to press or slide?). A small camera, like the Canon™ Elura™, can shoot scenes unobtrusively, while larger cameras stand out in a crowd. We recommend that you handle the camera you want to purchase in order to make sure it feels comfortable.

The features listed below are fairly common in all DV cameras. However, you should check with the manufacturer to get the specific statistics of the camera you want to purchase.

CCDs. The CCD is a charged-coupled device, an array of pixels—like the compound eyes of a bug—in which each pixel converts the light coming into the camera into electronic signals that are recorded digitally onto tape and presented as an image in the viewfinder or on the LCD display panel. More pixels mean increased resolution. A 1/3-inch CCD is 4.8 x 3.6 mm in size. A 1/4-inch CCD measures about 3.66 x 2.8 mm. Just for a comparison, 35 mm film is 36 x 24 mm. A single CCD chip is not going to provide color reproduction as good as the more expensive three-CCD chip camera, which offers a separate CCD for each of the red, green, and blue colors (the combination of which provides all the variety of colors you see on screen). While most DV cameras shoot pretty much the same quality of picture, you will probably notice the difference between a camera with three CCDs and a camera with only one.

Cameras with three-CCD chips shoot pictures with richer colors, less bleeding, and a slightly higher resolution than single-CCD chip cameras. To help compensate for this, some single CCD cameras use a RGB (red, green, blue) filter (what Canon calls their "Primary Color Filter") that splits the light into the red, green, and blue colors after it passes through the lens. This provides richer colors and better resolution of color gradations such as those you would see in a sunset. But it is not the same as a three-CCD chip, which allows each of the red, green, and blue light to be assigned their own CCD, providing the best image. (These are found on the more expensive cameras.) Canon, for example, uses a Primary Color Filter, which helps make the colors more rich. Despite their differences in overall image quality between the two types of cameras, one documentary filmmaker, Roger Richard, feels that there is no large difference between a higher-end Canon XL1™ three-CCD chip camera and Canon's Elura 1/4-inch single CCD chip camera, when scenes were shot in well-lit conditions (see www.digitaljournalist.org). Canon has since replaced the Elura with the Elura2™.

Progressive Scan CCDs. Canon claims that the Optura™ is the first DV camera to use a progressive-scan CCD, an enhanced charged-coupled device for increasing the imaging quality of digital video. With conventional non-progressive-scan CCDs, only half of the image is scanned in the output at a given moment: the first half provides half the information; the second half completes the scanned image—one line at a time. This comprises the interlace mode between scanned lines of video images from a computer monitor to a television screen. It is designed to help reduce onscreen flicker.

A progressive-scan CCD completes a full scan using all of its pixels (rather than half at a time) without the need to interlace half-scans. It provides a full-frame scanned image 60 times per second. This is advantageous when scanning fast-moving objects as well as providing a nonflickering image when the video is paused during playback (conventional CCDs flicker because of the interlacing). This also prevents any loss of resolution during output and printing of images and is thus useful when using DV cameras in digital still photo mode.

DVD Tapes. Most DV cameras use the miniDV tape, although Sony and Hitachi™ do make DV cameras that record a DV signal onto regular 8mm and Hi8mm tapes. There is also a DVCPro format tape. The main differences among these tapes is the size of the cartridge and the tape.

Zoom Lens. Most consumer DV cameras come with one zoom lens (although with the Canon XL1 you can attach different lenses) which allows you to attain various shot sizes while keeping the camera in one place. An optical zoom (as opposed to a digital zoom) occurs when the lens physically is adjusted to change the focal length, making objects appear closer or father away as you zoom in or pull back. You can also shoot a long shot of your subject, who is far away, then zoom in and shoot a close-up. It is not recommended that you shoot footage while zooming, unless you have a specific aesthetic reason to do so, because the shot may come across as seeming unprofessional. Instead, shoot your subject at the shot-size you want, then zoom in or pull out to reframe. In this way you can shoot the scene without adjusting the size of the shot while shooting it.

Digital Zoom. The digital zoom feature on DV cameras allows you to get extremely distant objects into close-up. As opposed to the optical zoom, which adjusts the focal length of the lens to attain different shot sizes, the digital zoom digitally enhances the image, allowing even more zoom power. However, at the extreme end of the spectrum, the image becomes pixelated, filled with video noise and boxy-looking artifacts that blur the image.

A "normal" lens on a camera offers the same perspective of objects as seen by the human eye (although the human eye can see more around the edges than a normal lens). Keep in mind, however, that longer focal-length lenses (telephoto and zoom-in mode) give you a shallow depth-of-field for focusing. In other words, when using these lenses, either the background or foreground will be out of focus. With shorter lenses (wide angle), almost everything within its vision will be in focus.

Exposure. The focal length of a lens is the distance from the lens to the point at which the image is focused; this point is known as the focal point. Behind the lens is an aperture, which allows you to adjust the amount of light coming into the camera to be exposed. When opened all the way, it lets in the most light. When closed all the way, it prevents light from entering. The aperture setting is called the f-stop (a lens set at $f1.6$ may be opened all the way, while if it is set at $f16$, it only allows a little light to enter). The smaller the number, the wider the aperture. A wider setting also means that the camera is more sensitive to light and can shoot in dimmer lighting set-ups. The same aperture number (measured in f-stops) allows the same amount of light to enter the camera for all lens sizes. For this reason, when you are shooting multiple shots in a scene and changing shot sizes (going from a medium shot to a close-up for example), you need to keep the same f-stop setting. Otherwise, if you either open or close the aperture, the shot looks different because it either has more light or less light in the scene, depending on how you adjusted the aperture.

Like a regular 35mm camera, you can set the aperture in digital video. The aperture opens and closes the iris of the lens to let in more or less light, making the scene brighter or darker. To achieve the same look throughout a scene, all of your shots should be locked at the same aperture setting. If you are shooting a scene that has 12 shots, for example, unless your aperture is uniform, you will have darker and lighter shots within the same scene. If you need to increase or decrease the amount of light in the scene, adjust the lights, not the aperture. Always use manual-control aperture priority settings on the camera. If your camera is left in automatic mode, then it may change the f-stop to adjust to lighting conditions. Some cameras have preset exposure controls, allowing you to shoot under different conditions. Some even allow you to program additional preset exposures, so you can program your exposure you want without having to set it manually every time you shoot.

Shutter Speed. Although there are no shutters on a DV camera as there are in regular film cameras, some DV cameras are programmed to simulate various shutter speeds. You should experiment with the various settings to see how changing the shutter speed changes the nuance of the footage.

Manual Focus. It is important that a camera have manual focus. This allows *you* to maintain control of what you are shooting. In automatic focus, the camera focuses on what *it* thinks should be the focus of the shot. In addition, manual focus allows you to use special techniques, such as rack focus, in which you focus on the foreground of your scene and then slowly shift the focus to the background as you shoot.

Image Stabilizer. Digital image stabilizers and optical image stabilizers both help compensate for any sudden movements or vibrations (such as shooting in a moving car), stabilizing any shakiness of the image that might occur. The digital image stabilizer removes unwanted jitter digitally as the movie is recorded. The optical image stabilizer prevents jitter through the lens housing itself, so the image is smoother before the shot is recorded. With the use of a tripod or a mounting device that steadies the movement of the camera as you move, however, these features are not as necessary.

Lux Level. The lux level is the amount of light the camera needs in order to record. One lux is the brightness of one candle at the distance of 1 meter.

White Balance. The white balance allows you to set the camera to record in true colors. You place a white sheet of paper or other white object in front of the lens and focus on it. The camera then corrects any changes of color in its chip and resets its color values. Be sure to manually reset your white balance when changing from indoor to outdoor shots and vice versa.

Built-in Light. Cameras with built-in lights may be fine for shooting home videos like birthday parties, but for most purposes they are not really useful. If you are shooting a movie and trying to attain a more professional look, you need to light your scenes with professional lights or halogen work lamps.

Viewfinder and LCD Panel. Most DV cameras come with a viewfinder and flip-out liquid crystal display (LCD) panel (the same technology used in laptop computers). Most viewfinders are in color (with a few in black and white). With the flip-out side color LCD panel, you may not want to use the viewfinder at all. However, if you are shooting outdoors, the sun may be too bright to see the LCD panel, making the viewfinder more useful. LCD side-panel imagers usually allow you to set the brightness and contrast, but they make it difficult to determine the actual lighting conditions on the set. Is it too bright or too dark? Black-and-white viewfinders allow you to determine how well a scene is lit, which is why professional cameras use black-and-white viewfinders.

Shooting Modes. Typically, DV cameras include three shooting modes: normal movie; digital photography, for still shots; and progressive scan, which allows you to record 30 full-frame still images per second. (Film is shot at 24 frames per second; PAL, the European, China, Australia, and South American video format, is 25 frames per second; and NTSC, the North and Central American and Japanese standard, is 29.97 frames per second.) In nonprogressive CCD cameras, the interlacing (or scan lines on the screen) of half-scanned video images prevents this feature from being fully realized due to the motion flicker that occurs during the interlaced scanning.

In progressive-scan mode, high-resolution images are received for each of the 30 frames being recorded each second. In other words, the camera captures each full frame and allows you to see images at 1/30 of a second. This allows you to capture each moment of a sporting event, or even a falling raindrop hitting a puddle, as if in slow motion.

Digital Photo Camera Mode. Most DV cameras come with a digital photo mode. This allows you to take still digital pictures. Some of these cameras record the image onto a memory stick (a recordable RAM chip that can be plugged into the camera). Others record the image onto a few seconds of tape. Recording onto tape gives you the advantage of recording audio commentary at the same time.

16 X 9 Mode. Some DV cameras allow you to set the image to a theatrical "letterbox" look, as opposed to the 4 x 3 television-screen dimension. This feature can be used for HDTV (high-definition television) and webfilms. Check to see if the camera presents true letterbox format or if it "squeezes" the image.

PCM Digital Stereo Audio. PCM stands for pulse code modulation. Instead of sound being recorded magnetically on tape, it is converted to a digital signal and recorded.

Firewire®, I-Link™, IEEE 1394 Digital Input/Output. IEEE 1394 is the industry standard DV input/output interface connecting your DV camera to a computer. (FireWire is Apple Computer's registered trademark for this, and I-Link is Sony's trademark.) It is what allows you to transfer your footage to your computer, so you can edit it, add sound effects and music, and then record it onto tape for storage and/or distribution.

Digital Effects. The digital-effects feature allows you to shoot your movie and play it back in effects beyond regular DV color. It also allows you to shoot scenes in strobe (digitally "freezing" a series of images), mosaic (turning the image into a mosaic watercolor-looking pattern), slim (expanding the image vertically), stretch (expanding the image horizontally), trail (forming multiple impressions of all images in motion which gradually fade out as the motion comes to a halt, creating a "trail" effect), monotone (playing the image back in black and white), or sepia (providing a sepia tone to give the work an old-movie look). Some cameras may also have digital zoom (enlarging the center of the playback image) and digital mirror (creating a mirror-like symmetrical image). Check the manufacturer's description for any special digital effects included with the camera that you want to purchase. We recommend that you put these kinds of effects in during postproduction and not while you shoot your scenes.

Scene Transitions. You will probably want to ignore this feature because you can always create your transitions on the computer during postproduction. If you do it on your camera, your footage is altered. But if you do it on the computer, you will always have your original footage, allowing you to experiment if you change your mind about a scene transition effect. In any case, we recommend you keep with simple fades and wipes. Avoid the glitzy transitions, unless you really need one for a certain aesthetic look. Otherwise your film may come across as having an unprofessional flashy look.

Microphone Input. Finally, you want to make sure that your camera has a microphone input so that you can connect a high-quality microphone to record your actors. Avoid using the built-in microphone, because your good-looking film will sound poor. If you want professional sound, purchase a professional microphone (see "Microphone" below).

TRIPOD AND STABILIZATION DEVICE

Tripods are designed to keep your camera steady. They are great for composing nonmoving shots. They are also good for locking down your shot and keeping your camera still. A pan shot is usually used with a tripod, allowing you to move the camera from side to side, from point A to point B within a shot. A tilt does the same thing, but moves from up to down or down to up. A pan shot might begin on an actor and then move to a car within the same shot. Although a tripod permits you to achieve these effects, we recommend that you do not use the pan or tilt on the tripod unless you have an expensive tripod head (which can cost thousands of dollars); cheap heads on the kinds of tripods that are within the home movie studio budget do not provide the bearings you need for smooth pans and tilts. Instead, there are some fairly inexpensive stabilization devices—such as a Mightywondercam Classic™, GlideCam™, or the higher-priced Steadicam™—that give you the smooth pan and tilt movements you require. These devices provide smooth motion, even when walking. They remove any unwanted jerkiness of movement that handheld causes. They are also good for creating tracking shots (also called a dolly shot). (A tracking shot is traditionally shot by placing the camera on a cart which is set on a tracks like those used for trains, so the camera can smoothly follow the action of actors, while a dolly shot is created by setting the camera tripod on a dolly with wheels to provide for smooth motion.) If actors are walking down a sidewalk, for example, a tracking shot follows alongside, moving with them. Some independent filmmakers have used skateboards and roller-blades. Remember that if you do use handheld or tracking shots, you still want to keep your shots tightly controlled and composed.

A crane allows you to give your scene a smooth, professional look when moving the camera towards or away from your actor as well as when moving a camera up and down.

Our recommendations:

- Skateboards or roller-blades are good if you cannot afford stabilization devices
- Tripods are great for composing and locking down your shots
- The Steadicam, Mightywondercam Classic, or Glidecam are good for pan, tilt, and tracking shots

MICROPHONE

Whether or not your movie sounds professional is determined by the quality of the microphone and the microphone's quality in recording the voices. The microphones built into cameras are the greatest cause for concern, because they do not provide professional sound, and can actually make your movie dialogue sound poor (unless the camera is just a few feet from an actor's face—and even then you won't be getting the richness of a wide dynamic range found on a good microphone). You need to compensate by either purchasing a good microphone or, at the very least, keeping the camera close to the actors when they are speaking. Unless the microphone is near the actor, it is difficult to achieve good clear sound.

Make sure that the camera you purchase includes a microphone input. Most professional microphones have large three-prong XLR connectors, one of which is a ground wire that helps prevent line noise, but there are some companies that make good microphones for a 1/8-inch microphone jack, standard with most DV cameras. Be aware that different microphones as well as cameras with microphone inputs have varying levels of impedance (or resistance to electrical flow). XLR microphones are low impedance, while most DV cameras have high impedance. You will need a low- to high-impedance adaptor; otherwise, you may pick up interference from other signals, such as radio stations. It is also important that the camera include a headphone input (so you can hear the sound) as well as manual adjusters of audio, so you can control the input signal of the microphone sound.

Microphones come in different styles: standard handheld (those that an interviewee holds or that can be attached to a microphone stand), wireless handheld (same as a standard microphone, except it uses a radio frequency to transfer the sound instead of using wires), wireless lavalier (small microphones that attach to the body of the actor and transfer sound to a radio receiver), and shotgun (standard for most camera-mounted microphones, but larger sizes can be placed on a boom and either mounted on a stand or held by a boom operator above an actor's head).

Microphones pick up sounds from different directions, depending on their design. Omnidirectional mikes pick up sounds from all directions: front, back, and sides. Cardioid unidirectional mikes pick up sound from the front and sides in a heart-shaped pattern, with the point of the heart towards the microphone. A hypercardioid pattern (typical for a shotgun mike) picks up sound from directly in front of it, as well as a little from behind. Bidirectional mikes record sound from the left and right sides of the microphone.

Microphones also come in two main design categories: dynamic and condenser. Dynamic microphones, like the reverse of a speaker, use a magnet and a diaphragm that vibrates when sound hits it, converting the sound waves into a signal through an attached coil. These mikes are sturdy. They don't require a battery or outside power, are relatively inexpensive, and can pick up a wide dynamic range of sound. Somewhat more accurate than dynamic mikes, condenser microphones have a capacitor containing two plates separated by space. One of the plates vibrates when sound waves hit it, and as it moves, it adjusts the voltage of the capacitor, which subsequently sends a signal converting it to audio.

It might be worth investing in a digital audio tape (DAT) or minidisc recorder. However, since your microphone would not be connected to the camera with either device, you will have to sync in the sounds after transferring them to the computer in separate files. If you decide to use a separate sound recorder, you need a clapper board, which is used to sync the sound with the visual.

LIGHTING

The eye can discern a contrast ratio of 800:1 (from black to white); film can record a ratio of 100:1; on good video, the contrast ratio is 40:1. To shoot good video, you must work within this limitation. If the contrast is too great, then the image looks too dark or too washed out. In addition, because each type of light burns at a different temperature, providing a different color contrast, a camera can only balance one light temperature at a time. For example, mixing a fluorescent with a halogen lamp causes a poorer realistic color representation, since the camera cannot balance both of them properly.

We recommend you use one kind of light in a shoot. When shooting outdoors, use a tinfoil or a white cloth sheet to reflect or bounce light onto your subject. Umbrellas also allow you to control the contrast ratio so that you can provide the best image possible for the camera. Without these tools, the contrast may be so high that the face gets washed out, or if it's too low the face may be in shadow. When shooting inside, halogen work lamps from Walmart™, Kmart™, or Home Depot™ provide you with enough bright light. It is also worth picking up an AC plug-in dimmer so that you can adjust the brightness of these work lamps. Professional video lamps allow you to use barndoors to adjust where the light flows into the scene. You could also attach color gels to the barn doors, allowing you to light scenes with different colors as desired.

POST-PRODUCTION

COMPUTER

The heart of the digital video revolution is the computer. No matter which one you choose, whether a Dell™, Gateway®, a Macintosh®iMac™, Power Mac G4, or if you build one from parts, the computer allows you to edit your film, mix in audio sound-effects and music, special visual effects, and so on. With the computer you can then transfer your final edited movie onto either tape or a recordable DVD, or you can put your movie directly up onto a web site.

CPU. The computer is run by the central processing unit (CPU). For example, a Pentium™ 4 chip is the computer's CPU. The chip is important, because it determines the computer's speed in translating your film into a format that can be viewed on the Internet, such as QuickTime or RealPlayer formats. Faster chips also shorten the time it takes to render special effects, titles, and scene transitions. For a PC, we recommend that you have at least a Pentium III 500MHz chip; the same for an iMac, but a Power Mac G4 is best.

RAM. The computer's memory is also important. You will want at least 128MB of Random Access Memory (RAM), but 256MB is even better. When software is opened, it buffers the application in the computer's RAM. If the application requires a lot of work (such as video), then it needs more memory to keep the application running smoothly. At the same time, it reads and writes data on the hard drive while using the memory to buffer the application so there is no disruption of the program. The less memory you have, the more the hard drive must swap data from the drive to memory, slowing down the overall operation of the application. A computer with more RAM requires less disk swapping, so the overall performance of the computer does not slow down.

Hard Drive. Hard drives for digital video are required to maintain a transfer rate of 3.9 megabytes per second (MB/s), which is different than megabits per second (mb/s). (A bit is one-eighth of a byte.) Anything slower affects the quality of the recording (frame drops) and its ability to stay synced with the sound. Larger hard drives are getting more and more inexpensive, and these days a 60GB hard drive is actually affordable. Larger hard drives allow you to store more movie footage on your computer. The general rule of thumb is 13GB of hard drive space allows you to store about one hour of DV footage. Standard hard drives are connected to the computer through EIDE cables. UltraDMA (UDMA) drives are twice as fast as regular drives, allowing more data to be written and read from the hard drive in the same amount of time. This data transfer is called throughput. For digital movie-editing you need high sustained transfer rates; otherwise, your movie could drop frames and the audio can go out of sync with the picture. If the throughput is too slow, you cannot make effective movies.

If you are planning to put a lot of special effects in your movie, then you should invest in a ultra-wide SCSI card and hard drive, the fastest around. It is also better to have two hard drives—one for your software, the other dedicated solely to your movie files. If you can only afford one, then you need to partition the hard drive into two sections. By getting the right hardware, you can also stack many hard drives together, giving you even more storage capacity (see "Video Storage" below).

Monitor. You want at least a 17-inch monitor so that you have enough room to edit your movie onscreen. It is important that you invest in a Trinitron flat-screen monitor, since it provides the sharpest resolution and is less stressful on the eyes. A low-end monitor may be inexpensive, but the image tends to be fuzzier than Trinitrons. Even better is a flat-panel LCD monitor, which provides the least eye strain.

CD-ROM and DVD. A CD-ROM and rewritable drive (CD-RW) allows you to record your movies onto a CD-R disk (recordable CD-ROM) so that you can store them, give them to friends, or even sell them. The movies can only be played on a computer, not on DVD players made for television sets. DVD-R/RW drives allow you to make DVDs that can be played on regular DVD players. DVD-RAM drives are DVD drives that allow you to record data and movies onto a DVD. They do not record in a DVD format that can be played on a DVD player for television. Discs recorded on DVD-RAM drives can only be played back on these drives.

Sound Card and Speakers. A soundcard and speakers are also essential components. They allow you to play and hear sound on your computer.

Modem and Network Card. Even though computers come with standard 56K modems, it is important that you eventually invest in a cable modem or DSL broadband connection. In order to upload and watch movies on the Internet, a high-speed connection is required. 56K speed can get you by in the short term, but it doesn't really offer the Web filmmaker sufficient speed. This is why you need a network card, which allows you to connect your computer to a cable modem. Many television cable companies provide cable modem service (which costs about $40 per month). Some telephone companies provide DSL service for about the same price.

Operating Systems. You can choose from several different operating systems, from Windows, Linux, or the Mac® OS. However, if you want to create an Internet server for distributing movies or setting up Internet broadcasts, you need to get Windows 2000® (the new name for the Windows NT®) or another server platform operating system (such as Linux). This allows your potential audience to access your movie directly from your server. Since it is a more expensive process for what we want to cover in this book, we recommend that you use an Internet service provider (ISP) to store your movies on the web, rather than trying to set up your own Web server.

Video Storage

We recommend that you invest in a separate hard drive for storing and editing your video footage. There are several different types of hard drive storage for video. The least expensive are external FireWire drives and FireWire adapter kits. The former is a hard drive that plugs into the FireWire port of a computer. The latter allows you to place a regular UDMA hard drive into the kit, which connects to the computer's FireWire port. Several of these devices can be connected or "chained" together. A more expensive device is a SCSI hard drive, which is connected to a SCSI card (placed in one of the motherboard PCI slots of the computer). This is the fastest hard drive on the market. It allows you to sustain a high throughput for the video and special effects of your movies. This more expensive drive bay is required for some capture cards. It is needed if you want to attain real-time processing of effects and real-time video compression rendering. Again, 13GB of hard drive space will give you about 1 hour of DV storage.

Capture Card

The capture card allows your camera to talk to your computer. Typically a piece of hardware that is placed inside the computer, the capture card is connected to your DV camera with a cable. Software for the card allows you to transfer your footage from the camera to the computer. You need to be aware of the compatibility of capture cards with computers. Before purchasing a capture card, do the research to make sure the manufacturer's card is compatible with your computer, with its graphics cards, and any other compatibility issues. Some questions you should ask include: Do certain cards work only with PCs or are there Mac versions? Do the cards limit file sizes of video files to 2GB? Do the cards have to render the movie before it can be outputted—a process that can take hours—or can it render the movie in "real time"?

The more advanced capture cards allow you to mark the in and out points on your video tape (called batch capturing) so that you can tell the computer to transfer only the marked footage to your hard drive—instead of bringing everything in at once. If the card includes timeline playback (which the mid-range cards do), then you can transfer your raw DV footage back to the DV camera directly from the timeline. Never jump in and buy a high-tech product. Do the research. It may save you a lot of problems.

EDITING SOFTWARE

After you have all the footage for your movie, you need to edit the various shots into a coherent narrative. Editing software allows you to put your shots together and trim them. It also allows you to input soundtracks. Different software packages have different interfaces and features; some are complex and more expensive; others are fairly intuitive. Most of the capture cards available include some kind of editing software.

MUSIC SOFTWARE

Music is important in movies—just as important, in many cases, as the images and dialogue. Music renders a scene with emotional clarity that can be felt in any language. You may want to put your favorite music into your movies. Be aware, however, that if you do this, you will be legally restricted from selling or publicly distributing your film due to copyright law. Since most filmmakers are not music composers, the best option is to buy music software that allows you to mix music into your movie using the software's royalty-free music. Or use musician friends who want to do the music for free.

SPECIAL EFFECTS SOFTWARE

Some cameras come with special-effects features that allow you to shoot your scenes in such modes as black and white, sepia, mosaic, and art looks. These effects are created digitally through software located in the camera. You can also buy special-effects software that allows you to add many other kinds of effects. For example, in many *Star Wars* fan-films, there are light-saber dueling scenes that are made with such software. With a blue or green screen, you can also import your actors into virtual sets that you build on your computer.

VIDEO AUTHORING SOFTWARE

After you make your movie, you will want to prepare it for Internet broadcasting and to transfer your movie onto various media. Video authoring software allows you to put your movie into one or more of the various video streaming formats: RealPlayer, QuickTime, and MediaPlayer, as well as CD-R/RW and DVD-R/RW formats. These formats allow others to watch your movie over the Internet.

Section II: The Cost Of Building Your Home Movie Studio

We'll now lay out a brief description of some of the various pieces of equipment you can purchase within a number of budgets. The range of equipment we discuss within each budget is not definitive. You can certainly combine components from different budgets. For instance, you can purchase a $1000 camera from the Budget #3 category, allowing you more money within that budget to purchase extra software or a more expensive capture card. You could also get a more powerful computer, on Budget #5 and purchase a more inexpensive camera, allowing you to get better post-production products without having to worry about spending $3700 on the Canon XL1 found in this category. Pick and choose from the different categories. Remember, due to the lead-time for getting a book into production, the prices and equipment models are current for the third quarter of 2001, so be sure to research the current prices and models. Also remember to check the manufacturer's information for any compatibility issues among specific computer products (hardware and software) before you purchase anything. Be sure to examine the technical specifications sheet for each product you buy in order to fully learn about it. We provide an overview and some of the highlights for each product. However, we cannot provide an in-depth analysis due to restrictions on book space.

NOTE: We provide the manufacturers suggested retail price (MSRP) as well as a street price (in parentheses), if available. If you want to take advantage of discounted street prices, you will have to shop around—call various retailers and check various electronic retail companies online. However, if you go with the street price, make sure that you receive some kind of warranty within each product category. Also, most of the PCs list Windows Me as the operating system, but they will likely be replaced by Windows XP at the time of this book's release.

BUDGET #1: $2500-3500 (street price)

Budget #1 section provides a brief overview of some of the equipment you can purchase to create your own DV movie studio for between $2500 and $3500. We list the equipment from least to most expensive, alphabetically by company.

OVERVIEW OF COSTS MSRP (street price)
Preproduction
   Books: $108
Production
   DV camera: $600–1000 ($600-750)
   Tripod and stabilization device: $102 ($90)

Microphone: $60–250
Lights: $100
Postproduction
Computer: $1370–1500
DVD-RW: $600
Video storage: $330–380
Video capture card: $0 (included with computer): $70–100
Editing software: $0 (comes with capture cards): otherwise $70
Music software: $0 (free download from Sonic Foundry)
Video authoring software: $0–150
Streaming media players: free downloads
Total Cost: $2700–3800 ($2600–3500)

PREPRODUCTION

BOOKS

If you do not know how to tell a narrative story on film, the first two books listed are an excellent start. They provide not only the fundamentals, but practical examples as well. The last two books are more technical. Purchase them if you want to learn the intricacies of getting better sound and light for your projects. These four are not the only books available. For other titles, we advise you to check with your local bookseller or try online booksellers.

On Directing Film, by David Mamet (Penguin, 1992; $12.95)

David Mamet is an independent filmmaker, screenplay writer, and playwright. His film work includes *The Winslow Boy* (1999), *The Spanish Prisoner* (1997), and *House of Games* (1987), among others. In addition to filmmaking, he and actor William Macy own the Atlantic Theater Company in New York City. *On Directing Film* grew out of a film-directing course Mamet taught at Columbia University. In his book, he lays out his basic theory of telling a film story through the juxtaposition of a series of uninflected shots, a process pioneered by Russian filmmaker Sergei Eisenstein. In other words, a movie is a story told through pictures and not dialogue. Mamet also explains how to develop a film through narrative logic. The book includes classroom dialogue between Mamet and his students, giving the reader first-hand examples of filmmaking from a storyteller's point of view.

Pros: Short, easy to read. Provides a walk-through of the process it requires to write a story with a logical structure.

Cons: Deals with linear narratives and is not really useful to those who want to deal with experimental filmmaking.

Writing Your First Play, by Roger Hall (Focal Press, 1998; $19.95)

Roger Hall teaches playwriting at James Madison University. His book is filled with examples of scenes written by his students. Why would a filmmaker want a text on playwriting? Like Mamet, Hall hearkens back to Aristotle's belief that at the root of drama is dramatic action. Simply put, dramatic action is created when characters face obstacles while attempting to attain their goals. (Notice that this dynamic is at the root of most films and television stories.) As in filmmaking, dialogue is one tool used by the characters in an attempt to attain their goals or desires. The book includes important exercises that clearly explain how to write a scene conveying dramatic action.

Pros: Down to earth and easy to read. If you actually follow all of the exercises in order, you will have a completed script by the end of the book. Teaches the essential knowledge of dramatic action of characters. Most of the examples are from students' writing, so you don't feel inadequate when writing your script. In our opinion, this is one of the best books on teaching the basics. When read in conjunction with Mamet's book above, it provides the beginner with everything you need to know to tell a solid dramatic story.

Cons: Designed for writing plays, and consequently it does not teach you how to convey that dramatic action to film.

Placing Shadows: Lighting Techniques for Video Production, by Chuck B. Gloman, Tom Letourneau (Focal Press, 2000; $39.95)

Gloman's and LeTourneau's book, Placing Shadows, describes what kind of lighting equipment and techniques to use when lighting various scenes—whether in the studio or on location. It includes theory as well as practical examples. Gloman is a videographer (a video photographer). LeTourneau is a lighting designer who gives seminars at the North American Television Institute.

Producing Great Sound for Digital Video, by Jay Rose (Miller Freeman Books, 2000; $39.95)

Jay Rose specializes in postproduction sound, although he has worked on production sound, as well. He is the Creative Director of the Digital Playroom, a postproduction studio. In *Producing Great Sound for Digital Video,* Rose explains the various sound techniques from recording dialogue to audio editing, including mixing and editing sound effects and music. The book provides tutorials and includes a CD-ROM, with sample sound tracks.

PRODUCTION

DV CAMERAS

SONY *DCR-TRV130 DIGITAL 8*™: $599 (MSRP)

Company Web site: **www.sony.com**

The DCR-TRV130 uses an 8mm digital format, as opposed to the more popular miniDV format. This allows people to continue to use the regular (nondigital) 8mm tapes that they may have from a previous purchase of an 8mm or Hi8mm video camera, as long ago as 1985. This camera has a 20X optical zoom and a 560X digital zoom. It can shoot in one-lux lighting conditions, and in NightShot™ mode it can shoot in zero-lux illumination. The camera also has 14 digital effects as well as auto-exposure control. It contains a black-and-white eyepiece viewfinder, and a 2.5-inch LCD swivel-screen. It has Sony's I-LINK digital video in and out (IEEE 1394), plus analog inputs and outputs. It can shoot in 16:9 mode. It also has an external microphone jack, as well a headphone jack. It has an "Intelligent" accessory shoe, so it can be used with Sony Intelligent accessories, such as a Sony tripod that allows some of its features to be controlled through buttons on the tripod's handle.

Pros: 20X optical zoom and 560X digital zoom. It can shoot in low light conditions. Has an external microphone input. 16:9 shooting mode for HDTV. Battery meter.

CANON® ZR20® MINIDV: $799 (MSRP) (~ $700 street price)

Company Web site: **www.canondv.com**

The Canon, ZR10. Used by Permission.

The ZR20 contains a 460,000-pixel 1/4-inch CCD. It includes a f1.8–2.9 lens, giving it a focal length of 4.2 to 42 mm. The ZR20 can focus at a minimum distance of 1 meter, but on maximum wide-angle it can focus at 1 centimeter. The ZR20 has a 10X optical zoom and a 200X digital zoom. The maximum shutter speed is 1/8000 of a second (meaning the shutter stays open for just that unit of time). In low-light mode, it can record in 2.5-lux illumination. It contains a LCD eyepiece- viewfinder, as well as a 2.5" flip-out screen. It also has a four-pin IEEE 1394 input/output. Furthermore, the ZR20 can operate as a digital still camera, able to hold up to 700 still pictures.

Pros: An inexpensive and small DV camera.

Cons: 460,000-pixel 1/4-inch CCD (as compared to the 680,000 pixels in the JVC models in the same class).

JVC™ GR-DVL300U DIGITAL CAMCORDER: $999.95 (MSRP)(~$700 street price)

The JVC GR-DVL300U.
Courtesy of JVC, Inc.

Company web site: **www.jvc.com**

JVC's GR-DVL300U has a 680,000-pixel 1/4-CCD. The 2.5-inch LCD viewing panel swivels, allowing you to position the panel in many different shooting angles. It contains a focal length f1.8 lens. It also has a black-and-white eyepiece-viewfinder. It has a 10X optical zoom, a 250X digital zoom, a 16X9 recording mode, PCM digital stereo audio, various digital effects and transitions (wipes and fades), and an IEEE DV input/output. The camera can double as a digital still camera as well. In addition, it has manual focus, exposure, and a variable-speed shutter (1/500, 1/250, 1/100, 1/60 of a second). And, importantly, it has a white balance mode, so you can set the camera to record in true colors (by having its imager record a white sheet, it corrects any changes in color and resets its color values). It includes a J-terminal (for connecting to VCRs with a similar input) and S-video analog output.

Pros: Inexpensive. Includes a white-balance feature for setting "true" colors of a scene. Swivel LCD panel. Manual settings for focus, exposure, and shutter speeds. 16 X 9 shooting mode for HDTV.

Cons: 1/4-inch CCD is not as good as the larger CCDs.

PANASONIC™ PV-DV401 DIGITAL PALMCORDER®: $999.95 (MSRP)

(~ $750 street price) Company web site: **www.panasonic.com**

The Panasonic PV-DV400 has a 20X optical zoom and a 300X digital zoom. It contains a color eyepiece-viewfinder as well as a 3-inch LCD swing-out panel. It has the standard IEEE 1394 DV input/output interface for connecting to your computer. It also has an infrared-filter shooting mode, allowing you to record in near total blackness in three color modes: black and white, blue, or green. It contains digital effects for wipes and fades and auto-exposure program modes. This camera also has dual digital stabilization for both recording and playback modes. It has a built-in external microphone jack as well as a headphone jack. Infrared night shooting mode can give you some interesting shooting

The Panasonic PV-DV400; courtesy Panasonic Consumer Electronics Company

options in low light conditions, especially for science-fiction films. It includes many standard digital effects, such as digital zoom, digital mirror, strobe, mosaic, slim, stretch, trail, black and white, and sepia. Furthermore, it includes a digital still camera mode (Pansonic's PhotoShotÆ™), allowing you to record approximately 1,000 still images on an 80-minute DV tape (in LP mode). Panasonic's PhotoVU Link allows you to easily transfer images to the PC with an RS-232C serial cable. In addition, these images can be transferred with Panasonic's 8MB MultiMedia Card™.

Pros: Contains a 3-inch LCD swing-out panel. 300X digital zoom. External microphone input. Infrared shooting mode.

STABILIZATION DEVICES

VELBON™ VIDEOMATE 404 VIDEO TRIPOD: $41.95 (MSRP) (~ $30 street price)

Company Web site: **www.velbon.com**

This is a standard suggested tripod. Any tripod will work just fine. Like all tripods, the Velbon allows you to adjust its height by adjusting the legs, and provides different angles of shooting when you adjust the legs at various heights. The head allows for the adjustment of the camera angle. Remember, inexpensive tripods should only be used for locking down a shot, not for pan and tilt movements. We suggest you purchase one for no more than $100 because quality is not a deciding factor when all you need to do is to lock your camera into position for the shot. The difference comes in the strength of the tripod legs, its durability, and how the legs are adjusted (do you have to unscrew the legs to adjust them, or can you just lift a lever to let gravity make the adjustment when you lift the leg off the ground?) It is best that you examine the tripod you want and make sure your camera and tripod have the proper mounting plates. The camera store will have tripods for your examination. For $90 you could get both an inexpensive tripod and Glidecam's Campal (see product below).

Pros: Inexpensive.

Cons: Will not be stable with heavy cameras.

Glidecam's Campal is an inexpensive way for getting stable handheld shots.
Photographed by Martin P. Stevens.

GLIDECAM™ CAMPAL™: $59.95 (MSRP)

Company Web site: **www.glidecam.com**

The Glidecam Campal allows you to shoot steadier handheld shots. The handle system adjusts so you can shoot in various modes: shoulder mount, extra-steady and supportive handle grip, monopod mode (for getting the camera still by resting it on a surface), and low (for low-angle moving shots). The handle is foam padded, preventing it from damaging certain surfaces. It even includes a rain cover stored in the handle.

Pros: An inexpensive and portable way to give you steadier shots when you want to move the camera. It can be steady enough that you won't need to use a tripod in certain shooting circumstances.

Cons: It doesn't provide the smoothness of shots while moving as the Glidecam 2000. For small cameras only.

MICROPHONES

AUDIO-TECHNICA™ ATR55 UNIDIRECTIONAL SHOTGUN MICROPHONE:

($60 street price) Company Web site: **audio-technica.sony.com**

The ATR55 unidirectional shotgun microphone is designed to pick up sound from the direction in which the microphone is pointed, in most cases at the person the camera is recording. It has two settings, "normal" for picking up audio at close and medium range, and "tele" for picking up sound at long range. The normal mode is unidirectional, while the "tele" mode is supercardioid (making it focused on the subject). This microphone will mount on DV cameras with standard mounts, but this is only recommended if you're shooting close to your actors. Otherwise you will need a microphone operator—someone to hold the microphone near the subject as you film. Alternately, if you're shooting close-ups or medium shots, you can mount the microphone on a tripod and set it near your actors (just be sure that it is not in the line of the camera's shooting angle). The ATR55 has a miniplug connector, a 3-foot cable, a microphone stand clamp, camera mount, a foam windscreen, 1/4-inch plug adapter, and a battery. It has a frequency response of 70–18,000 Hz (from low frequency to high).

Pros: Unidirectional is good for pointing the microphone at the subject and picking up focused sound. It includes a miniplug which connects to the microphone inputs on DV cameras. The windscreen is useful on windy days if you are shooting outside. It is also good for softening speech when people are talking close to the microphone. Contains a camera mount.

Cons: The microphone is not good for picking up ambient sounds or talk from other subjects. The microphone must be pointed at the person who is speaking. You will need to purchase a boom and have a boom operator handling it. The 3-foot cable is too short, but if you add an extension cable, you may pick up radio signals because of the microphone's high impedance.

SONY MINI GUN ZOOM MICROPHONE ECM-HS1: $70 (MSRP)

Company web site: **www.sony.com**

This microphone mounts on top of your DV camera. It can switch between omnidirectional and cardioid. A suspension piece helps to reduce camera noise while it is recording. It includes a windscreen. The frequency range is 150–120,000 Hz.

Pros: Small and lightweight. Can switch between omnidirectional to cardioid.

Cons: The frequency response does not pick up lower-end sounds.

AZDEN WLX-PRO LAVALIER MIC WITH TRANSMITTER & RECEIVER:

$240 (MSRP) Company Web site: **www.azdencorp.com**

The Azden model is a standard lavalier microphone system, which includes an omnidirectional microphone/transmitter (that attaches to the subject with a belt-clip) and a receiver, which can be attached to the camcorder with a shoe-mount or velcro. This system offers two VHF frequencies (in case there is interference on one channel, the other channel can be used). It has a more than 200-foot range.

Pros: All receivers and transmitters in the "PRO" Series are on the same two frequencies (169.445MHz and 170.245MHz) and use the same circuitry. This makes them interchangeable, and allows you to add to the system.

Con: Only one subject can use it. You have to be alert to frequency interference.

SENNHEISER™ MKE 300 BOOM MICROPHONE: $249.50 (MSRP)

(~ $160 street price) Company Web site: **www.sennheiserusa.com**

This 2.1 ounce Sennheiser microphone is designed to be mounted on the DV camera (with shoe-mount attachment). It uses a supercardioid design. The microphone can also be placed on a boom and/or tripod. It has a suspension mount, which eliminates noise when holding it. The windscreen helps reduce wind noise.

Pros: Attaches directly onto the camera, so you don't need a boom for close-range shooting. Supercardioid design.

Cons: Does not give you the freedom of wireless, where the actor can be a good distance from the camera and still transmit good sound through a lavalier microphone.

LIGHTS

REGENT™ 500-WATT PORTABLE LIGHT: ~ $10 each

Purchase at any department or hardware store

This is the cheapest way to get a lot of light for video shoots. It comes with a 500-watt quartz halogen lamp. You access the housing with a screwdriver, but you should never touch the lamp with your fingers, which leave behind a residue that can cause the lamp to burn out or explode. It can illuminate an area of up to 10,000 square feet and contains a safety wire screen as well as a tempered glass.

Pros: Cheap. Provides a no-nonsense, bright intense light.

Cons: In order adjust the height or angle, you have to manually place it. It is not attachable to any kind of tripod for this purpose. There are no barn-door attachments for "sculpting" the light. A gel sheet can be placed behind the wire guard to get color, but be alert to overheating because the gels will start to melt.

REGENT™ 500-WATT QUARTZ LIGHT: ~ $30 each

Purchase at any department or hardware store

The 500-watt quartz light is an inexpensive way to provide lighting for your shoots. Two of these lamps provide enough lighting for most situations. You may want to use a "bounce" board to provide reflected light or to help soften it. For this effect, you can also use a lamp umbrella or place a white sheet in front of the lamp (but never on the light). The light includes a 5-foot grounded 18-gauge 3-wire cord, chrome-plated safety guard, a foam-grip handle, as well as tempered glass. It includes a 500-watt quartz halogen lamp.

Pros: This light is attached to its own stand, allowing you to adjust the height and angle of the lamp. A gel sheet can be placed behind the wire guard to get color, but be alert to overheating because the gels will start to melt.

Cons: Provides harsh white light. There are no barn-door attachments for "sculpting" the light.

DIMMER SWITCH: ~$25 each
Purchase at any department or hardware store

A dimmer is important if you want to adjust the intensity of your lights. In this way you can still apply adequate lighting to certain scenes and you can make the scenes more moody or darker by hooking up this device to your lamps. You need one dimmer per light. The light plugs into the dimmer box, which plugs into the wall outlet.

GELS: ~$5 per sheet
Purchase at theatrical lighting supply stores, some of which are located online

If you want to filter your light with different colors, then lighting gels are what you need. For example, you can use a yellow sheet in front of two 500-watt lamps at a low angle to provide the illusion of sunlight coming in on a kitchen table in the morning. Typically, gels are attached to a gel holder which slides in front the lamp housing. But the lights in this budget category do not have such devices, so you need to either tape the gel sheet to the lamp housing or slide a proper-sized sheet behind the light guard. They tend to melt in the high heat of 500-watt halogen lamps, but they can still be used. You just have to pay attention to them.

Pros: Excellent way to add vibrant and moody color to your movies.

POSTPRODUCTION

COMPUTERS

SONY VAIO DIGITAL STUDIO™ PC (PCV-RX462DS): $1450 (MSRP)
Company website: **www.sony.com**

This Sony computer makes for an excellent home postproduction studio. It includes an Intel® Pentium®4 1.3GHz CPU, 128MB RAM, a 40GB UltraDMA-66 hard drive, a 16X DVD-ROM drive, CD-RW drive (8X 4X 32X), a 17-inch Trinitron monitor, a 1394 IEEE DV card, USB connectors, a network card (for connecting your computer to a cable modem as well as to other computers), a 56K modem (for dial-up Web access), 16MB video graphics card, external speakers, Windows Millenium® (Windows Me), and the following software: Microsoft Word® 2000, Adobe Photoshop®, and Premiere® LE.

Pros: Has everything you need to do postproduction on a Pentium III system. You will want to add a hard drive dedicated to video storage (see below, "Video Storage").

DELL DIMENSION 4100 SERIES: $1369 (MSRP)

Company Web site: **www.dell.com**

Dell allows you to configure your own system on their interactive Web site. One configuration at this price includes a Pentium III 1GHz CPU, 256MB RAM, 60GB UltraDMA-100 7200 RPM hard drive, a CD-RW rewritable drive (with 8X write speed, 4X rewrite speed, and 32X read speed). It also includes a 17-inch monitor, a 32MB video or graphics card, a Microsoft Internet keyboard, mouse, 56K modem, network card, Windows Me, Sound Blaster™ sound card, Harman Kardon speakers, Microsoft Works and Money 2001, as well as The Norton Antivirus™. It also comes with a DV FireWire card (IEEE 1394) with editing software.

Pros: It includes almost everything you need for post-production, and for the price, this is one of the most affordable systems around. Note, you still want to add a hard drive dedicated to video storage (see below, "Video Storage").

Cons: Microsoft Works is a poor substitute for Microsoft Office.

iMAC: $1499 (MSRP)

Company Web site: **www.apple.com**

This iMac computer has a 700MHz CPU and comes with 256MB SDRAM, a 60GB hard drive, 56K internal modem, network card, two FireWire ports, two USB ports, a 15-inch monitor, keyboard, CD-RW drive, network card, Rage 128 Pro graphics card, video editing software, Harman Kardon speakers with subwoofer, both the Mac OS 9 and OSx operating system, and the following software: iMovie 2™, AppleWorks 6, Microsoft Internet Explorer, QuickTime 4, Microsoft Outlook Express, Netscape Communicator, Quicken 2000 Deluxe, Palm Desktop, FAXsft, and thirty days of free Internet access through EarthLink.

Pros: The famous Macintosh ease-of-use interface and general operation. The two FireWire ports. Aesthetically pleasing look. Easy to jump right in and use.

Cons: The iMac cannot hold a DVD-R/RW drive. You will need to get a Power Mac G4. However, ADS Pyro 1394 drive kit may hold a DVD-R/RW drive, and you can connect it externally through the FireWire port. Double-check compatibility.

HEWLETT-PACKARD 100i DVD+RW: $599

Company Web site: **www.hp.com**

HP's 100i drive is similar to Pioneer's, except that it uses RW discs, which allows for both writing and rewriting of data and has a 2.4x write speed. Included with HP drive is Sonic Solution's MyDVD, software that allows you to drag and drop movie files (from both digital and analog devices in AVI and QuickTime formats), converting them to MPEG-2 files. (The software is also available separately for $149 from Sonic Solutions and can be used to burn CDs, as well—see description in Budget #1.) A single 4.7GB DVD can recordabout 133 minutes of video.

Pros: 2.4X write speed and the inclusion of MyDVD.

VIDEO STORAGE

ADS TECHNOLOGIES™ PYRO 1394 DRIVE KIT: $169 (MSRP)

($150 street price) Company Web site: **www.adstech.com**

The Pyro 1394 Drive Kit allows you to place a regular IDE hard drive or a DVD-R/RW drive into it and then externally connect it to the FireWire port of your computer. It provides 16MB of sustained throughput (DV requires only 3.9MB). It can convert a hard drive (UDMA 66 as well as the earlier 33s), but you can also attach a regular CD-ROM, CD-RW, DVD-ROM, DVD-RAM, or DVD-R/RW drive into this FireWire drive kit to give them FireWire throughput capability. The hard drive (or one of the other devices) plugs into the ADS Native Bridge Board inside the kit enclosure. It is also a "plug-and-play" hot-swappable device. It includes a 50-watt power-supply that plugs into an outlet. In order to use this kit, you need a 1394 IEEE FireWire card attached to your PC with Windows Me or Windows 2000. For Macintosh, you need a FireWire card with Mac OS 9.0 or X operating system.

Pros: Just add a UDMA hard drive to this kit and you have what you need for video storage. You can hook this hard drive to any computer with a FireWire port. It is stackable, so you can daisy-chain more kits with hard drives for even more storage. Also useful for holding an internal DVD-R/RW drive, so you can have external portability.

Cons: Because it is designed to hold 5.25-inch bay CD-ROM drives, this kit is big (7.5 inches by almost 11 inches, and over 2 inches high), so it is not convenient for portable computers and should not be mistaken for a small portable device. You will need to purchase an internal hard drive and format it before putting it into the drive kit.

LaCIE SE2100 FIREWIRE 60GB: $329

Company Web site: **www.lacie.com**

An affordable FireWire drive, LaCie's drive comes in several sizes, from 20–75GB. The drives have a 50MB/s throughput, allowing for DV storage and editing. The ATA100 drives run at 7200 rpm and have a 2MB cache. Up to 63 units can be daisy-chained together, for those who really need extra video space. The hot-swappable hard drive plugs directly into your computer's FireWire port and it includes another port in back, acting as an extender of the FireWire card so you can connect other FireWire devices to it.

Pros: An affordable FireWire drive for video storage.

MAXTOR® 1394 (FIREWIRE) EXTERNAL STORAGE 80GB: $379.95
Company Web site: **www.maxtordirect.com**

An affordable FireWire drive, Maxtor's drive can store 80GB of video. The drives have a 50MB/s throughput, allowing for DV storage and editing. For those who are working on really large projects, the drive includes add up to 63 units can be daisy-chained together. The hot-swappable hard drive plugs directly into your computer's FireWire port and it includes another port in back, acting as an extender of the FireWire card so you can connect other FireWire devices to it.

Pros: An affordable FireWire drive for video storage.

CAPTURE CARDS

Capture cards are included in the cost of the Dell system (part of the configuration set-up on the Web, so make sure you do choose it) as well as the iMac and Sony. If your computer does not include a capture card, you can get one for under $100.

ADS PYRO BASIC DV: $69
Company Web site: **www.adstech.com**

The ADS Pyro video capture card allows you to transfer your video footage from your DV camera to your computer. It has three FireWire ports (multiple ports come in handy when you want to add additional products that use the FireWire port, such as external hard drives). The software included with this product lets you control the camera through the computer (using a virtual interface). It comes with Ulead VideoStudio™ as well. When you have finished editing the movie you can format the film as a Windows audio/video file (.avi), as Real Video so it can be seen over the Internet with RealPlayer, as well as in MPEG, and QuickTime video formats. You can also send the edited movie back to the DV camera so you can store and distribute the film on tape. This product can only use Ulead video editor.

Pros: Comes with Ulead VideoStudio™ Pro VE. Has three FireWire ports. You can record and preview in real time. MPEG-2 support.

Cons: Can only use the Ulead video editor. Windows .avi files have a 2GB file-size limitation.

DAZZLE DV-EDITOR: $69.99 (MSRP)
Company Web site: **www.dazzle.com**

This combination capture card and video editor includes three DV (IEEE 1394) input/output ports. It includes the Ulead editor, allowing you to edit your movie, add titles and transitions, as well as special effects. You can record your movie onto DV tape or a CD-R disk with a CD-RW drive.

An additional feature allows you to convert the movie into a compressed MPEG-1 or MPEG-2 (the standard format for DVDs).

Pros: Includes three ports and video editing software. MPEG-2 conversion.

PINNACLE SYSTEMS STUDIO DV: $99 (MSRP)
Company Web site: **www.pinnaclesys.com**

Like other capture cards, Studio DV lets you transfer your movie footage to the computer. What makes this board unique in its class is how it captures the movie through its "Smart Capture" feature. The board transfers footage in a low-resolution mode, allowing you to store an hour's worth of video on 150MB of hard drive storage. Once you edit your video, Studio DV recaptures only your edited footage in full resolution mode (which comes out to about 240MB per minute). It includes three FireWire IEE 1394 ports and has the ability to output the final movie to tape or format it for the Internet or email. Also included are TitleDeko (a titling software package) and SpiceRack (for special effects transitions).

Pros: Three FireWire ports and Smart Capture, allowing you to dump a lot of your footage in low-resolution mode onto your hard drive, edit it, and then later compile it in full DV mode. In the end, it saves you space on the hard drive. Includes a video editor.

Cons: Windows .avi files have a 2GB file size limitation.

EDITING SOFTWARE

The ADS Pyro and Studio DV capture cards come with their own video editors for no additional cost. These no-frills editors are fairly intuitive and are a good option if you cannot afford the higher-end editors (Vegas® Video, Premier, EditDV, and FinalCut Pro™). However, free editors are available in iMac DV computers, Macintosh PowerBooks™, and the Power Mac™G4.

iMOVIE: $49 ($0 with purchase of computer)
Company Web site: **www.apple.com**

Apple's iMovie is an elegant and easy-to-use capture and editing software package. It is designed for beginners, but it includes the design of more costly editing software. You can control the DV camera through an on-screen interface, allowing you to capture your footage with a press of a button. Your clips are placed in a clip area window, and you can drag-and-drop your clips into the timeline. The software even includes transitions, wipes and fades, as well as an titler (so you can title your movie and add credits). Apple is including iMovie 2 with a new purchase of an iMac DV and the Power Mac G4. The program can also be downloaded for $49. This program will format your movie in QuickTime format. (You can also output the movie back to your DV camera for recording on tape.)

Pros: Free. Easy to use. Includes wipes, fades, and title creator.

WINDOWS MOVIE MAKER®: $0
Company web site: **www.microsoft.com**

Windows Me comes with a free version of Windows Movie Maker. It is a simple to use capture and editing software package that allows to import your movie from a DV camera or existing files. It includes drag-and-drop features.

Pros: Free. Fairly easy to use.

Cons: Does not export to DV camera. Does not have built-in fades, wipes, or title creator.

VIDEOFACTORY™: $59.97
Company Web site: **www.sonicfoundry.com**

VideoFactory is the low-end version of Vegas Video, one of the best digital editing software packages out there. Instead of the unlimited number of audio and video tracks you're allowed in Vegas Video, VideoFactory limits you to two video tracks and three audio tracks. It has an easy-to-use interface, automatic cross-fades of video and audio, as well as multiple audio effects and video transitions. The software allows you to capture video, use widescreen and normal ratio video images, and open and mix video and audio formats, among other advanced features. Furthermore, you can preview effects in real time without rendering the project first.

Pros: Multiple file-format support. Easy-to-use interface. Despite its limitations, it is one of the best products out there.

Cons: Limited to a set number of video and audio tracks. Can't do composite video work, such as blue screen effects. PC only.

ULEAD VIDEOSTUDIO 4.0 (INCLUDED WITH ADS PYRO AND DAZZLE DV-EDITOR): $79.95 (download), $89.95 (box)
Company Web site: **www.ulead.com**

Ulead Video Studio Pro allows you to edit as well as compress your movies into various formats, including those for the web (such as RealPlayer, QuickTime, and regular MPEG compression). You can also upgrade to the full version, where you can get MPEG-2 support.

Pros: It comes for no additional cost with ADS Pyro.

Cons: It doesn't have the professional feel of other editors. Not quite as intuitive as Windows Movie Maker or Studio DV.

STUDIO DV EDITOR (INCLUDED WITH STUDIO DV): $0
Company Web site: **www.pinnaclesys.com**

This intuitive editor included with Studio DV allows you to drag-and-drop scenes, titles, voice-over narration, music, and sound effects, and scene transitions.

Pros: A very simple interface allows you to drag and drop your footage into the timeline, where you can add titles and transition effects. Playback mode lets you view the edited movie.

Cons: Not as advanced as other systems, such as Apple's Final Cut Pro or Vegas Video.

MUSIC SOFTWARE

ACID™ *XPRESS:* $0
Company web site: **www.sonicfoundry.com**

You can download the free version of ACID Xpress from SonicFoundry's Web site. Acid Xpress uses repeatable loops to create music that contains an interface similar to the ones seen on video editors. You can create your own music or use existing software libraries that can be purchased (such as rock music or ambient soundscapes libraries), or you can use some of the samples available on their site. Using a point-and-click method, you can pull in various music and sound tracks, and ACID Xpress matches the pitch and tempo. This is royalty-free music. If you use existing music from CDs for your movie soundtracks and put them up on the Internet or sell your movie on a CD-ROM that contains copyrighted music, you are in violation of copyright, unless you pay a royalty—which can be expensive. ACID Xpress lets you be creative in your own composition of music and sound effects tracks on your movies.

Pros: Free product. Royalty free. You can record your own audio into ACID Xpress.

Cons: You are limited eight tracks of sound.

VIDEO AUTHORING SOFTWARE

REALSYSTEM PRODUCER™ *BASIC:* $0
Company Web site: **www.realnetworks.com**

RealProducer is RealNetworks' web publishing software that enables you to convert your movie file into a RealPlayer format. RealProducer Basic is offered as a free download from www.realnetworks.com. (Giving you such added features as an editor and a bandwidth simulator, RealProducer Plus is the upgraded version of RealProducer Basic.) Both versions of this product are powerful tools for converting the following file types into RealPlayer format: audio files (.au and .wav), video for Windows (.avi), QuickTime for Windows (.mov), and MPEG-1 (.mpg).

Pros: Free. Easy-to-use interface.

Cons: RealProducer cannot convert or a file larger than 2GB.

SONIC SOLUTIONS MYDVD: $149

Company Web site: **www.sonic.com**

Sonic Solution's MyDVD software allows you to drag and drop movie files (from both digital and analog devices in AVI and QuickTime formats), converting them into MPEG-2 files. You can also edit DVD movie files off the DVD. It also records the file in faster-than-real time. It also acts as a capture card, allowing for the transfer of video footage from your computer to the hard drive in MPEG-2 format. Video clips can also be recorded directly to DVD or CD, creating a menue and thumbnail image of the clip. This product is similar to Sonic's DVDit! profiled in Chapter 3.

Pros: Easy-to-use. Comes free with Pioneer AO3 and HP 100i DVD-R/RW drive.

STREAMING MEDIA PLAYERS

Streaming media players let you view movies on the computer (from your hard drive) and over the Internet (through live video streaming). If your operating system does not come with either Windows Media Player, QuickTime, or RealPlayer, download free versions of these from their company's respective web sites. Essentially, they all do the same thing— they allow you to view and have your movies viewed over the Internet. They also let you listen to Internet audio radio programs as well as news broadcasts and other broadcast shows, like the JenniShow (see Chapter 8).

Picture from left to right, Apple QuickTime, RealNetworks RealPlayer, Microsoft's Windows Media Player. Images used with permission.

APPLE QUICKTIME™ MOVIE PLAYER: $0

Company web site: **www.apple.com**

The QuickTime movie player provides a straightforward interface. When downloading movies, it buffers the movie into temporary hard drive space as it plays. If net congestion slows down the movie, QuickTime pauses the movie before resuming play. It has an intuitive interface design.

REALNETWORKS REALPLAYER: $0
Company web site: **www.realnetworks.com**

RealNetworks includes broadcast channels within the window interface. This is currently the most popular video streaming software. It is a standard format for you to use in converting your movies.

WINDOWS MEDIA PLAYER: $0
Company web site: **www.microsoft.com**

Below the main window of Windows MediaPlayer, there's a list of information about the movie that is playing, including the title, director's name, and running time. It comes free with Windows Me. Its straightforward interface is easy to use.

RECOMMENDED SYSTEMS

Below are three studio systems priced for a certain budget. These are not the only systems to consider. You might decide to add the most expensive camera to the "least-expensive system," which will adjust the price. Configure it how you want, but keep in mind that before purchasing any system, you should double-check with the manufacturer to make sure that the hardware and software you select are compatible with each other (especially when purchasing products that need to go either with a Mac or PC)! Also, in the list below, if there is a list of items in the same category, choose only one of the various brands. (Obviously, the price does not include two items of the same category.)

#1: LEAST EXPENSIVE SYSTEM ~$2700 (~$2600)
Books: $108
DV Camera:
 Sony DCR-TRV130 Digital 8: $600
Tripod:
 Velbon Videomate 404 Video Tripod: $42 ($30)
Stabilization device:
 Glidecam Campal: $60
Microphone:
 Audio-Technica ATR55 Unidirectional Shotgun Microphone: ($60)
 Sony Mini Gun Zoom Microphone ECM-HS1: $70
Lights:
 Two 500-watt portable work lamps, a set of gels, and two dimmers: ~$100
Computer:
 Dell Dimension 4100: $1369
Video storage:
 LaCie SE2100 FireWire 60GB hard drive: $329
Video capture card:
 Included with computers: $0

ADS Pyro Basic DV: $70
Dazzle DV Editor: $70
Editing software:
  Included with these computers: $0
  VideoFactory: $60
Music software:
  ACID Xpress: (free download version): $0
Video authoring software:
  RealSystem Producer Basic: $0
  Sonic Solutions MyDVD: $149
Streaming media players:
  (free download versions): $0

#2: MIDRANGE SYSTEM~$2900 (~$2800) ($3500 W/DVD-R/RW DRIVE)

Books: $108
DV Camera:
  Canon ZR20: $800 ($700)
Tripod:
  Velbon Videomate 404 Video Tripod: $42 ($30)
Stabilization device:
  Glidecam Campal: $60
Microphone:
  Sony Mini Gun Zoom Microphone ECM-HSI: $70
Lights:
  Two 500-watt work lamps, a set of gels, and two dimmers: $125
Computer:
  Dell Dimension 4100 Series: $1369
  HP 100i DVD + RW: $600
Video storage:
  Maxtor 1394 External Storage 80 GB: $380
Video capture card:
  Included with computers: $0
  ADS Pyro Basic DV: $70
  Dazzle DV-Editor: $70
Editing software:
  Included with these computers
  VideoFactory: $60
Music software:
  ACID Xpress (free download version): $0
Video Authoring Software:
  RealSystem Producer Basic: $0
  Some Solutions M4DVD: $149
Streaming media players:
  (free download versions): $0

#3: MOST EXPENSIVE SYSTEM ~$3800 (~$3500)

Books: $108
DV Camera:
   JVC GR-DVL300U Digital Camcorder: $1000 (~ $700 street price)
   Panasonic PV-DV401 Digital Palmcorder: $1000 ($750)
Tripod:
   Velbon Videomate 404 Video Tripod: $42 ($30)
Stabilization device:
   Glidecam Campal: $60
Microphone:
   Azden WLX-PRO Lavalier Mic with Transmitter & Receiver: $240
   Sennheiser MKE 300 Boom Microphone: $250 ($160)
Lights:
   Two 500-watt halogen work lamps, a set of gels, and two dimmers: ~ $125
Computer:
   Sony VAIO Digital Studio: $1450
   iMac : $1499
   HP 100i DVD + RW: $600
Video storage:
   ADS Technologies Pyro 1394 portable drive kit: $170
   Maxtor 1394 External Storage 80 GB: $380
Video capture card:
   included with computers: $0
   Pinnacle Systems Studio DV: $100
Editing software:
   Included with the computers and included with Studio DV capture cards: $0
   VideoFactory: $60
Music software:
   ACID Xpress: $0 (free download version)
Video authoring software:
   RealSystem Producer Basic: $0
   Sonic Solutions MyDVD: $149
Streaming media players:
   $0 (free download versions)

BUDGET #2: $3500–5000 (street price)

Budget #2 provides a brief overview of some of the equipment you can purchase to create your own DV movie studio for between $3500 and $5000.

OVERVIEW OF COSTS
Preproduction
   Books: $108
Production
   DV cameras: $1300–1600 ($900–1200)

Tripods: $80–170 ($70–100)
Stabilization device: $60
Microphones: $250–450 ($160–335)
Lights: $400 ($280)
Postproduction
Computers: $1450–1560
Video storage: $380
Capture cards: $0-300 ($0-230)
Editing software: $0 (included with capture cards)
Music software: $0 (free download from Sonicfoundry)
Video authoring software: $0–150
Streaming media players: free downloads
Total Cost: $4500-5775 ($3900-4900)

PREPRODUCTION

BOOKS

See descriptions in Budget #1.
On Directing Film by David Mamet (Penguin, 1992; $13)
Writing Your First Play by Roger Hall (Focal Press, 1998; $20)
Producing Great Sound for Digital Video by Jay Rose (Miller Freeman
   Books, 2000; $40)
Placing Shadows, Lighting Techniques for Video Production by Chuck B.
   Gloman, Tom Letourneau, (Focal Press, 2000; $35)

PRODUCTION

DV CAMERAS

PANASONIC PV-DV600 DIGITAL PALMCORDER: $1299.95 (MSRP)
(~ $900 street price) Company Web site: **www.panasonic.com**

Panasonic PV-DV600; courtesy
Panasonic Consumer Electronics Company

The Panasonic PV-DV600 includes a 18X optical zoom. Also included is a 300X digital zoom, which digitally enhances the image. Panasonic offers an electronic image stabilization system, in which motion jitter is corrected during recording as well as during playback. The infrared (IR) filter is one of the unique features of this camera (and the PV-DV400 and PV-DV800). It allows you to shoot in darkness (0 lux), but it cannot record in color. You have the option of recording in black and white, blue, or green. The range of the infrared light is 10 feet. Analog inputs let you record other works you might have on VHS onto miniDV tape. The photograph feature of this camera can record on the tape or onto a memory stick called a MultiMediaCard. It records 60 images at 640X480 resolution or 240 images in 320X240 resolution mode (with space for 7 seconds of audio narration for each picture). In digital still camera mode, approximately 1000 images can be recorded onto an 80-minute DV tape (in LP mode). Panasonic's PhotoVU Link allows you to easily transfer images to the PC with an RS-232C serial cable.

Pros: 3-inch LCD flip-out monitor. Infrared shooting capability. Analog inputs. Audio recording of still images.

Sony DCR-TRV830 Digital 8: $1399 (MSRP) (~ $900 street price)
Company Web site: **www.sony.com**

The DCR-TRV820 has a built-in color printer that allows you to print pictures in digital still-shot mode. It uses the 8mm digital format. It has a 1/4-inch CCD with 1.07K pixels (690K actual). This camera has an 18X optical zoom and a 500X digital zoom, and it can shoot in one-lux lighting conditions (zero lux in NightShotÆ mode). The camera also has 14 picture effects as well as a seven-mode auto-exposure control. It contains a color eyepiece-viewfinder, and a 4-inch LCD swivel screen. It has Sony's I-LINK digital video in and out (IEEE 1394), plus analog inputs and outputs. It can shoot in 16:9 mode. It also has an external microphone jack, as well a headphone jack. It has an "Intelligent" accessory shoe, so it can be used with Sony Intelligent accessories such as a Sony tripod that allows some of its features to be controlled through buttons on the tripod's handle.

Pros: Color printer. 3.5-inch LCD screen. It can shoot in low light conditions. Has an external microphone input. 16:9 shooting mode for HDTV. Battery meter.

Panasonic PV-DV800 Digital Palmcorder: $1399.95 (MSRP)
(~ $1100 street price) Company Web site: **www.panasonic.com**

The Panasonic PV-DV800 includes an 18X optical zoom. Also included is a 300X digital zoom, which digitally enhances the image. Panasonic offers an electronic image stabilization system, in which motion jitter is corrected during recording as well as during playback. The IR filter is one of the unique features of this camera (and the PV-DV400 and PV-DV600) that allows you to shoot in darkness (0 lux), but it cannot record in color. You have the option of recording in black and white, blue, or green. The range of the infrared light is 10 feet. Analog inputs let you record other works you might have on VHS onto miniDV tape. The photograph feature of this camera can record on the tape or onto a memory stick called a MultiMediaCard. It records at 60 images at 640X480 resolution or 240 images in 320X240 resolution

The Panasonic PV-DV800; courtesy Panasonic Consumer Electronics Company

mode (with space for 7 seconds of audio narration for each picture). In digital still camera mode, approximately 1000 images can be recorded onto an 80-minute DV tape (in LP mode). Panasonic's PhotoVU Link allows you to easily transfer images to the PC with an RS-232C serial cable.

Pros: 3.5 inch LCD flip-out monitor. Infrared shooting capability. Analog inputs. Audio recording of still images.

CANON ELURA2 MC: $1599 (MSRP) (~ $1200 street price)
Company Web site: **www.canondv.com**

The main features of this camera are its lightness and portability. Weighing less than a pound and standing just over 4 inches tall, it is a great portable field camera. It's especially ideal for guerilla filmmaking

and news gathering, because it lets you shoot and move quickly. It comes standard with the optical image stabilizer for its $f1.6$–2.6 (3.5–35mm) 10X zoom lens (and 40X digital zoom). The standard movie, photo, and digital motor drive is also available on the Elura2. It also uses a progressive scan CCD, as well as an RGB Primary Color Filter. It has a 1/4-inch CCD with 680,000 pixels (360,000 effective) and a 2.5-inch flip-out color viewscreen (as well as a color viewfinder). It includes a 16:9 wide-screen mode, which allows you to shoot in a letter-box format. In addition to the IEEE 1394 DV

The Canon, Elura,2 MC. Canon and Elura are registered trademarks of Canon Inc. All rights reserved. Used by Permission.

input/output port, it includes both composite RCA and S-video input/output. Plus, the camera includes a speaker so you can listen to footage without using headphones. Furthermore, it comes with such standard digital effects as faders, in which you can fade into and out of black using wipes, scrolls, or mosaic fades; as well as allowing you to record in standard art, black-and-white, sepia, and mosaic effect modes. The headphone and external microphone inputs are on a separate docking unit (included).

Pros: Small and light. Progressive-scan CCD. An on-camera speaker. You can store still images on a MultiMediaCard.

TRIPODS/STABILIZATION DEVICES

SONY VCT-570RM TRIPOD: $80 (MSRP)
Company Web site: **www.sony.com**

This Sony tripod can be adjusted from a 17.5-inch to a 45-inch height. It includes a handgrip that has remote-control buttons for controlling Sony camera zoom, record, start/stop, and lock/standby modes.

Pros: Handgrip buttons for Sony camera control: zoom, record, start/stop and lock/standby modes.

Cons: Not recommended for pan and tilt camera movements.

VELBON VIDEOMATE 607 WITH CASE: $104.95 (MSRP) (~ $60 street price)
Company Web site: **www.velbon.com**

Designed for full-size, heavier video cameras. It features the standard tripod capabilities: leg adjustment, pan and tilt head, vertical shaft adjuster.

Pros: Includes carrying case.

Cons: Screw attachment for legs. Not recommended for pan and tilt camera movements.

SLIK 300DX: $169.95 (MSRP) (~ $100 street price)
Company Web site: **www.tocad.com/slik.html**

This tripod can hold up to 11 pounds and has a black anodized finish. It can be adjusted from 25.75 inches to 61.25 inches. It includes a quick-release camera mount. The tripod legs have "D" shaped leg segments, so the legs won't twist or move. It has rubber leg-tips to protect surfaces and weighs 5.5 lbs.

Pros: This is a solid tripod that should meet most of your shooting needs. D-shaped leg connectors.

Cons: Not recommended for pan and tilt camera movements.

GLIDECAM CAMPAL: $59.95 (MSRP)
See picture and description in Budget #1 (page 38).

Pros: An inexpensive and portable way to give you steadier shots when you want to move the camera. It can be steady enough that you won't need to use a tripod in certain shooting circumstances.

Cons: It doesn't provide the same smoothness of moving shots as the Glidecam 2000. For small cameras only.

MICROPHONES

SENNHEISER MKE 300 BOOM MICROPHONE: $249.50 (MSRP)
(~ $160 street price) Company web site: **www.sennheiserusa.com**

See description in Budget #1 (page 40).

Pros: Attaches right onto the camera, so you don't have to have a boom for close-range shooting. Supercardioid design.

Cons: Does not give you the freedom of wireless, where the actor can be a good distance from the camera and still pick up good sound through a lavalier.

SONY ECM-MS957: $299.99 (MSRP) (~ $230 street price)
Company web site: **www.sony.com**

This handheld includes a 1/8-inch stereo jack (or miniplug), which is useful for recording to your DV camera as well as to a minidisc recorder. This microphone can be mounted on a stand or placed on a hand-held boom.

Pros: You don't have to worry about RF or UHF interference because it is a wired microphone. Includes a 1/8-inch jack for quick attachment to DV cameras.

Cons: You won't have the freedom of a wireless. Since it is high impedance, you may pick up interference if you use an extension cable. You will have to purchase a boom and a boom mount.

Nady™ Duet Lavalier system: $479.95 (MSRP) (~ $335 street price)
Company web site: **www.nadywireless.com**

This is a two-channel wireless microphone system with two independent lavalier microphones. It has Nady's120dB dynamic range microphone, as well as a 250-foot range (500 feet if within line of sight of the receiver). The batteries last about 16–20 hours.

Pros: Two independent microphones let you have two different actors speaking into the microphone. Two channels allow you to switch channels if one line does pick up interference.

Cons: Wireless microphones may pick up interference.

LIGHTS

Smith-Victor Two-Light Attaché Kit K102: $275 (MSRP)(~ $185 street price)

Barn doors: $64.50 each (~ $44 each street price)
Web site for product catalog: **www.catalogcity.com**

This Smith-Victor two-light kit gives you 600 watts of quartz lighting power per light. It is a compact way to make your lighting portable. The lights can be stored in the included attaché-style case. It includes two Model S6R 6-foot light stands which break down to just 17.5 inches, making it possible to pack these systems in a 18x12.5-inch hard-shell carry case. The kits come with two DYH 600-watt lamps. Barn doors are worth getting so you can sculpt your scene with light.

Pros: The portability makes this an excellent choice for this budget.

Cons: You need to purchase the barn doors, adding $88 to the cost.

Dimmer switch: ~ $25
Purchase at a hardware or lighting store. See description in Budget #1.

Gels: ~ $5 per sheet
Purchase at theatrical lighting supply stores, some of which are located online.

See description in Budget #1.

Pros: Excellent way to add vibrant and moody color to your movies.

POSTPRODUCTION

COMPUTERS

SONY VAIO DIGITAL STUDIO PC (PCV-RX462DS): $1450 (MSRP)

Company Web site: **www.sony.com**

See description in Budget #1

iMac DV SPECIAL EDITION: $1499 (MSRP)

Company Web site: **www.apple.com**

See description in Budget #1 (page 42).

GATEWAY PERFORMANCE 1500: $1563

Company Web site: **www.gateway.com**

Gateway's Pentium IV 1.5GHz computer with Windows Me is a solid set-up for a home postproduction studio. It includes 256MB of RAM, an 80GB hard drive (UltraDMA), 56K modem, SoundBlaster soundcard, speakers, a 17-inch monitor, 32MB graphics or video card, a midtower case (with five PCI and 1 AGP slots), a standard keyboard, 3.5-inch floppy drive, Logitech VSB optical mouse, and a CD-RW drive (12X write, 8X rewrite, and 32X read).

Pros: This system provides almost everything you need to get started.

Cons: You need to add a capture card and a dedicated hard drive video storage.

HP 100i DVD+RW: $599 (MSRP) (~ $150 street price)

Company Web site: **www.adstech.com**

See description in Budget #1 (page 42).

VIDEO STORAGE

ADS TECHNOLOGIES PYRO 1394 DRIVE KIT: $169 (MSRP)

(~ $150 street price) Company Web site: **www.adstech.com**

See description in Budget #1 (page 43).

MAXTOR™1394 FIREWIRE EXTERNAL STORAGE 80GB: $379.95

Company Web site: **www.maxtor.com**

See description in Budget #1 (page 44).

VIDEO CAPTURE CARDS

ADS PYRO: $69

Company Web site: **www.adstech.com**

See description in Budget #1 (page 44).

PINNACLE SYSTEMS STUDIO DV: $99 (MSRP)

Company Web site: **www.pinnaclesys.com**

See description in Budget #1 (page 45).

INTRODV™ (CAPTURE AND EDIT): $149

Company Web site: **www.media100.com**

This is a simple but elegant capture and editing product. It lays out the various editing windows in an uncluttered, easy-to-see manner. See "Editing Software" below for a description of the editor.

   Pros: An easy-to-use digital video capture and editing tool. Allows you to export movies to the web. It can be upgraded to the EditDV 2.0 product.

   Cons: For digital video only. Does not give you timeline playback.

DAZZLE DIGITAL VIDEO CREATOR II: $299 (MSRP) (~ $230 street price)

Company web site: **www.dazzle.com**

This capture device is designed to be used both with movie footage on video cameras and with movies stored on regular VCR tapes, converting them into MPEG-2, the DVD format. For VHS and S-video footage, you should use the Dazzle external capture card to get your movies onto your computer. The device allows you to import your movies from VHS tape (through component RCA audio/video and S-video input/outputs). It includes a 1/8-inch microphone input. It includes Dazzle MovieStar editing software. The software includes steps for converting the movie into RealPlayer and Windows Media formats and also lets you transfer the film to a Web site. We include this item in the book as a supplement to those who may have nondigital footage that they would like to edit or send to the web. Also, this product includes Sonic Solutions DVDit! (light edition), allowing you to create DVD movies on a CD-R/RW and DVD-R/RW drives.

   Pros: For nondigital films you might have stored on VHS or S-video tape as well as non-DV cameras. The software allows you to convert your movies to RealPlayer and Windows Media formats and includes steps for creating a Web page and uploading your movies to the Web through your ISP. Encodes your movies in MPEG-2 format (which is the DVD standard).

   Cons: The term "Digital Video" in this product's title is a misnomer. It can be used with DV cameras, but only through its S-video jack. If you want to use a DV camera's FireWire port, get Dazzle's Hollywood DV-Bridge, which uses similar hardware, but it does not include the same software.

EDITING SOFTWARE

INTRODV EDITOR: $0 (integrated with the IntroDV capture card)

Company Web site: **www.media100.com**

This product, lays out the various editing windows in an uncluttered easy-

-to-see manner. IntroDV includes a Library, Cutting Room, Story windows, and an Effects window, which appears on the screen until you are ready to place effects such as transitions into your movies. The Story window shows the location of your video clips, text and transitions, and audio clips on a timeline. The Library holds all video clips imported from your DV camera. The Cutting Room contains two windows. The first, the Clip Player, allows you to play clips from the library (you can also set the beginning and end points of these clips here). The second window, the Story Player, lets you play your edited movie, including all the shots edited together, as well as titles and transitions.

Pros: A fairly easy-to-use digital video editing tool.

Cons: For digital video only. Does not give you timeline playback.

ULead VideoStudio: (comes with ADS Pyro)

See description in Budget #1 (page 46).

Vegas Video: $559.96 (packaged); $489.97 (download)(~ $370 street price)
Company web site: **www.sonicfoundry.com**

If you can get this product at its street price, this book recommends that you purchase it. It is one of the best valued video editing software packages. Created by the same company that publishes Acid Music and Sound Forge, Vegas Video is also one of the most powerful and easiest to use editing tools on the market today. It has an intelligently designed and intuitive interface and allows you to use multiple layers of different types of video and audio. Vegas gives you the ability to edit video and audio, composite layers (including blue screen effects), titles, transitions (such as fades and cross-fades), video and audio effects (including video sepia, black-and-white conversion, and so forth), letterbox capabilities, as well as streaming video creation. This is one of our favorites.

Pros: One of the best video editing tools on the market.

MUSIC

ACID Xpress: (Free download)
Company web site: **www.sonicfoundry.com**

See description in Budget #1 (page 47).

VIDEO AUTHORING SOFTWARE

Sonic Solutions MyDVD: $140
Company web site: **www.sonic.com**

See description in Budget #1 (page 48).

REALSYSTEM PRODUCER BASIC: $0 (Free download)

Company web site: **www.realnetworks.com**

See description in Budget #1 (page 47).

STREAMING MEDIA PLAYERS

QUICKTIME MOVIE PLAYER, REALNETWORKS REALPLAYER, AND WINDOWS MEDIA PLAYER.

See descriptions in Budget #1 (page 48).

RECOMMENDED SYSTEMS

See explanation in Budget #1 (page 48).

#1: LEAST EXPENSIVE SYSTEM ~$4500 (~$3900)

Books: $108

DV Camera:
   Panasonic PV-DV600 Digital Palmcorder: $1300 ($900)

Tripod:
   Sony VCT-570RM Tripod: $80
   Velbon Videomate 607 with case: $105 ($60)

Stabilization device:
   Glidecam Campal: $60

Microphone:
   Sennheiser MKE 300 Boom Microphone: $250 ($160)

Lights:
   Smith-Victor Video Two-Light Kit with barn doors: $400 ($280)

Computer:
   Sony VAIO Digital Studio PC: $1450

Video storage:
   Maxtor 1394 External Storage 80 GB: $380

Video capture card:
   Included with Sony: $0
   ADS Pyro: $69

Editing software:
   Included with capture card

Music software:
   ACID Xpress (free download version): $0

Video Authoring Software:
   RealSystem Producer Basic (free download): $0
   Sonic Solutions MyDVD: $150

Streaming media players (free download versions): $0

#2: MIDRANGE SYSTEM ~$4800 (~$4300)

Books: $108

DV Camera:

Sony DCR-TRV830 Digital 8: $1400 ($1200)
Panasonic PV-DV800 Digital Palmcorder: $1400 ($1100)
Tripod:
Sony VCT-570RM Tripod: $80
Velbon Videomate 607 with case: $105 ($60)
Stabilization device:
Glidecam Campal: $60
Microphone:
Sennheiser MKE 300 Boom Microphone: $250 ($160)
Sony ECM 957 handheld: $300 ($230)
Lights:
Smith-Victor Video Two Light Kit with barn
doors: $400 ($280)
Computer:
Sony VAIO Digital Studio PC: $1450
iMac DV Special Edition: $1500
HP 100i DVD + RW: $600
Video storage:
ADS Technologies Pyro 1394 portable drive kit: $170
Maxtor 1394 External storage 80GB: $380
Video capture card:
Included with iMac and Sony
IntroDV (capture and edit) $150
Dazzle Video Creator II: $300
Editing software:
Included with IntroDV and Dazzle, as well as Sony and iMac.
Music software:
ACID Xpress (free download version): $0
Video authoring software:
RealSystem Producer Basic (free download): $0
Sonic Solutions MyDVD: $150
Streaming media players (free download versions): $0

#3: MOST EXPENSIVE SYSTEM ~$5775 (~$4900)

Books: $108
DV Camera:
Canon Elura 2MC: $1600 ($1200)
Tripod:
Slik 300DX: $170 ($100)
Stabilization device:
Glidecam Campal: $60
Microphone:
Sennheiser MKE 300 Boom Microphone: $250 ($160)
Sony ECM 957 handheld: $300 ($230)
Nady Dual Microphone System Lapels: $458 ($275)

Lights:
  Smith-Victor Video Two Light Kit with barn doors: $400 ($280)
Computer:
  Gateway Performance 1500: $1563
  HP 100i DVD + RW: $600
Video storage:
  ADS Technologies Pyro 1394 portable drive kit: $170
  Maxtor 1394 External Storage 80GB: $380.
Video capture card:
  Included with Sony
  IntroDV: $150
  Dazzle Video Creator II: 370 ($230)
Editing software:
  Included with Sony
  Vegas Video: $490 ($370)
Music software:
  ACID Xpress (free download version): $0
Video authoring software:
  RealSystem Producer Basic (free download): $0
  Sonic Solutions MyDVD: $150
Streaming media players (free download versions): $0

BUDGET #3: $5,000-$7500 (street price)

Budget #3 provides a brief overview of some of the equipment you can purchase to create your own DV movie studio for around $5,000-7,500.

OVERVIEW OF COSTS

Preproduction
  Books: $108
Production
  DV cameras: $1100–2000 ($900–1000)
  Tripods: $80–170 ($80–100)
  Stabilization device: $60–510
  Microphones: $300–1210 ($230–380)
  Lights: $475–640 ($45–-600)
Postproduction
  Computer: $2000–2050
  Video storage: $380–900
  Capture card: $0–600 ($0–480)
  Editing software: $0–490
  Music software: $0–60
  Video authoring software: $600 ($500)
  Streaming media players: free downloads
Total Cost: $6000–8400 ($5500–7000)

PREPRODUCTION

BOOKS

On Directing Film, by David Mamet (Penguin, 1992; $13)
Writing Your First Play, by Roger Hall (Focal Press, 1998; $20)
Producing Great Sound for Digital Video, by Jay Rose (Miller Freeman Books, 2000; $40)
Placing Shadows, Lighting Techniques for Video Production, by Chuck B. Gloman, Tom Letourneau (Focal Press, 2000; $35)

PRODUCTION

DV CAMERAS

SONY DCR-TRV17 MINIDV: $1099.95 (MSRP) (~ $900 street price)

Company Web site: **www.sony.com**

One of the best cameras in its class, this 1.5-pound Mini DV camera comes with a 1/4-inch 680,000-pixel CCD and a Carl Zeiss™ lens (10X optical/120X digital zoom lens). TRV17 has a color eyepiece-viewfinder, a 3.5-inch swivel LCD panel, as well as the standard Sony "Intelligent" accessory shoe, USB port, S-video out, I-LINK IEEE 1394 DV input/output, and microphone and headphone inputs. It includes such features as white balance, digital video converter, and pass through, which allows you to convert analog movies to digital video format, and white balance.

Pros: Has a manual-focus ring on the lens (rather than a button as in many other DV cameras). Built-in analog to digital converter. Includes a microphone input, white balance capabilities, microphone input, a Memory Stick® for digital still-picture mode, and a battery meter.

SONY DCR-PC9 DIGITAL HANDYCAM®: $1299.95 (MSRP)

(~ $1000 street price) Company Web site: **www.sony.com**

The compact DCR-PC5 has a 1/4-inch, 680,000-pixel CCD with a 10X optical and 120X digital zoom lens. Its features include a 2.5-inch color LCD swivel screen, infrared Nightshot mode, I-LINK (IEEE-1394) DV input/output as well as analog composite inputs (for converting VHS movies to DV format). It can shoot in a digital still camera mode (with a Memory Stick). Also, it has 16:9 wide-screen mode.

Pros: Compact size. InfoLithium battery for monitoring the battery level. Infrared NightShot recording capability.

SONY DCM-M1 DISCAM™ MD DIGITAL CAMCORDER: $1299.95 (MSRP)

Company Web site: **www.sony.com**

The DCM-M1 is the first video camera to record in the minidisc format

(MD-650A type). A minidisc is like a small CD-ROM. It records data in MPEG-1 format (the same as used in DVDs). It also has a 64MB buffer, so if you jar the camera, it won't skip or knock off-track what you're recording. However, it can only record 20-minutes of footage before you have to replace it. In digital still photo mode, you can store 4,500 images on the minidisc (in 640X480 image size mode). It uses a 1/4 inch CCD that contains 680,000 pixels. The 3.5-inch color LCD touchscreen allows you to navigate through the menu by touching the screen, rather than using buttons. And with the stylus, you can draw on your images and the drawing transfers to the recording. It also has a color viewfinder. The lens has a 10X optical zoom and 40X digital zoom (f1.7–2.2). It has the standard digital effects, exposure settings, headphone and microphone inputs, as well as white balance and manual focus capabilities. Instead of the I-LINK (IEEE 1394) input/output, it uses an Ethernet port to transfer the data to your computer. It uses your Web browser as the interface (either Netscape or Internet Explorer).

Pros: Compact size. Manual focus ring on the lens. White balance. It uses minidisc technology, allowing you to access scenes without have to fast-forward or rewind through tape. Records in MPEG-2 DVD format.

Cons: Only 20 minutes of video footage can be stored on a minidisc. It does not record in raw DV format (it is compressed in MPEG-2 format).

JVC GR-DVM90U MiniDV: $1699.95 (~ $740 street price)
Company Web site: **www.jvc.com**

The GR-DVM90U camera contains a 1/4-inch, 680,000-pixel CCD with an f1.8 focal-length lens and a 10X optical zoom. It has a 2.5-inch flip-out LCD display panel and a black-and-white CRT eyepiece viewfinder. It also has manual control of focus, exposure, and white balance. The camera has the

standard preprogrammed automatic exposure setting and scene transitions, including wipes and fades. It has a 16:9 wide-screen mode (for HDTV). The camera doubles as a digital still camera, with 8MB of removable flash memory for storing pictures. The standard IEEE 1394 DV input/ouput port comes standard. The docking station for this camera includes a J-terminal (for a JVC VCR), S-video output. It also includes the following software: MultiMedia Navigator, JLIP™ Video Capture and Video Producer, Picture Navigator, Card Navigator, Video Player, JVC Video Decoder, Mr. Photo, Photo Album, and Image Folio.

Pros: The CRT viewfinder gives you a truer sense of the brightness or darkness of your lighting. (LCD screens do not provide as sharp an image for this purpose.) White balance.

The JVC GR-DVM90U.
Courtesy JVC. Inc.

Cons: Requires the docking station for use of all of its features.

Canon Optura Pi (miniDV: $1599 (MSRP) (~ $1000 street price)

Company Web site: **www.canondv.com**

This camera, like other Canon DV cameras, has a progressive-scan CCD (380,000 pixels) with a 12X optical zoom lens (48X digital zoom) with a focal-length of 4.1–49.2mm, which is the equivalent of 39–472mm in a 35mm camera, with an optical image stabilizer. It has the standard IEEE 1394 DV input/output (as well as an analog composite in/out) and digital effects for filming and transitions. It also has a 3.5-inch color LCD screen as well as a color eyepiece-viewfinder. The Optura Pi can shoot digital still pictures.

The Canon, Optura, Pi. Canon and Optura are registered trademarks of Canon Inc. All rights reserved. Used by Permission.

    Pros: Small. Composite video inputs allowing conversion of analog movies to digital.

JVC GR-DVL9800U miniDV: $1999.95 (MSRP) (~ $1000 street price)

Company web site: **www.jvc.com**

This JVC DV camera includes a progressive scan 680,000 1/4-inch CCD with a 10X optical and 200X digital zoom. Coupled with a progressive color filter and a high-band process, it is designed to provide full image resolution. The camera has a high speed recording mode, allowing you to record up to four times the normal speed—providing a smooth, broacast-level slow-motion playback. The camera also allows you to shoot in digital still mode (recorded on a memory stick or multimedia card). It uses a digital image stabilizer. The GR-DVL9800 comes with a 3.5 inch color LCD screen and a color eyepiece viewfinder. During playback, you can zoom in on a section of an image through its 10x digital poinpoint zoom function, allowing you to reframe your shots during editing. Also included are the standard digital effects for wipes and fades, as well as black and white, sepia, classic film, video echo, cinema, and strobe playback modes.

JVC GR-DVL9800U. Courtesy JVC Inc.

    Pros: High speed recording mode for slow motion effects. 3.5 inch LCD swing out panel.

    Cons: Doesn't have an eyepiece focus ring.

Sony DCR-PC110 miniDV: $1799.95 (MSRP) (~ $1400 street price)

Company Web site: **www.sony.com**

The Sony PC110 is the first DV camera to has a megapixel imager—a 1/4-inch CCD with 1,070,000 pixels (in digital still camera mode; actual video mode is 690,000 effective pixels). It is lightweight and compact (1 1/4 pounds). Combined with Sony's HAD technology (designed to reduce noise in the video signal-to-noise ratio), this CCD increases detail, clarity, and color (providing a 520-line resolution). The camera comes with a $f1.8$–2.2 zoom lens (10X optical; 120X digital enhanced zoom), providing a focal distance of 4.2–42mm (which is equivalent to 48–480mm in a 35mm camera). The Sony camera has a 2.5-inch swivel LCD color panel, as well as a color eyepiece-viewfinder. It comes with such DV features as digital effects for picture (black and white, sepia, negative art, solarization, pastel, slim, stretch, and mosaic) as well as wipes and fades. Furthermore, it also has the standard IEEE 1394 DV input/output, a miniplug audio/video, and an S-video connector. The camera also has a 4MB Memory Stick for digital still camera storage. The battery includes a meter, viewed on the viewfinder or LCD screen, which shows how many minutes of recording time you have remaining. Like some of the other Sony cameras, it also includes the zero-lux NightShot infrared system (10 foot range); however, in noninfrared mode, the minimum lighting illumination required is 7 lux. The camera comes with the "Intelligent" accessory shoe as well, allowing it to be controlled by Sony's Intelligent tripod, for example.

Pros: Compact size. Manual focus ring on the lens. White balance. Battery time in minutes. Infrared night shooting capabilities.

TRIPODS/STABILIZATION DEVICES

SONY VCT-570RM TRIPOD: $80 (MSRP)
Company Web site: **www.sony.com**

See description in Budget #2 (page 54).

SLIK 300DX: $169.95 (MSRP) (~ $100 street price)
Company web site: **www.tocad.com/slik.html**

See description in Budget #2 (page 55).

GLIDECAM CAMPAL: $59.95 (MSRP)
Company web site: **www.glidecam.com**

See picture and description in Budget #1 (page 38).

Pros: An inexpensive and portable way to give you steadier shots when you want to move the camera. It can be steady enough that you won't need to use a tripod in certain shooting circumstances.

Cons: It doesn't provide the smoothness of shots while moving as with the Glidecam 2000. For small cameras only.

MIGHTYWONDERCAM CLASSIC: $229 (MSRP); (~ $190 street price)
Company Web site: **www.videosmith.com**

This shoulder-mounted camera stabilizer is useful for several purposes. It not only stabilizes your handheld pan and tilt movements, but it gives your arm a rest since the device is mounted on your shoulder. The camera can be adjusted along five axes. Additionally, you can mount up to three other accessaries such as microphones, small lights, or Mighty-wondercam Classic can also be mounted on a tripod, if needed.

The Mightywondercam Classic. Courtesy Videosmith, Inc.

Pros: Inexpensive camera stabilizer, with more shooting options than a tripod/handheld combination.

Cons: It doesn't have an independent free-floating gimbal to absorb shocks, as provided with the Glidecam 2000, for instance.

GLIDECAM 2000 PRO™: $369 (MSRP) (~ $320 street price)

Company Web site: **www.glidecam.com**

BODYPOD ATTACHMENT: $139 (MSRP); (~ $120 street price)

The Glidecam 2000 provides you with a relatively inexpensive way to shoot smooth shots for pans, tilts, and in-scene movement (the equivalent of dolly or track shots), allowing you to follow actors or pass through them within a scene. Furthermore, this stabilization device provides you with smooth shots when walking and even running. The Glidecam covers everything else, from hand-held to smooth pans, preventing you from having to purchase an expensive tripod and dolly combination. The Glidecam can be attached to an optional body-pod, which helps against fatigue, especially if you're doing any all-day shoots. The Glidecam has a handle which is attached to a free-floating gimbal, allowing your hands to move (whether up and down or side to side) without causing unwanted camera jarring or movement. Since the handle moves up and down, the Glidecam prevents the camera from moving up and down. The platform for the camera moves forward and back as well as side to side, allowing you to adjust the horizontal balance of the camera. Counterweight disks on the bottom platform of the device let you adjust the vertical balance of the camera. When everything is balanced properly, the camera should feel as if it is floating. The optional body-pod supports the weight of the Glidecam 2000, displacing the weight from your hands and arms to your waist and shoulders. However, since it is a rigid support system, it does not absorb shocks and sudden movements (such as running). For this reason it does not provide as smooth a shot under

Glidecam 2000. Copyright 2000, Glidecam Industries, Inc. Photographed by Martin P. Stevens.

certain conditions if you were to shoot with the Glidecam 2000 in hand-held mode. Even the mounted mode, however, still provides smoother shots than the Mightywondercam Classic or with unaided hand-held shots.

Pros: Provides you with a relatively inexpensive means for achieving aesthetically pleasing smooth-looking shots. It will handle cameras weighing up to six pounds.

Cons: You may have to purchase the bodypod, which does not provide as smooth shots under certain conditions as without it.

MICROPHONES

SONY ECM 957: $299.99 (MSRP) (~ $230 street price)
Company Web site: **www.sony.com**

See description in Budget #2 (page 55).

NADY DUET-LT LAVALIER SYSTEM: $479.95 (MSRP) (~ $275 street price)
Company Web site: **www.nadywireless.com**

See description in Budget #2.

SENNHEISER SHOTGUN MICROPHONE AND POWERING MODULE (ME 66/K6):
$565 (MSRP)(~ $430 street price)
Company Web site:**www.sennheiserusa.com**

The Sennheiser boom shotgun microphone includes the microphone and powering module. The microphone itself has microphone capsules so you can attach different kinds of microphones within it (such as bidirectional or omnidirectional, for example). It has a low impedance for the current (200ohms), so it can be used only with a low impedance camera (unless you purchase an adapter to adjust for the impedance). The frequency range of the microphone is 50-20,000 Hz. It is 15 inches long (with the powering module) and has a XLR connector. It runs off a 1.5-volt AA battery (which will last 150 hours), or it can be powered by a camera supplying "phantom" power. It also has an LED indicator for the on/off switch. A further feature is a bass roll-off switch, which helps to flatten the sound by subtracting 11 decibels.

Pros: A solid shotgun microphone that allows you to change the type of microphone capsule used. It has a 50-20,000 Hz range.

Cons: You'll need a XLR-to-1/8-inch mini-jack adapter to use on most DV cameras. Also, since the microphone is low impedance, you'll need a low to high impedance converter adaptor.

VAN DEN BERGH MICROPHONE FISHPOLES/BOOMS
SVDBBCC BABY COIL CABLED: (~ $400 street price)
Available at several online dealers.

This is a mini carbon-fiber boom pole designed to have a shotgun microphone attached to it. It has six sections, so it can be adjusted to various sizes. It is coated with a special material designed to help reduce handling noise (which a microphone could pick up as it records). This boom also includes

XLR cable that passes through the pole. It is 16 inches long when closed. It can extend out to a length of 5 feet 4 inches, and it weighs 9 ounces.

NADY 401 FOUR-CHANNEL WIRELESS LAVALIER MICROPHONE SYSTEM: $1210 (MSRP) (~ $700 street price)
Company Web site: **www.nadywireless.com**

This system comes with four lavalier microphones with bodypack transmitters. Each microphone is independent, so up to four actors can speak at once. The microphones have a 25–20,000Hz dynamic range. Each transmitter uses a 9-volt battery, which lasts 16–20 hours, with a low-battery LED indicator. The receiver uses an AC adapter. The range can go up to 250 feet.

Pros: Four channels so you can mike four actors in a scene. This is the microphone system to get if you have multiple actors in a scene. It provides a 25–20,000Hz dynamic range.

Cons: It is a wireless system, so it can pick up interference.

LIGHTS

SMITH-VICTOR SV-1800 3-LIGHT KIT: $475 (MSRP) (~$450 street price)

BARN DOORS: $64.50 each (MSRP) (~ $44 each street price)

The same as the Smith-Victor two light kit [described in Budget #2 (page 56)], but with the addition of one more light and stand.

Pros: The portability makes this an excellent choice for this budget.

Cons: You have to purchase the barn doors separately, adding $132 to the cost.

LOWEL ViP V1-90 EASY V LIGHTING KIT: $575 (~ $500 street price)

GDA DUAL END LOW PRESSURE 3150K 120V/500W LAMP: $22 (each)

T1-20 TOTA-FRAME: $33
Company Web site: **www.lowel.com**

The Lowel lighting kit includes two lights and two stands as well as an umbrella for softening harsh light, a frame for holding gels, a set of gels, a case for holding spare lamps, and a shoulder case for the whole kit.

Pros: A fairly inexpensive kit that includes almost everything you need for a decent two-light lighting set-up: lights, stands, umbrella, and gels.

Cons: You will need to purchase an additional frame for the second light if you want to attach gels to it.

NRG POWER PRODUCTS (51803) 1800W, 3-LIGHT ALL-FOCUSING QUARTZ KIT: $639.95 (MSRP) (~ $555 street price)
Company Web site: **www.nrgresearch.com**

The kit includes three 600-watt quartz halogen lamps, light heads (for holding the lamps), three stands that can be adjusted to a height of 8 feet, a durable hard case with foam interior for holding the light heads, and an instruction manual. The light heads include an adjustable focus so you can go from a narrow beam to a wide wash. The kit includes three barn doors.

Pros: Adjustable focus lights, allowing you to change the beam angle of the light (from narrow beam to wide wash). Hard case for transporting the lights.

Cons: Does not include an umbrella or gels.

DIMMER SWITCH: ~$25
Purchase at a hardware or lighting store.

See description in Budget #1 (page 41).

GELS: ~$5 per sheet
Purchase at theatrical lighting supply stores, some of which are located online.

See description in Budget #1.

Pros: Excellent way to add vibrant and moody color to your movies.

POSTPRODUCTION

COMPUTERS

DELL DIMENSION 8100: $1947
Company Web site: **www.dell.com**

This Dell Dimension 8100-series come with a Pentium 4 1.5GHz CPU, 256MB RDRAM, 60GB hard drive, a 17-inch Trinitron monitor, 56K modem, a CD-RW drive (8X4X32X), a IEEE 1394 FireWire card, SoundBlaster soundcard, Harman Kardon speakers, a 32MB NVIDIA GeForce2 Go™ video graphics card, 3.5-inch floppy drive, a standard keyboard, Microsoft Intellimouse, Windows Me XP upgrade.

Pros: A nice overall system that provides you with almost everything you need for a home postproduction studio. 17-inch Trinitron monitor.

Cons: You need to purchase an extra hard drive for video storage (see "Video Storage," below).

POWER MAC G4: $2007

This G4 contains a 733 MHz CPU, 256 MB of RAM, a 60GB hard drive, a CD-RW drive, 32 MB 3D graphics card, network card, 56K modem, Ethernet network, card, Ultra wide SCSI card (so you can connect a VideoRAID hard drive video storage), keyboard and mouse, and speakers. It comes with two FireWire ports and two iMovie 2, a video editing software package. Price does not include a monitor.

Cons: The Apple store lists three flat screen monitors for this product, with the cheapest one (15-inch display) costing about $600. It is recommended that you purchase a regular 17-inch monitor for $300 or get a 17-inch flat screen monitor from another company (which costs around $600).

SONY VAIO DIGITAL STUDIO PC (PCV-RX470DS): $2050

Company Web site: **www.sony.com**

This Sony computer makes for an excellent home postproduction studio. It includes a Pentium IV 1.5GHz CPU, 256MB RAM, a 60GB UltraDMA-100 hard drive, a 16X DVD-ROM drive, a CD-RW drive (12X/8X/32X), a 17" Trinitron monitor, a 1394 IEEE DV card, USB connectors, a network card (for connecting your computer to a cable modem, as well as to other computers), a 56K modem (for dial-up web access), 16MB video graphics card, external speakers, Windows Me, and the following software: Microsoft Word 2002, Adobe PhotoDeluxe, and Premiere LE.

Pros: Has everything you need to do postproduction on a Pentium 4 system. You will want to add a hard drive for video storage.

PIONEER DVR-AO3 DVD-R/RW: $995 (~ $600 street price)

Company Web site: **www.pioneerelectronics.com**

The Pioneer DVD-AO3 is an ideal product for a home movie studio. A consumer-level affordable DVD player/recorder that records movies in the same media as professional DVD movies, the DVDs you make with the AO3 can be played on home DVD players. (This is the same hardware that comes in Compaq's Presario 7000 and PowerMac G4 computers.) In addition to recording DVD discs (both recordable DVD-R and rerecordable DVD-RW at 2X speed), it can also record onto regular compact discs (CD-R and CD-RW). You can also use the DVDs to record 4.7GB (actual 4.37) of data. The DVD-AO3 comes with three separate software: one for authoring software for building DVD menus, another for playing DVDs on your computer, and one for recording data onto DVD-R/RWs and CD-R/RWs. This all-in-one drive also reads the following formats: DVD-ROM/DVD-Video, DVD-R, DVD-RW, CD-ROM, CD-R, CD-RW, photo CD, and audio CD. Included with this drive is Sonic Solution's MyDVD, software that allows you to drag and drop movie files (from both digital and analog devices in AVI and QuickTime formats), converting them to MPEG-2 files. [The software is also available separately for $149 from Sonic Solutions and can be used to burn CDs, as well—see description in Budget #1 (page 48)] A single 4.7GB DVD can record about 133 minutes of video.

Pros: This is *the* product to have if you want audiences to view your films offline (perfect for audiences who might not have a computer, but have a DVD player). It can record and re-rewrite CD-R/CD-RWs.

Cons: It records slowly, so it takes some time to make multiple copies. Also, at an average price of $15 per DVD-R and $30 for DVD-RW, it is too expensive when making a lot of copies.

Video storage

ADS Technologies Pyro 1394 Drive Kit: $169 (MSRP)
(~$150 street price) Company Web site: **www.adstech.com**
See description in Budget #1 (page 43).

Maxtor 1394 (FireWire) External Storage 80GB: $379. 95;
(~$200 street price) Company Web site: **www.maxtor.com**
See description in Budget #1 (page 44).

VideoRaid™ 2-bay 60GB hard drive (SCSI card included):
$899 (MSRP); $800 street price Company Web site: **www.medeacorp.com**

The two-bay hard drive connects to a ultra-wide SCSI controller that connects inside your computer. Together, the drives provide about 3 hours of storage. What sets these hard drives apart from other drives that can be set in an array is VideoRaid's Zone Stripe Technology. When recording video onto other hard drives, the speed of the data rate drops 40 percent when the drive begins to fill up—this results in frames of the movie being dropped out. But through Zone Stripe Technology, VideoRaid drives sustain high throughput on their data, even when full. This means that full-motion video will be maintained on these hard drives without any frame drop-outs. Ultra-wide SCSI cards main a throughput rate of 20MB per second. (The more expensive four-bay drives have a throughput of 40 MB per second.) The drives can be daisy-chained together, so you can have plenty of storage possibilities.
   Pros: One of the best ways to store video. A good value for its features. With the ultra-wide SCSI, you get sustained throughput of 20MB per second.
   Cons: Fairly expensive.

Video capture cards

All of these video capture cards include video editing software.

ADS Pyro ProDV: $329 (MSRP)
Company Web site: **www.adstech.com**

The ADS PYRO ProDV capture card (with three IEEE 1394 DV ports) supports DV, MPEG, MPEG-2, RealVideo, and QuickTime formats, among others. It includes the full version of Ulead Media Studio Pro 6.0 video editor, titling software with Piexelan-SpaceMaster Lite with 50 effects from Video Spice Rack, Boris FX 4.0 for special effects and compositing, Hash's Animation Master 2000 for 3-D character creator and animation, music creation and sound editing with Acid Style 2.0 and Sound Forge XP 4.5.
   Pros: A lot of good software is included with this package. The card supports a wide range of video capture and compression.

PINNACLE SYSTEMS DV200: $329 (MSRP)
Company Web site: **www.pinnaclesys.com**

The Pinnacle Systems DV200 is a digital video editing card with the standard IEEE 1394 DV ports. This card includes Pinnacle Systems' DVTools, a software package that scans each scene on your DV tape automatically, allowing you to mark the in and out points for each scene and essentially telling the computer exactly what footage you want sent to the hard drive, a process called batch capturing. It also lets you control your DV camera's functions through the software. You can also output the movie directly from the timeline without having to fully render it as a separate movie file (it renders the transitions and effects only, not the whole movie, saving hard drive space. The package includes the full version of Adobe Premiere 6.0 for video editing, the ACID package for creating music, and Title Deko (useful for creating titles for your movies).

Pros: Comes with Adobe Premiere 6.0 and ACID Music. A reasonably priced capture card that includes some excellent software.

Cons: Doesn't provide MPEG-2 support.

CANOPUS™ DVRAPTOR-RT: $599 (MSRP) (~ $470 street price)
Company web site: **www.canopuscorp.com**

With the DVRaptor-RT, you can render your video projects in real time. It includes CD, DVD, and Web streaming encoding in MPEG-1 and MPEG-2 formats. It also processes the video in YUV 4:2:2 format, allowing for increased video quality. Supports 16:9 widescreen format. As with other capture boards in its class, DVRaptor allows you to batch-capture your footage. It puts all of your scenes into a catalog which you can arrange and edit. After this is done, the computer transfers and stores only the selected scenes to the hard drive. The Raptor includes the capture card, RaptorNavigator (for automatic or manual batch capture), RaptorEdit (video editing software), SoftXplode (special effects), and the Adobe Premiere 6.0 video editor (alternatively, you can get the Raptor software bundled with a different video editor, such as MS Pro or EditDV). It has RCA, S-Video, and IEEE 1394 inputs/outputs.

Pros: One of the best capture cards in its class. Real time processing and MPEG-2 support. Choice of editing software bundled with the hardware. Can be used on Windows 98, Windows 2000, and Windows NT operating systems.

EDITING SOFTWARE

ADOBE PREMIERE 6.0 (INCLUDED WITH DV200 AND DV RAPTOR):
$549 (MSRP) Company Web site: **www.adobe.com**

Adobe Premiere 6.0 lets you edit your movies and insert and edit audio, titles, fades, and effects within the timeline. It uses a three-point window editing display. Within the timeline editor, you select the in and out points of the length of the video you want to insert. You select the first or last frame of the footage to be inserted, and Premiere automatically adjusts the length of the footage to match the length you indicated in the timeline. You can also trim scenes within the timeline by using a mouse to drag and extend clips with "handles." Premiere also allows for DV capture and web export of your movie.

Pros: This is a solid choice for video editing. Gives you the power and control to easily edit long movies (up to 3 hours). It can be integrated with other Adobe software, such as After Effects (special effects), Photoshop, and Illustrator.

SONIC FOUNDRY VEGAS VIDEO: $489.97; (~ 370 street price)
Company web site: **www.sonicfoundry.com**

See description in Budget #1 (page 59).
Pros: One of the best video editing tools on the market.

MUSIC SOFTWARE

ACID MUSIC 3.0: $59.97 (MSRP)
Company Web site: **www.sonicfoundry.com**

See description of ACID XPress in Budget #1 (page 47). The main difference between ACID XPress and ACID Music 3.0 is the fact that you can have unlimited audio tracks in ACID Music, while XPress is limited to eight tracks. Use a source of libraries to mix and create your own soundtrack for your movies. The files you create can be saved in a WAV, WMA, MP3, AIF, and RM formats.

Pros: Easy to use loop-based music creator. Royalty-free music.

Cons: You're paying the extra money just for having more than eight tracks of audio.

VIDEO AUTHORING SOFTWARE

CLEANER 5 (MAC AND WINDOWS): $599 (MSRP)
(~ $500 street price) Company Web site: **www.terran.com**

Media Cleaner Pro 5 is designed solely for compression of your video so you can output it into almost any other format: QuickTime, RealMedia, Media Player, MPEG-1, MPEG-2, MP3, AVI, and DV for delivery to the Web, broadband network, CD-ROM, and DVD format, as well as broadband, kiosk, and presentation (such as through Microsoft PowerPoint, for instance). Editing packages do include video compression, but they do not offer the wide range of compression options and features of Media Cleaner Pro (such as variable bit-rate encoding, so streaming media can detect the different speeds of the connection). It includes cross-platform support so you can use it for Macintosh and Windows 95/98/NT operating systems. You use the compression software after the movie has been edited and its effects and transitions put into place.

Pros: Covers nearly all of your compression needs for your movies in whatever format you need to deliver them.

STREAMING MEDIA PLAYERS

QUICKTIME MOVIE PLAYER, REALNETWORKS REALPLAYER, AND WINDOWS MEDIA PLAYER.

See description in Budget #1 (page 48).

RECOMMENDED SYSTEMS

See explanation in Budget #1 (page 49).

#1: LEAST EXPENSIVE SYSTEM ~$6000 (~$5500)

Books: $108
DV Camera:
    Sony DCR-TRV17 miniDV: $1100 ($900)
    Sony DCR-PC9 miniDV: $1300 ($1000)
    Sony DCM-M1 MD Discam Digital Camcorder: $1300
Tripod:
    Sony VCT-570RM Tripod: $80
Stabilization mount:
    Glidecam Campal: $60
Microphone:
    Sony ECM 957 handheld: $300 ($230)
    Nady Systems Duet Receiver 2-Channel Wireless Lavalier: $480 ($275)
    Sennheiser shotgun microphone and powering module (ME 661/K6): $565 ($430)
Lights:
    Lowel ViP V1-90 Easy V Lighting Kit: $575 (~ $500 street price)
    Smith-Victor SV-1800 1800W Three-Light Kit: $475 ($450)
Computer:
    Dell Dimension 8100: $1950
    Power Mac G4: $2007
    HP 100i DVD + RW: $600
Video storage:
    ADS Technologies Pyro 1394 portable drive kit: $170
    Maxtor1394(FireWire) External Storage 80 GB: $380
Video capture card:
    Included with Dell and Power Mac
    ADS Pyro ProDV: $330
    Pinnacle Systems DV200: $330

Editing software:
  Ulead Media Studio Pro 6.0 (included with Pyro ProDV): $0
  Premiere 6.0 (included with DV 200): $0
  Vegas Video: $490 ($370)
Music software:
  ACID Music: $60
Video authoring software:
  Cleaner 5 (Mac and Windows): $600 ($500)
Streaming media players (free download versions): $0

#2: MIDRANGE SYSTEM ~$6800 (~$5800)
Books: $108
DV Camera:
  Canon Video Optura Pi: $1600 ($1000)
  JVC GR-DVM90U miniDV: $1700 ($740)
Tripod:
  Sony VCT-570RM Tripod: $80
  Slik 300DX: $170 ($100)
Stabilization device:
  Glidecam Campal: $60
  Mightywondercam Classic: $230 (~$190)
Microphone:
  Sony ECM 957 handheld: $300 ($230)
  Nady Systems Duet Receiver 2-Channel Wireless Lavalier:
    $480 ($275)
  Sennheiser shotgun microphone and powering module (ME 66/K6):
    $565 ($430)
Lights:
  Lowel ViP V1-90 Easy V Lighting Kit: $575 ($500)
  NRG Power Products 51803 1800-Watt, Three-light Kit: $640 ($555)
Computer:
  Dell Dimension 8100: $1950
  Power Mac G4: $2007
  HP100i DVD + RW: $600
Video storage:
  ADS Technologies Pyro 1394 portable drive kit: $170
  Maxtor 1394 (FireWire) external storage 80GB: $380
Video capture card:
  Included with Dell and Power Mac
  Pinnacle Systems DV200: $330
Editing software:
  Premier 6.0 (included with DV 200 and DV Raptor): $0
  Vegas Video: $490 ($370)
Music software:
  ACID Music: $60

Video authoring software:
   Cleaner 5 (Mac and Windows): $600 ($500)
Streaming media players (free download versions): $0

#3: Most Expensive System ~$8400 (~$7000)
Books: $108
DV Camera:
   Sony DCR-PC110: $1800 (~ $1400)
   JVC GR-DVL9800U miniDV: $2000 ($1400)
Tripod:
   Slik 300DX: $170 ($100)
Stabilization device:
   Glidecam 2000 (w/ body-pod): $510 (~ $490)
Microphone:
   Sennheiser shotgun microphone and powering module (ME 66/K6):
      $565 ($430)
   Nady 401-LT Four-Channel Wireless Lavalier Microphone System:
      $1210 ($625)
   Van Den Bergh microphone boom: (~ $400)
Lights:
   Lowel ViP V1-90 Easy V Lighting Kit: $575 ($500)
   NRG Power Products 51803 1800-Watt, Three-light Kit: $640 ($555)
Computer:
   Power Mac G4: $2007
   Sony VAIO Digital Studio: $2050
   Pioneer DVD-A03: $1000 ($600)
Video storage:
   Maxtor 1394 (FireWire) external storage 80 GB: $380
   VideoRaid 2-bay 60GB hard drive (includes SCSI card): $900
Video capture card:
   Included with Sony and Power Mac
   Canopus DVRaptor-RT: $600
Editing software:
   Premier 6.0 (included with DV 200 and DVRaptor-RT): $0
   Vegas Video: $490 ($370)
Music software:
   ACID Music: $60
Video authoring software:
   Cleaner 5: $600 ($500)
Streaming media players (free download versions): $0

BUDGET #4: $7,500–10,000 (street price)

Budget #4 provides a brief overview of some of the equipment you can purchase to create your own DV movie studio for between $7,500–10,000.

Preproduction
   Books: $108
Production
   DV cameras: $2000–3000 ($1600–2500)
   Tripod: $170 ($100)
   Stabilization device: $510–$850 ($460–850)
   Microphone: $565–1210 ($430–930)
   Lights: $575–1530 ($500–1250)
Post Production
   Computer: $2040–2900
   Video storage: $380–1000 ($380–900)
   Capture card: $650–1000 ($550–900)
   Editing software: $0–1000
   Special effects software: $650 ($620)
   Music software: $0–460
   Video authoring: $0–500 ($0–450)
   Streaming media players: free downloads
Total Cost ~ $9000–13,500 (~ $7800–11,000)

PREPRODUCTION

BOOKS: $108

See description in Budget #1.
On Directing Film, by David Mamet (Penguin, 1992; $13)
On Writing Your First Play, by Roger Hall (Focal Press, 1998; $20)
Producing Great Sound for Digital Video, by Jay Rose (Miller Freeman
   Books, 2000; $40)
Placing Shadows, Lighting Techniques for Video Production, by Chuck B.
   Gloman, Tom Letourneau (Focal Press, 2000; $35)

PRODUCTION

DV CAMERAS

SONY DCR-TRV900: $1999.95 (MSRP) (~ $1600 street price)
Company Web site: **www.sony.com**

The Sony TRV900 has three 1/4-inch CCDs with 380,000 pixels each (dedicated for red, green, and blue), with progressive-scan capability. It has a 12X optical zoom and 48X digital zoom lens (which has an optical image stabilization system), with a four-lux minimum illumination. The lens is a f1.6–2.8mm providing a focal length of 4.3–51.6mm (equivalent to a 41–492mm lens on a 35mm camera). It includes a 3.5–inch flip-out swivel LCD color screen and a color eyepiece-viewfinder. It also has the standard digital picture effects and transitions, as well as IEEE 1394 DV input/output and analog inputs for converting non-DV movies into the DV format. It can shoot in digital still camera mode, images of which can be recorded onto a floppy disc (with supplied adapter) or put on a Memory Stick (with optional adapter). In addition, it has the Sony "Intelligent" accessory shoe. The battery provides a read-out for the remaining minutes of recording time. It provides manual control of focus, aperture, shutter, white balance, and gain.

Pros: Three CCDs. Manual-focus ring. White balance. Analog inputs for converting non-DV movies into DV format.

Canon GL1 miniDV: $2499 (MSRP) (~ $1700 street price)
Company Web site: **www.canondv.com**

Canon GL1. Used by Permission.

This three 1/4-inch CCD DV camera contains 270,000 pixels per CCD. Canon claims that with their pixel-shift technology, the CCDs match the image quality of a CCD containing 410,000 pixels, giving this camera the equivalent combined image resolution quality of 1,230,000 pixels. Since the green component of the image in a CCD contains 60 percent of the detail in the image, the red and blue contain the remaining 40 percent. To compensate, Canon shifts the green CCD half a pixel from the red and blue, causing the green to be read more frequently and thus providing a sharper picture. Since there are less pixels in the CCD, the pixels are larger in size, allowing them to gather more light and offer a wider dynamic range within lights and shadows (and preventing less color "noise" and reducing vertical smear). The GL1 has a *f*/1.6–2.9 20X zoom lens, providing a 4.2–84mm focal length (with a 100X digital zoom enhancement and an optical image stabilization system). Additionally, the lens uses a broadcast-quality lens made of Fluorite material, helping to provide increased resolution, contrast, and color. In normal glass lenses, color aberration occurs, reducing the sharpness, contrast, and color of the light. The Fluorite material helps prevent this problem, resulting in increased picture quality. The camera comes with a 2.5-inch LCD screen and a color eyepiece-viewfinder. Its minimum lighting illumination is six lux. In addition to the standard IEEE 1394 DV input/output, the camera has inputs for converting analog movies to DV format. As well as digital effects and transitions, preprogrammed auto-exposure modes, and digital still-camera mode, it includes white balance for setting true color and zebra pattern so you know when you have over-exposed shots. It also has a microphone input.

Pros: Pixel-shift technology on the CCDs for increasing picture quality. Fluorite lens increases sharpness of detail. White balance for setting true color. Zebra pattern for setting exposure. Microphone input. Full manual operation. Manual focus ring. Can convert non-DV movies into the DV format.

Cons: 2.5-inch LCD screen could be larger.

PANASONIC PV-DV950: $2699.95 (MSRP) ($1600 street price)

Company Web site: **www.panasonic.com**

Panasonic PV-DV950; courtesy
Panasonic Consumer Electronics Company.

The Panasonic PV-DV950 has three CCD chips. It includes a 12X optical zoom and a 120X digital zoom. The photograph feature of this camera can be recorded on the tape or onto a memory stick called a MultiMediaCard. It records 60 images at 640X480 resolution or 240 images in 320X240 resolution mode (with 7 seconds of audio narration space allowed for each picture). In digital still camera mode, approximately 1000 images can be recorded onto an 80-minute DV tape (in LP mode). It has white balance control, digital effects (wipe/mix, strobe, still, and black and white), high-speed shutter (1/60 to 1/8000 of a second), and a manual focus ring. It also has the standard IEEE 1394 digital input/output, as well as a docking station that contains analogue inputs and outputs.

    Pros: Three CCD chips. Also see the DV951 on the company Web site, listed at $2500 ($1600 street price).

SONY DSR-PD100A DVCAM: $2725 (MSRP) ($2500 street price)

Company Web site: **www.sony.com**

Sony's DSR-PD100A uses the DVCAM tape format, which can store 40 minutes of footage on one tape. It has three 1/4-inch CCDs (with 380,000 pixels). It has a 12X optical zoom and 48X digital zoom lens (*f*4.3–51.6mm). It also has a 3.5-inch LCD screen and a color viewfinder (with zebra pattern capability—so you know when you have overexposed a shot). This camera has white balance, shutter speed (1/4 to 1/1000 of a second), and exposure controls. It also has a Memory Stick adaptor for storing still digital photos. One of its special features is the XLR microphone adaptor, so it can use professional XLR microphone (as opposed to the stereo minijack microphones). Overall, this camera contains a lot of features seen in professional cameras.

    Pros: XLR adaptor, three CCDs, and zebra pattern for exposure control.

SONY DCR-VX2000 MINIDV: $2999 (MSRP) (~ $2300 street price)

Company web site: **www.sony.com**

The VX2000 uses three 1/3-inch CCDs with 380,000 (340,000 effective) pixels each, with progressive-scan capability. The CCD uses Sony's HAD technology, helping to reduce video noise. This gives this camera the ability to record up to 530 lines of horizontal resolution, making it sharper than lower-end cameras (the Sony TRV900 provides up to 500 lines of resolution, for example). It has a *f*1.6–2.4 12X zoom lens with a 6.0–72.0mm focal length (equivalent to 43.2–518.4mm in a 35mm camera). It includes a 48X digital zoom enhancement and an optical image stabilization system.

The minimum illumination for shooting is four lux. A 2.5-inch swivel LCD color screen and color eyepiece-viewfinder is included. The camera comes with the standard digital picture-effects as well as wipes and fades. It can also record in 16:9 wide-screen format. It has a zebra pattern setting and white balance control. In addition, it comes with a manual microphone level control, battery meter (showing minutes of remaining record time), an "Intelligent" accessory shoe, the standard IEEE 1394 DV input/output, S-video, as well as analog inputs and pass-through capabilities, converting nondigital movies to the DV format.

Pros: Three 1/3-inch CCDs. Microphone level control and microphone input. Battery meter. White balance and zebra settings. Analog inputs for converting non DV movies into the DV format. Manual control of aperture, shutter, and focus. Focus ring.

TRIPODS/STABILIZATION DEVICES

SLIK 300DX: $169.95 (MSRP) (~ $100 street price)
Company Web site: **www.tocad.com/slik.html**

See description in Budget #2 (page 55).

GLIDECAM 2000: $369 (MSRP) (~ $320 street price)
BODY-POD ATTACHMENT: $139 (~ $120 street price)
Company Web site: **www.glidecam.com**

See picture and description in Budget #3 (page 67).

GLIDECAM CAMCRANE 200: $549 (MSRP) (~ $410 street price)
Company Web site: **www.glidecam.com**

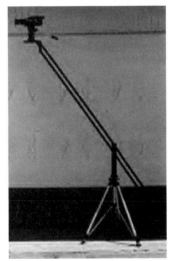

Glidecam's Camcrane is essentially a boom arm that mounts onto a tripod (not included). It allows for fluid smooth motion in a full 360 degree circle as well as up and down. It is made out of anodized black aluminum. There are four possible boom lengths: 3 feet 3 inches, 4 feet 10 inches, 6 feet 6 inches, and 8 feet 1 inch. At its longest extension, the boom can travel from the floor to a height of up to 10 feet. It can hold a camera that weighs up to 30 pounds. The crane weighs 16 pounds and collapses down to a 3-foot 3-inch length. It mounts on a 3/8-inch standard tripod bolt. Note, however, you will need a tripod that can sustain the crane and camera's combined weight. The head of the crane contains a 3/8-inch mounting hole for mounting the head of a tripod which connects to the camera. It also includes counterbalance weights for fine-tuning the balance.

Pros: A fairly inexpensive way to devise some professional-looking shots. Compact size.

The Glidecam Crane for crane shots. Copyright 2000 Glidecam Industries, Inc. Photographed by Martin P. Stevens.

Cons: You will need to get a hefty tripod to handle the weight of the crane and camera.

STEADICAM JR.: $849 (MSRP)
Company Web site: **www.steadicam.com**

The Steadicam Jr. is the smallest stabilization device from Steadicam. It supports cameras weighing up to 4 pounds. The handle/gimbal attachment provides you with smooth motion shots as you move. The gimbal absorbs the shock of the movement so the camera records smooth shots.

Pros: Includes an on-mount LCD color monitor (2.9 inches).

Cons: Limited to camera weights of up to 4 pounds. Does not have a body-pod attachment.

MICROPHONES

SENNHEISER SHOTGUN MICROPHONE AND POWERING MODULE (ME 66/K6):
$565 (MSRP) (~$430 street price)
Company Web site: **www.sennheiserusa.com**

See description in Budget #3 (page 68).

Pros: A solid shotgun microphone that allows you to change the type of microphone capsule used. It has a 50-20,000 Hz range.

VAN DEN BERGH MICROPHONE FISHPOLES/BOOMS SVDBBCC BABY COIL CABLED: (~$400 street price)
Available at several online dealers.

See description in Budget #3 (p. 68).

NADY 401 FOUR CHANNEL WIRELESS LAVALIER MICROPHONE SYSTEM:
$1210(MSRP) (~$625 street price)
Company Web site: **www.nadywireless.com**

See description and picture in Budget #3 (p. 68).

LIGHTS

LOWEL VIP V1-90 EASY V LIGHTING KIT: $575 (~$500 street price)
Company Web site: **www.lowel.com**

See description in budget #3 (p. 69).

NRG POWER PRODUCTS (51803) 1800W, 3-LIGHT ALL-FOCUSING QUARTZ KIT:
$639.95 (MSRP) (~$555 street price)
Company web site: **www.nrgresearch.com**

See description and picture in Budget #3 (p. 69).

NRG Research Three-Light Location Lighting Pro (51903):

$989.95 (MSRP) Company web site: **www.nrgresearch.com**

This kit contains three lights, with each lighting head containing an alloy-etched reflector, that provides naturally smooth illumination. Each head also has an adjustable 8:1 focusing mechanism, so the light can be adjusted from narrow beam to a wide wash. Furthermore, each head can hold either a 500-, 750-, or 1000-watt quartz lamp (a removable metal scrim provides protection). The kit includes barn doors, so you can control where the light goes. They include mounting clips for gels as well. Each light has an adjustable 9-foot stand with detachable power cables. The kit includes a hard transport case.

Pros: You get three adjustable focus lights with stands, barn doors, and gel clamps.

Cons: Does not include the quartz lamps.

Cool-Lux Cool-Kit Location Kit LK2201: $1530 (MSRP)

(~ $1250 street price) Company web site: **www.cool-lux.com**

This lighting kit from Cool-Lux contains three lights: two Mini-Cool lights with 150-watt and 75-watt lamps, as well as a Micro-Lux light and lamp, which can be attached to the camera. It also includes a light stand, stable-cam, stand adapters, camera adapter, hand-hold handle, light bracket, umbrella, umbrella mount, clamp, dimmer, daylight filter, frosted diffusion lens, DC-to-AC adapter, and case.

Pros: Portable case containing a wide variety of lighting equipment.

Cons: Only one light stand is included. Does not include gel mounts for the lights.

Dimmer switch: ~ $25

Purchase at a hardware or lighting store.

See description in Budget #1 (p. 41)

Gels: ~ $5 per sheet

Purchase at theatrical lighting supply stores, some of which are located online.

See description in Budget #1 (p. 41).

Pros: Excellent way to add vibrant and moody color to your movies.

POSTPRODUCTION

COMPUTERS

Compaq Presario 7000: $2041(MSRP)

Company Web site: **www.apple.com**

The Compaq Presario contains Pioneer's DVD-R/RW drive, as well as a

Pentium IV 1.6 GHz CPU, 256 MB of RAM, a 40 GB hard drive, 64 MB 3D graphics card, network card, 56K modem, Ethernet network card, 17" Trinitron monitor, keyboard, and mouse, speakers, as well as an inkjet printer (for no additional cost). It also comes with a FireWire port, and two USB ports. It uses Microsoft Me OS. It is bundled with Microsoft Home Suite, Studio DV editor, and Sonic's DVDit! software.

Pros: The Pioneer DVD-R/RW drive allows you to record your movies onto a DVD that can be viewed on a standard television DVD player.

POWERMAC G4 ULTIMATE: $2907
Company Web site: **www.apple.com**

Apple broke the budget barrier for DVD-R drives with the inclusion of their Super Drive in this Power Mac G4 Ultimate, which contains an 867 MHz CPU, 256 MB of RAM, a 80 GB hard drive, a DVD-R/CD-RW drive, 64 MB 3D graphics card, network card, 56K modem, Ethernet network card, Ultra wide SCSI card (so you can connect a VideoRAID hard drive video storage), keyboard and mouse, and speakers. It comes with two FireWire ports and two USB ports. It has both the Mac OS 9 and OS X operating systems and includes iMovie 2, a video editing software package.

Pros: The DVD-R Super Drive allows you to record your movies onto a DVD that can be viewed on a standard television DVD player.

Cons: The Apple store lists three flat screen monitors for this product, with the cheapest one (15" display) costing about $600. It is recommended that you purchase a regular 17" monitor for $350 or get a 17" flat screen monitor from another company (which costs around $600).

PIONEER DVR-A03 DVD-R/RW: $995 (~ $600 street price)
Company Web site: **www.pioneer.com**

See description in Budget # 3 (p. 71).

Pros: A version of this drive is included in the Compaq Presario 7000 and Power Mac G4 Ultimate.

VIDEO STORAGE

MAXTOR 1394 (FIREWIRE) EXTERNAL STORAGE 80GB: $379
Company Web site: **www.maxtor.com**

See description in Budget #1 (p. 44).

VIDEORAID 2-BAY 80 GB HARD DRIVE (SCSI CARD INCLUDED):
$999(MSRP) ($900 street price) Company Web site: **www.medeacorp.com**

See description in Budget #3 (p. 72). This model has 80GB.

CAPTURE CARDS

PINNACLE SYSTEMS DV 500 PLUS: $649 (MSRP) (~ $550 street price)
Company Web site: **www.pinnaclesys.com**

This is one of the best-value capture-card boards you can purchase. This card does what lower-value cards do (such as video log and batch capture). However, in addition to these standard features, it provides you with the ability to do real-time editing through its dual-stream feature (one stream for video and audio; the other stream for special effects, titling, and transitions). In non real-time editing situations, if you insert a title or transition, the computer would have to render these effects before you can play them back and see how they look in your movie—which can take some time. With real-time effects, the process occurs in "real time" (if the transition is 3 seconds, the DV500 renders it in 3 seconds, as opposed to several minutes in a non real-time editor). Furthermore, this card allows MPEG-2 output for DVD and CD-Rs as well as giving you the ability to do web streaming. Additionally, this card not only has IEEE 1394 DV input/ output, but it has a box that includes component video and audio and S-video input/ouput, so it meets your diverse editing needs, including transfering your non-DV movies into DV format. The DV500 includes Adobe Premiere 6.0, TitleDeko (so you can create professional-looking titles for your movies), Hollywood/FX™ Copper (both for creating 3D transition effects).

Pros: One of the best video capture cards. It lets you edit and do effects in real-time. It includes software for editing, titles, transition effects, music, and CD/DVD authoring. It captures files at their proper length, instead of in 2GB segments in lower-end PC capture cards.

MATROX RT2500: $999 (MSRP) (~ $900 street price)
Company Web site: **www.matrox.com**

This system is in the same class as the DV500. It provides standard capture-card features with real-time three-layer effects and editing capabilities. And if you don't have a good graphics card, this is a good product to get. It also provides MPEG-2 output to DVD, CD-R, and web streaming. It has a box with analog composite and S-video input/output as well as the standard IEEE 1394 DV input/output. Software includes: Premiere 6.0, Inscriber Title Express, and Video Spicerack Lite, (a titling program for 3D and animated titling effects), SonicFoundry's ACID Music, and Sonic DVDit!™ (for CD and DVD authoring).

Pros: An excellent, top-of-the-line graphics card. It includes software for editing, titles, transition effects, music, and CD/DVD authoring. It captures files at their proper length, instead of in 2GB segments of lower-end PC capture cards.

Editing software

Adobe Premiere 6.0 (included with DV 500 and Matrox RT2000):
$549 (MSRP) Company Web site: **www.adobe.com**

See description and picture in Budget #3 (p. 73). Includes a real-time plug in for the DV500 and RT2000, providing you with real time rendering of effects.

Pros: This is a solid choice for video editing. Gives you the power and control to easily edit long movies (up to 3 hours). It can be integrated with other Adobe software, such as After Effects (special effects), Photoshop, and Illustrator.

Vegas Video: $559.96 (~ $370 street price)

Company Web site: www.sonicfoundry.com

See description in budget #2 (p. 59).

Pros: One of the best video editing tools on the market.

Final Cut Pro 2.0: $999 (MSRP)

Company Web site: www.apple.com

A powerful capturing and editing software for Power Mac G4s and PowerBooks. It includes an easy-to-use software interface, as well as the capability to output movies for Internet broadcast and to record them onto CDs in DVD format.

Pros: Powerful and easy to use.

Cons: Expensive when compared to other software in its class (such as Vegas Video, Premiere, and EditDV). It needs the processing power of a G4 system processor, so it will not run as well on an iMac.

Music software

ACID Music 2.0: $59.97 (MSRP)

Company Web site: **www.sonicfoundry.com**

See description in Budget #3 (p. 74).

Sonic Desktop SmartSound® for Multimedia: $199 (MSRP)
Company Web site: **www.sonicdesktop.com**

SmartSound presents a music-making process that allows you to create compositions without having any prior experience in creating music. It walks you through a step-by-step process for creating your sound track. It prompts you to select how you plan to use the music (background, transition, an opening or closing segment), its length, and the style (action, romantic, ethnic, jazz, and so forth). There are dozens of songs and musical selections you can choose from the audio libraries, and you can also select whether a song will be looped or if it will end at a certain point. You can import your own music and sounds as well. SmartSound includes Audio Palette 1, which has music and audio effects in the following categories: ambiences, animals, cartoon, office, people, and sports.

Pros: Royalty-free music. It is a lot cheaper to purchase this software and audio libraries than it would if you had to purchase music rights.

Cons: The software libraries are expensive ($70 for 22K 16-bit samples or $130 for 44K 16-bit audio sampling), so if you want a large library, it could become fairly expensive.

SOUND FORGE™ 5.0: $399 (MSRP) (~ $300 street price)
Company Web site: **www.sonicfoundry.com**

Sound Forge 5.0 is a digital audio editor. Along with the computer's sound card, you can create, record, and edit audio files. It comes with dozens of audio effects and processing tools in order to manipulate and shape the sound you want, from eerie-sounding vocal effects to removing unwanted sound with such audio effects as amplitude modulation, chorus, delay/echo, distortion, dynamics, envelopes, flange/wah-wah, gapper/snipper, noise gate, pitch bend/shift, reverb, and vibrato. With Sound Forge, you can cut, paste, move, delete, mute, reverse, fade, and cross-fade audio, and you can preview audio changes before you save the file. Additionally, you can also control the sound with equalizers. The time compress/expand feature allows you to squeeze or stretch sound within a given time segment without altering the pitch of the sound. Files can be saved in the following formats: WAV, WMA, RM, ASF, and MP3. It has built-in video support.

Pros: An excellent audio tool. Coupled with Sonic Foundry ACID Music, you will have nearly everything you need for sound designs for your movies.

Cons: It is more expensive than it needs to be.

SPECIAL EFFECTS SOFTWARE

ADOBE AFTER EFFECTS 5.0: $649 (MSRP) (~ $620 street price)
Company Web site: **www.adobe.com**

Adobe After Effects is a software package that will allow you to create visual still and motion special-effects that can be integrated with your video footage. You can create flying spaceships in space, light saber effects from *Star Wars*, or even a car. You can import images into your footage as well manipulate your existing footage. It includes such plug-in effects as ColorsQuad, which allows you to mix colors together; Radial Shadow, for creating shadows from a nearby light point, even if it moves; and Noise Turbulent, which uses a fractal-based technology to simulate cloud movement or even lava flows.

Pros: It is integrated with Adobe Premiere 6.0, so there are no compatibility issues when editing and importing your effects.

Cons: Like all effects packages, there is a high learning-curve involved in creating the effect you want.

VIDEO AUTHORING

DVDit!™ *SE:* $499 (MSRP) (~ $450 street price)
Company web site: **www.dvdit.com**

Sonic DVDit! allows you to record your movies onto a CD-ROM (with a CD-RW drive) in a DVD format. It lets you see menu controls, add comments, and insert links for director's and actors' comments into separate menu portions on the CD (just like regular DVDs movies). It uses a fairly easy drag-and-drop style interface for placing buttons and text on a menu screen. There is also real-time preview of the DVD, so you can see it before it is processed. Additionally, the product includes a slideshow creator for presentations. (See Chapter 3, "Transferring Your Film onto CD-ROM and DVD," for a detailed walk-through of this product.)

Pros: An inexpensive way to record your movies onto recordable CDs through your CD-RW or DVD-RAM drive. In this way you can give your movies away or sell them.

Cons: Movie files larger than 650–700MB cannot be recorded onto a CD-ROM. You need a DVD recorder (costing thousands of dollars) to record onto a DVD that you can play on a television DVD player.

MEDIA CLEANER 5 (MAC AND WINDOWS): $599 (MSRP) (~ $500 street price)
Company Web site: **www.terran.com**

See description and picture in Budget #3.

STREAMING MEDIA PLAYERS

QUICKTIME MOVIE PLAYER, REALNETWORKS REALPLAYER, AND WINDOWS MEDIA PLAYER.

See description in Budget #1 (p. 48).

RECOMMENDED SYSTEMS

See explanation in Budget #1 (p. 49).

#1: LEAST EXPENSIVE SYSTEM ~$9000 (~$7800)
Books: $108
DV Camera:
Sony DCR-TRV 900: $2000 ($1600)

Tripod:
   Slik 300DX: $170 ($100)
Stabilization device:
   Glidecam 2000: $510 ($450)
   Glidecam Crane: $550 ($410)
Microphone:
   Sennheiser Shotgun Microphone and Powering module (ME 66/K66):
      $565 ($430)
Lights:
   Lowel ViP V1-90 Easy V Lighting Kit: $575 ($500)
   NRG Power Products 1800W, Three-Light All-Focusing Quartz Kit:
      $640 ($555)
Computer:
   Compaq Presario 7000: $2041
Video storage:
   Maxtor 1394 (FireWire) External Storage 80GB: $380
   VideoRaid Two-bay 80GB hard drive: $1000 ($900)
Video capture card:
   Pinnacle Systems DV500: $650 ($550)
Editing software:
   Adobe Premiere 6.0 (included with DV 500): $0
   Vegas Video: $490 ($370)
Special-effects software:
   Adobe After Effects 5.0: $650 ($620)
Music software:
   ACID Music 2.0: $60
   Sonic Desktop Smartsound: $200
   Sound Forge 5.0: $400 ($300)
Video Authoring software:
   DVDit! SE: $500 ($450)
   Media Cleaner 5: $600 ($500)
Streaming media players (free download versions): $0

#2: MIDRANGE SYSTEM ~$12,000 (~$9900)

Books: $113
DV Camera:
   Canon GL1: $2500 ($1700)
   Panasonic PV-DV950: $2700 ($1600)
   Sony DSR-PD100A DVCAM $2725 ($2500)
Tripod:
   Slik 300DX: $170 ($100)
Stabilization device:
   Glidecam 2000: $510 ($450)
   Glidecam Crane: $550 ($430)
Microphone:

Sennheiser Shotgun Microphone and Poweringmodule (ME 66/K6): $565 ($430)
Nady 401-LT Four-Channel Lavaliere system: $1210 ($625)
Van Der Bergh Microphone Boom: $400
Lights:
   Lowel ViP V1-90 Easy V Lighting Kit: $575 ($500)
   NRG Power Products 1800-watt, Three-light Kit: $640 ($555)
   NRG Research Three-Light Location Lighting Pro: $990
Computer:
   Compaq Presario 7000: $2040
   PowerMac G4 Ultimate: $2900
Video storage:
   VideoRaid 2-bay 80GB hard drive: $1000 ($900)
Video capture card:
   Pinnacle Systems DV500: $650 ($550)
   Matrox RT2500: $1000 ($900)
Editing software:
   Adobe Premiere 6.0 (included with DV 500 and RT2500): $0
   Vegas Video $490 ($370)
   Final Cut Pro 2.0: $1000
Special effects software:
   Adobe After Effects 5.0: $650 ($620)
Music software:
   ACID Music 2.0: $60
   Sound Forge: $400 ($300)
Video Authoring software:
   Media Cleaner 5: $600 ($500)
   DVDit! SE: $500 ($450)
Streaming media players (free download versions): $0

#3: MOST EXPENSIVE SYSTEM ~$13,500 (~$11,000)

Books: $113
DV Camera:
   Sony DCR-VX2000 MiniDV: $3000 ($2300)
Tripod:
   Slik 300DX: $170 ($100)
Stabilization device:
   Glidecam 2000: $510 ($450)
   Glidecam Crane: $550 ($410)
   Steadicam Jr: $850
Microphone:
   Nady 401-LT Four-Channel Lavaliere system: $1210 ($625)
Lights:
   NRG Research Three-Light Location Lighting Pro: $990
   Cool-Lux Cool-Kit Location Kit LK2201: $1530 ($1250)

Computer:
    Power Mac G4 Ultimate: $2900
Storage:
    VideoRaid 2-bay 80GB hard drive: $1000 ($900)
Video capture card:
    Pinnacle Systems DV 500: $650 ($550)
    Matrox RT2500: $1000 ($900)
Editing software:
    Adobe Premiere 6.0 (included with DV 500 and RT2500): $0
    Vegas Video: $490 ($370)
    Final Cut Pro 2.0: $999
Special effects software:
    Adobe After Effects 5.1: $650 ($620)
Music software:
    ACID Music 2.0: $60
    Sound Forge: $400 ($300)
Video Authoring software:
    Media Cleaner 5: $600 ($500)
    DVDit! SE: $500 ($450)
Streaming media players (free download versions): $0

BUDGET #5: over $10,000 (street price)

Budget #5 provides a brief overview of some of the equipment you can purchase to create your own DV movie studio costing between $10,000–20,000.

OVERVIEW OF COSTS

Preproduction
    Books: $108
Production
    DV cameras: $3700–5000 ($3500–4700)
    Tripod: $170 ($100)
    Stabilization device: $550–1400
    Microphone: $565–1210 ($430–830)
    Lights: $1300–2000 ($900–1500)
Post Production
    Computer: $3650–4050
    Video storage: $1650–2400
    Capture card: $2000–3000 ($1800–2800)
    Editing software (included with capture cards): $0
    Special effects software: $2500–3500
    Music software: $100–500
    Video authoring software: $600–3000 ($480–3000)
    Streaming media players: free downloads
Total Cost ~ $18,000–25,000 (~ $16,600–25,000)

PREPRODUCTION

BOOKS: $108

See description in Budget #1.
On Directing Film, by David Mamet (Penguin, 1992; $13)
Writing Your First Play, by Roger Hall (Focal Press, 1998; $20)
Producing Great Sound for Digital Video, by Jay Rose (Miller Freeman
   Books, 2000; $40)
Placing Shadows, Lighting Techniques for Video Production, by Chuck B.
   Gloman, Tom Letourneau (Focal Press, 2000; $35)

PRODUCTION

DV CAMERAS

CANON XL1S: $4699 (MSRP) (~ $4200 street price)
Company Web site: **www.canondv.com**

The XL1S is a professional-looking camera that gives you professional results for a reasonable price. The XL1S has 3 1/3-inch CCDs with 270,000

Canon XL1. Canon is a registered trademark of
Canon Inc. All rights reserved. Used by Permission.

pixels, each with pixel-shift technology, providing better clarity of image (see description under GL1 in
Budget #4). The key feature of the XL1S is the ability
to attach multiple lenses. From wide-angle to telephoto—you're not limited to the supplied lens-size given
on other DV cameras that do not have interchangeable lenses. The camera does include a 16X zoom lens
with a focal length of *f*5.5–88mm and an optical image
stabilization system. Additionally, you can use 35
EOS lenses with an EF adapter. The XL1S provides
full manual control of exposure, audio, focus (with
the focus ring on the lens), and white balance. It also
has a zebra pattern setting so you can set your exposure range. It has a microphone with 3.5 mm stereo minijack. The minimum illumination is two lux. It comes with a color LCD eyepiece-
viewfinder, but it does not have a swing-out LCD screen. It includes an
IEEE 1394 DV connector, an S-video terminal, and a stereo microphone
mini-jack input. Additionally, the camera can shoot digital still pictures. It
weighs over 6 pounds with the lens and battery.

   Pros: Interchangeable lens. Three 1/3-inch CCDs. White balance. Manual focus
ring on lens. Can shoot in 16:9 wide angle mode.

   Cons: No swing-out LCD panel. It does not have the special digital picture effects found in the new lower-end cameras (such as sepia and black-
and-white modes, for example).

Sony Pro DSR-PD150 MiniDV: $4400 (MSRP) (~ $3200 street price)
Company Web site: **www.sony.com**

Sony's DSR-PD150 is offered as a "pro" camera. It is in the same class as Canon's XL1. It uses three 1/3-inch CCDs with 380,000 pixels, providing the camera with sharp, clean pictures (with 530 lines of horizontal resolution). The lens has a 12X optical zoom and 48X digital zoom enhancement capabilities. Besides the standard IEEE 1394 DV input/output, and S-video input (for conversion of analog movies to DV format), it also has the ability to record in digital-component video and audio. It can shoot in 16:9 wide-screen format. The camera has manual controls of focus and exposure. The eyepiece viewfinder is black and white, but with a high resolution, and it also includes a swing-out 2.5-inch LCD color screen. The camera includes two XLR inputs for microphones. It also has a built-in speaker, so you can listen to audio during playback without using headphones. Additionally, it includes a 64MB Memory Stick for digital still pictures. This camera comes with the standard digital picture effects and fades found in the lower-end DV cameras, as well as the professional zebra pattern for exposure control. Along with all this it also has manual control of shutter speed, recording levels, white balance, iris, and focus. The camera weighs just over 3 pounds.

Pros: Three 1/3-inch high-resolution CCDs (380,000 pixels each). Manual control of exposure and shutter speeds. White balance. Focus ring on lens. 16:9 wide screen mode.

Cons: Does not have interchangeable lenses as found in the Canon XL1 or the JVC GY-DV500.

JVC GY-DV500: ~ $4635 (MSRP); $4300 street price; without lens
Company web site: **www.jvcpro.com**

This is a miniDV professional camera that gives you the ability to change lenses (with a bayonet lens mount). It comes with three 1/2-inch CCDs with 380,000 pixels each. It uses a 14-bit digital signal processor, providing the capability of higher-end cameras. The combination of these two factors helps eliminate vertical smear or blurring. In addition, this camera can shoot in 3/4-lux illumination. The camera comes with the standard IEEE 1394 DV input/output terminal. The camera also allows you to set full auto-shooting mode so you can move from a dark to a light setting without being required

JVC GY-DV500. Courtesy of JVC Inc.

to change the manual settings. It gives you full manual control for exposure, shutter, gain, white balance, and focus, and it provides sync-lock mode so you can set the camera for a multicamera set-up. The camera has built-in phantom power to provide power to microphones that need them.

Pros: Interchangeable lens system. Three 1/2-inch CCDs with 380,000 pixels each, increasing the color quality and image sharpness. Manual control over exposure, shutter, white balance, gain, and focus.

Cons: Does not have 16:9 wide screen mode. Weighs 11 pounds.

TRIPODS

SLIK 300DX: $169.95 (MSRP) (~ $100 street price)
Company Web site: **www.tocad.com/slik.html**

See description in Budget #2 (p. 55).

GLIDECAM CRANE: $550 ($410)
Company Web site: **www.glidecam.com**

See description and picture in Budget #4 (p. 81).
Pros: A fairly inexpensive way to devise some professional-looking shots. Compact size.

Cons: You will need to get a hefty tripod to handle the weight of the crane and camera.

GLIDECAM 2000: $369 (MSRP) (~ $320 street price)

BODYPOD ATTACHMENT: $139 (MSRP) (~ $120 street price)
Company Web site: **www.glidecam.com**

See picture and description in Budget #3 (p. 67).

MICROPHONES

SENNHEISER SHOTGUN MICROPHONE AND POWERING MODULE (ME 66/K6):
$565 (MSRP) (~ $430 street price) Company Web site: **www.sennheiser.com**

See description in Budget #3 (p. 68).
Pros: A solid shotgun microphone that allows you to change the type of microphone capsule used. It has a 50–20,000 Hz range.

VAN DEN BERGH MICROPHONE FISHPOLES/BOOMS SVDBBCC BABY COIL CABLED:
(~ $400 street price) Available at several online dealers.

See description in Budget #3 (p. 68).

NADY 401 FOUR CHANNEL WIRELESS LAVALIER MICROPHONE SYSTEM:
$1210 (MSRP) (~ $625 street price)
Company Web site: **www.nadywireless.com**

See description in Budget #3 (p. 68).

NRG RESEARCH 4-LIGHT (51904): $1299.95 (MSRP)
Company Web site: **www.nrgresearch.com**

This kit contains four lights, with each lighting head containing an alloy-etched reflector, which provides naturally smooth illumination (see picture in Budget #4). Each head has an adjustable 8:1 focusing mechanism, so the light can be adjusted from narrow beam to a wide wash. Furthermore, each head can hold either a 500-, 750-, or 1000-watt quartz lamp (a removable metal scrim provides protection). The kit comes with barn doors, so you can control where the light goes, and mounting clips for gels to add color to your scenes. Each light has an adjustable 9-foot stand with detachable power cables. The kit includes a multicompartment hard transport case.

Pros: You get four adjustable focus lights with stands, barn doors, and gel clamps, so you can meet almost any lighting situation.

Cons: Does not include the quartz lamps.

COOL-LUX COOL-KIT STUDIO KIT LK2202:
$2394 (MSRP) (~ $1900 street price)
Company web site: **www.cool-lux.com**

This lighting kit from Cool-Lux contains five lights (see similar picture in Budget #4): four Mini-Cool lights with four 150-watt lamps, as well as a Micro-Lux light and lamp, which can be attached to the camera. It also includes two light stands, stable-cam, four stand adapters, one camera adapter, two spring clamps, three scissor clamps for T-bars, hand-hold handle, light bracket, two umbrellas (with two umbrella mounts), two barn doors, two dimmers, daylight filter, three frosted diffusion lens (to soften harsh light), DC-to-AC adapter, and case.

Pros: Portable case containing a wide variety of lighting equipment.

Cons: Only two light stands and two dimmers included. Does not include gel mounts for the lights.

DIMMER SWITCH: ~ $25
Purchase at a hardware or lighting store.

See description in Budget #1 (p. 41).

GELS: ~ $5 per sheet
Purchase at theatrical lighting supply stores, some of which are located online.

See description in Budget #1 (p. 41).

Pros: Excellent way to add vibrant and moody color to your movies.

POSTPRODUCTION

COMPUTERS

DELL DIMENSION 8100 SERIES: $3446
Company web site: **www.dell.com**

This Dell Dimension comes with a Pentium 4 1.8GHz CPU, 512MB RAM, 80GB hard drive, a 19-inch Trinitron monitor, 56K modem, and a combination DVD/CD-RW drive. It includes a IEEE 1394 input/output card. It also has a Sound Blaster soundcard, Altec Lansing TXH certified speakers and subwoofer, a 64MB NVIDIA GeForce AGP video/graphics card, 3.5-inch floppy drive, a keyboard, Microsoft Intellimouse, Windows Me, Microsoft Office Professional, and Norton Antivirus software. It also includes a 3-year next-business-day on-site parts and labor warranty, as well as 2 years labor, 3 years parts warranty, and lifetime phone support.

Pros: A nice overall system that provides you with almost everything you need for a postproduction studio. The 733MHz Pentium III should give you more than enough power. 19-inch Trinitron monitor.

Cons: You need to purchase a capture card and a hard drive for video storage. The DVD/RW drive is read only. However, by the printing of this book, DVD-R/RW should become more standard.

POWER MAC G4 ULTIMATE: $3807
Company web site: **www.apple.com**

Same as the G4 Ultimate as described in Budget #4 (p. 84), except this model is configured with dual 800 MHz processors and 512 MB of RAM.

Pros: The DVD-R Super Drive allows you to record your movies onto a DVD that can be viewed on a standard television DVD player.

Cons: The Apple store lists three flat screen monitors for this product, with the cheapest one (15-inch display) costing about $600. It is recommended that you purchase a regular 17-inch monitor for $350 or get a 17-inch flat screen monitor from another company (which costs around $600).

DVLINE EDITING WORKSTATION/MATROX RT2500: $4491
Company web site: **www.dvline.com**

This editing workstation has a Pentium III 1GHz dual-processor CPU, 1GB of RAM, a 60GB hard drive, 19-inch Viewsonic monitor, SoundBlaster Live, a Pioneer A03 DVD-R/RW drive, and a Matrox RT2500 graphics/video card. Software includes: Windows 2000 operating system, Adobe Premiere 6.0, Minerva Impression (for CD authoring), TitleDeko (for creating titles), and ACID Music. The system has a 3-year warranty.

Pros: Comes with just about everything you need for postproduction work.

Cons: Even though it includes a 60GB hard drive, you need to purchase another one for video; in any case, we recommend that you purchase a VideoRAID hard drive for dedicated video storage.

PIONEER DVR-A03 DVD-R/RW: $995 (~ $600 street price)
Company web site: **www.pioneer.com**

See description in Budget #3.

VIDEO STORAGE

VIDEORAID 2-BAY 80GB STORAGE (INCLUDES SCSI CARD): $999 (MSRP)
(~ $900 street price) Company web site: **www.medeacorp.com**

The same as the two-bay VideoRaid (see description in Budget #3).

Pros: One of the best ways to store and edit your video, providing you with 4.5 hours of storage. A good value for its features. If you can afford this video storage system, buy it, because it's one of the best out there. It provides you with enough throughput for real time effects. With the ultra-wide SCSI, you get sustained throughputs of 20MB per second.

Cons: You're paying a fair amount of money for the hard drive, compared to regular internal hard drives.

VIDEORAID RT 4 BAY 160GB (INCLUDES SCSI CARD): $1999 (MSRP)
(~ $1800 street price) Company web site: **www.medeacorp.com**

Similar to the VideoRAID, the VideoRAID RT gives you 120GB of DV storage (over 9 hours) and has a throughput of 55MB per second—this will meet all of your video and special effects throughput needs.

Pros: Provides a lot of storage with a high throughput. Worth the investment.

Cons: More expensive than regular hard drives, but if you need the extra throughput, this gives you what you need.

CAPTURE CARDS

PINNACLE SYSTEMS DV 500: $650 (MSRP) (~ $550 street price)
Company web site: **www.pinnaclesys.com**

See description in Budget #4 (p. 84).

Pros: This is one of the best video capture cards you can get. It lets you edit and do effects in real-time. It includes software for editing, titles, transition effects, music, and CD/DVD authoring. It captures files at their proper length, instead of in 2GB segments of lower-end PC capture cards.

MATROX RT2500: $1000 (MSRP) (~ $900 street price)
Company web site: **www.matrox.com**

See description in Budget #4 (p. 85).

Pros: An excellent, top-of-the-line graphics card. It includes software for editing, titles, transition effects, music, and CD/DVD authoring. It captures files at their proper length, instead of in 2GB segments of lower-end PC capture cards.

DC1000: $1300 (~ $1200 street price)
Company Web site: **www.pinnaclesys.com**

The DC1000 is a top-of-the-line capture card. The editor provides real-time dual-stream in MPEG-2 format. It includes the full version of Adobe Premiere 6.0 for editing, TitleDeko for creating titles, Smart Sound Quicktracks, and Pinnacle CD-Pro video authoring (the authoring can be output to videotape, CD-RW, DVD-R/RW drives, as well as Web-streaming production). Like the DV500, it has a IEEE 1394 DV input/output terminal as well as an external box with analog composite and S-video input/output terminals.
   Pros: MPEG-2 support in real time.

EDITING SOFTWARE

ADOBE PREMIERE 6.0 (INCLUDED WITH DC1000 AND DC2000):
$549 (MSRP) Company Web site: **www.adobe.com**

See description in Budget #3 (p. 73).

VEGAS VIDEO: $490 (~ $370 street price)
Company Web site: **www.sonicfoundry.com**

See description in Budget #2 (p. 59).
   Pros: One of the best video-editing tools on the market.

FINALCUT PRO: $999 (MSRP)
Company Web site: **www.apple.com**

See description in Budget #4 (p. 86).

SPECIAL EFFECTS SOFTWARE

ADOBE AFTER EFFECTS 5.1: $649 (MSRP) (~ $620 street price)
Company Web site: **www.adobe.com**

See description in Budget #4 (p. 87).

LIGHTWAVE 3D 7.0: $2250 (MSRP)
www.newtek.com

LightWave 3D is the special effects software that was used on the television series *Babylon 5.* Like other special effects software, LightWave 3D is designed to enhance your movie with special effects, whether you want to manipulate an image by giving a character glowing eyes or placing images of beads of water on a surface.

3D STUDIO MAX: $3495 (MSRP)
www.discreet.com

3D Studio Max is another special effects package that allows you to enhance your film with visual still and moving effects, from importing laser blasts to shadow and color effects manipulation within your footage.

MUSIC SOFTWARE

ACID MUSIC 3.0 (INCLUDED WITH DC1000 AND DC2000): $59.97 (MSRP)
Company Web site: **www.sonicfoundry.com**

See description in Budget #3 (p. 74).

SOUND FORGE 5.0: $399 ($300 street price)
Company Web site: **www.sonicfoundry.com**

See description in Budget #4 (p. 87).

VIDEO AUTHORING SOFTWARE

CLEANER 5 (MAC AND WINDOWS): $599 (MSRP) (~ $480 street price)
Company web site: **www.terran.com**

See description and picture in Budget #3 (p. 74).

IGNITER™ FOR MAC: $1149 (MSRP) (~ $1100 street price)
Company Web site: **www.auroravideosys.com**

A product for the Macintosh, the Igniter provides video compression to a low ratio of 1.5:1 with a speed of 13.3MB per second. It includes fully synchronized audio (up to 16-bit 48kHz stereo). Igniter is fully compatible with QuickTime MJPEG-A format and with FinalCut Pro.

MEDIA 100 iFINISH™ V20DV: $2995 (MSRP)
Company Web site: **www.media100.com**

This is an all-in-one product that includes video capture, editing, visual effects audio editing, media compression, and authoring. It allows you to present your movies in all the major formats (RealPlayer, QuickTime, and Media Player). The capture card lets you bring movies into your computer through an IEEE 1394 DV terminal, as well as S-video and composite terminals. Furthermore, you can integrate all of the editing, effects, and audio into QuickTime-based format.

    Pros: If you want to be a web producer, this is the product to get.

DVDIT PE: $749 (MSRP)
Company web site: **www.dvdit.com**

The Professional Edition is the same as the Standard Edition [see Budget #4 (p. 88)], but it has 99 support menus (instead of ten), has Dolby Digital encoding and file import, and contains DLT mastering support (so you can do mass duplication). It also includes a timeline editor, so you can trim scenes, if needed.

Pros: A good product for putting your movies onto DVDs and CDs in DVD menu format.

Cons: Cannot record movie files larger than 650-700MB onto a CD-ROM.

STREAMING MEDIA PLAYERS

QUICKTIME MOVIE PLAYER, REALNETWORKS REALPLAYER, AND WINDOWS MEDIA PLAYER.

See description in Budget #1 (p. 48).

RECOMMENDED SYSTEMS

See explanation in Budget #1 (p. 49).

#1: LEAST EXPENSIVE SYSTEM ~$15,000 (~$13,000)
Books: $108
DV Camera:
   Sony Pro DSR-PD150 MiniDV Camcorder: $4400 ($3200)
   Canon XL1S: $4700 ($4200)
Tripod:
   Slik 300DX: $170 ($100)
Stabilization device:
   Glidecam 2000 (with bodypod): $510 ($440)
   Glidecam Crane: $550 ($410)
Microphone:
   Sennheiser shotgun microphone and powering module (ME 66/K6): $565 ($430)
   (Add ~$400 for a boom)
   Nady 401 Four Channel Wireless Lavalier Microphone
System: $1210 ($625)
Lights:
   NRG Research Four-Light Kit: $1300
   Cool-Lux Cool-Kit Studio Kit LK2202: $2394 ($1900)
Computer:
   Dell Dimension 8100 series: $3446
Video storage:
   VideoRaid 2 bay 80 GB Storage (includes SCSI card): $1000 ($900)

Video capture card:
   DV 500 included with workstation: $650 ($550)
   Matrox RT2500: $1000 ($900)
Editing software:
   Premier 6.0 included with DV 500 and RT2000: $0
   Vegas Video: $490 ($370)
Special effects:
   Adobe After Effects: $650 ($620)
Music software:
   Acid Music 3.0: $60
   Soundforge: $400 ($300)
Video Authoring Software:
   Cleaner 5 (Mac and Windows): $600 ($480)
Streaming media players (free download versions): $0

#2: MIDRANGE SYSTEM ~$18,500 (~$17,000)

Books: $108
DV Camera:
   Sony Pro DSR-PD150 MiniDV Camcorder: $4400 ($3200)
   Canon XL1S: $4700 ($4200)
Tripod:
   Slik 300DX: $170 ($100)
Stabilization device:
   Glidecam 2000 (with bodypod): $510 ($440)
   Glidecam Crane: $550 ($410)
Microphone:
   Sennheiser shotgun microphone and powering module (ME 66/K66):
      $565 ($430)
      (Add ~$400 for a boom)
   Nady 401 401-LT Four-Channel Wireless Lavalier Microphone
      System: $1210 ($625)
Lights:
   NRG Research Four-Light Kit: $1300
   Cool-Lux Cool-Kit Studio Kit LK2202: $2394 ($1900)
Computer:
   DVLine Editing Workstation/Matrox RT 2500: $4491
Video storage:
   VideoRAID Two Bay 80GB (includes SCSI card): $1000
      ($900)
   VideoRAID RT Four bay 160 GB: $2000 ($1800)
Video capture card:
   DC1000: $1300 ($1200)
Editing software:
   Adobe Premiere 6.0 (included with DC1000): $0
   Vegas Video: $490 ($370)

Music software:
    ACID Music 3.0: $60
    Sound Forge: $400 ($300)
Special effects software:
    LightWave 3D: $2250
Video authoring:
    Cleaner 5 (Mac and Windows): $600 ($480)
    DVDit PE: $750
    Igniter (for Mac): $1150 ($1100)
    Pinnacle Impression for CD authoring (included with DC1000): $0
Streaming media players (free download versions): $0

#3: MOST EXPENSIVE SYSTEM ~$20,000 (~$18,000)
Books: $108
DV Camera:
    Sony Pro DSR-PD150 miniDV Camcorder: $4400 ($3200)
    JVC GY-DV500 miniDV: $4635 ($4300)
    Canon XL1S: $4700 ($4200)
Tripod:
    Slik 300DX: $170 ($100)
Stabilization device:
    Glidecam 2000 (with body-pod): $510 ($440)
    Glidecam Crane: $550 ($410)
Microphone:
    Sennheiser shotgun microphone and powering module (ME 66/K6):
        $565 ($430)
        (Add ~$400 for a boom)
    Nady 401 401-LT Four Channel Wireless Lavalier Microphone
        System: $1210 ($625)
Lights:
    NRG Research Four-Light Kit: $1300
    Cool-Lux Cool-Kit Studio Kit LK2202: $2394 ($1900)
Computer:
    Power Mac G4 Ultimate: $3807
Video storage:
    VideoRAID RT 4 bay 160GB: $1999 ($1800)
Video capture card:
    DC1000: $1300 ($1200)
Editing software:
    Adobe Premiere 6.0 (included with DVLine Matrox RT2500 and
        DC2000): $0
    Vegas Video: $490 ($370)
    Final Cut Pro: $1000
Special effects software:
    LightWave 3D: $2250

3D Studio Max: $3500
Music software:
    ACID Music 3.0: $60
    Sound forge: $400 ($300)
Video authoring:
    Pinnacle Impression for CD authoring (included with DC1000): $0
    Media 100 iFinish: $3000
Streaming media players (free download versions): $0

Video Streaming Your Films onto the Web

Until relatively recently, independent filmmakers had to rely on art houses, film festivals, and video stores to get their work shown to an audience. Out of the many films produced, only a few would ever make it to film festivals and the art-house circuit. Today, filmmakers no longer need to rely on these three limited outlets to get films seen. Through computer technology developed over the past few years, audiences worldwide can watch films that you, the independent or hobby filmmaker, have made. This chapter shows how you can participate in the online independent cinema movement.

In this chapter we lay out, step by step, the process of getting your film online so that people can view it with *video streaming* technology (by which a film is broadcast over the Internet and viewed on a computer screen without requiring audiences to wait for the film to download) as well as with downloads. First we show you how your film can be recorded from a videotape or DV camera to a computer using Windows Movie Maker and iMovie. Both of these are free software programs that come with the Windows Millennium (Windows Me) and Windows XP operating systems and the iMac and Power Mac G4 computer, respectively. They allow you to import your movie into your computer and edit it. Next, we describe how to convert your movie into three of the most popular video streaming viewers for Internet media broadcasting: *Media Player, QuickTime,* and *RealPlayer.* We take you through the steps involved in sending your movie to an existing Web site, and finally we show you how to create your own Web site using Microsoft FrontPage®. Note that the principles explored in this chapter can be applied using any software product. Read through the material and get familiar with the terminology. Use the specific product's manual if you have questions beyond the scope of this chapter.

After you shoot your movie, you will need to put it on your computer. This is done through the use of a *capture card.* Like an interpreter arranging a meeting between two people who speak different languages, the video capture card interprets the movie on videotape and translates the information into a form that the computer fully recognizes and understands the digital language. The same principle applies to both *analog video* (video information magnetically recorded) and *digital video* (video information digitally converted and recorded). The only difference between the two is the clarity of the translation, allowing for better understanding and communication. Apple's trademarked FireWire or Sony's I-LINK are the same thing: an IEEE 1394 four- or six-pin terminal allows for a pure translation from a DV camcorder to the computer. They speak the same language (digital), and there is nothing inhibiting the translation of information between the two. The information can go back and forth without any degradation of picture and audio clarity. With analog video (composite RCA and S-video connectors), information gets lost in the translation: the computer speaks digital, while the composite RCA and S-video speak analog. The computer translates the information into a digital format and thus understands and has available the information on your original film. But the clarity of the information, the fully realized fluency between an analog camcorder and computer, is much less than that of digital video translators because as the video is *compressed*—made smaller so as to allow more information to be stored onto a hard drive—the image becomes less clear.

If your movie is on film, then the first step is to get the film transferred to video tape. In our examples, we use a DV recording of a play produced at the Massachusetts Institute of Technology in August 2000, Kurt's Web site project, and a short film, *Intruder,* shot on 16mm black-and-white film in March 1996 by Scott Lancaster.

In the rest of this chapter we show you how to transfer a movie from videotape to your computer (Section I), how to convert the movie to a video streaming player (Section II), and how to place your movie onto the Web, whether uploading your movie to an existing site or building your own web site (Section III).

SECTION I—TRANSFERRING YOUR FILM FROM VIDEO TAPE TO COMPUTER

To transfer your film from videotape, you need to get an interpreter (the capture card) and install it on your computer. Once your DV camera or VCR is hooked up to the capture card's inputs and outputs, follow the steps outlined below to transfer the movie onto your computer. We use a Canon DV camera when explaining the steps used in Windows Movie Maker and a Sony DV camera for iMovie. In all cases, the same principles apply whether you are using a FireWire card from a camcorder to your computer or another analog video capture card.

USING MICROSOFT WINDOWS MOVIE MAKER

Windows Movie Maker comes as a standard feature of the Windows Me operating system, as well as W/Windows XP, the latest upgrade from Windows 98. The operating system is designed to meet the demands of Internet and digital video use. Its Movie Maker program allows you to import movies from a DV camera and from files on your hard drive. You can then edit your movie, add music and sound, and export it to the web either as an email file or directly to a web server. Furthermore, the movie file it creates is designed to be read by Windows Media Player, Microsoft's video streaming viewer. (You will need a IEEE 1394 capture card if you plan to import footage from your DV camera into Windows Movie Maker.)

The layout of Windows Movie Maker (see Figure 2.1) includes on the left side a list of files and folders called "Collections." The central window is the "Collections area," a list of your clips from the folder selected in the left window. To the right is the "Monitor," the window that allows you to see footage of your movie on the computer. Below the Monitor is a set of buttons that enable you to view and control the footage as on a VCR. The yellow bar above the buttons with a triangle pointing down shows your progression through the movie as it plays. You can also drag the triangle to move through the footage quickly. The first of the two buttons to the right of the VCR-style control buttons is the full-screen button, which displays your footage on the entire monitor screen. The button just to the right allows you to split your clip into pieces after you drag it into the timeline, the horizontal bar on the bottom of the screen. We explain these in more detail after showing you how to record your footage from your DV camera to Windows Movie Maker.

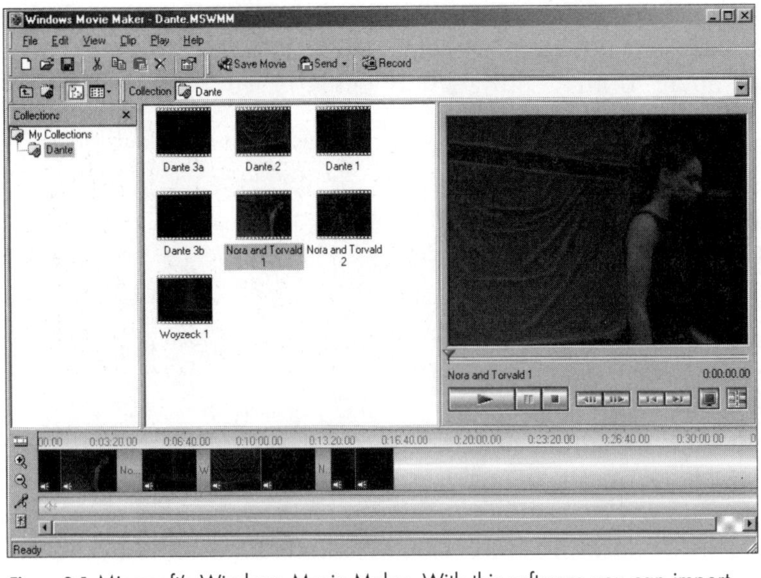

Step: 1. After you have loaded your software and plugged your DV camera into the FireWire port on the computer, Windows Movie Maker automatically detects the presence of your camera. Press the "Record" button, located on the top menu bar, just right of center. A pop-up menu appears, asking you, "What would you like to do?" (See Figure 2.2.) You are given three options:

Figure 2.1 Microsoft's Windows Movie Maker. With this software you can import your movie files, controlling it with VCR-like control buttons. Screen shot reprinted by permission from Microsoft Corporation. Trademark owned by Microsoft. Use of movie image courtesy of Kurt Lancaster. Kortney Adams as Nora.

"Automatically start recording my video from the beginning of my tape"; "Begin recording my video from the current position on my tape"; or "Do not record at this time."

You will be taken to the screen showing you Movie Maker's "Record" window, listing several options for you to consider before recording (see Figure 2.3). Starting on the upper left-hand side, the "Record" mode shows either "Video and audio" (for video recording) or "Audio" (if you're recording audio from a CD player, for example). Below the Record window are listed the types of "Video device" and "Audio device" attached to the computer. In our case it lists the Canon DV camera for both ("Canon DV Device"). The "Change Device"

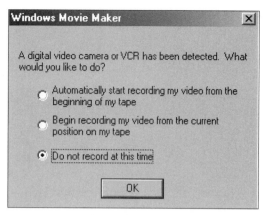

Figure 2.2 Microsoft's Windows Movie Maker. With this software you can import your movie files, controlling it with VCR-like control buttons. Screen shot reprinted by permission from Microsoft Corporation. Trademark owned by Microsoft.

button gives you the option of choosing the recording device, provided you have more than one device attached to your computer, such as a VCR.

Step: 2. In the middle left-hand side of the "Record" window (Figure 2.3) are listed three options you can select to tell the computer how to record your clips: "Record time limit" (the computer automatically records only a certain number of minutes); "Create clips" (the computer cuts your recording into small-sized clips); and "Disable preview while capturing" (for slower computers, so your computer's resources are not used up while it records your clips). Set your three choices. (We choose to unclick "Record time limit" so we can record any length. Since we don't want the computer to cut our scene into smaller clips, we also unclick "Create clips." We want to preview our movie as it records, so we do not choose "Disable preview while capturing.")

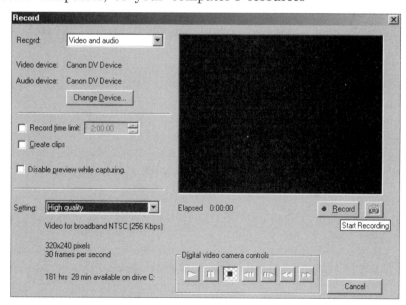

Step: 3. Next, choose the quality of the recording by selecting your capture "Setting" (as shown

Figure 2.3 The record screen for Windows Movie Maker allows you to control the settings of your file you want to record. Screen shot reprinted by permission from Microsoft Corporation. Trademark owned by Microsoft.

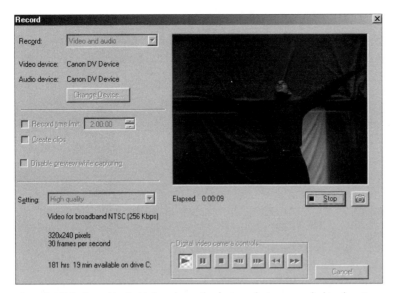

Record dialog window showing capture settings

Figure 2.4 Windows Movie Maker shows the footage being recorded in the view screen area. Screen shot reprinted by permission from Microsoft Corporation. Trademark owned by Microsoft. Use of movie image courtesy of Kurt Lancaster. Anand Sarwate as Dante.

near the bottom left side of Figure 2.3). You are given a choice of "Low quality," "Medium quality," "High quality," and "Other," each determining the quality of your capture. The higher quality setting requires more hard drive space, while the lowest setting requires the least amount of space. "Other" allows you to choose from a preselected menu providing optimized settings, depending on how you want to output your movie to the Web. Such choices include whether to send it so it can be viewed by someone with a 28.8K modem, all the way up to "video for broadband 768K" (for people with cable modems). (We choose "High quality" so our movie will look the best it can on the Web.) Below these choices is a summary of what you have chosen. At "High quality," the computer will capture the footage at "Video for broadband NTSC (256Kbps)," meaning that it is set for broadcast in North America (NTSC) at a bit rate of 256K (requiring a high speed-modem for viewing using video streaming; someone could still download it and watch it from her computer without worrying about the streaming rate, since it would be recorded to the hard drive before playing). Below this information is the frame size and frame rate of the movie: "320X240 pixels" (size of the screen the movie will stream—each pixel is one dot on your computer monitor) and "30 frames per second" (the standard video rate of images broadcast on video and on television, as opposed to 24 frames per second of film.) On the next line is the computer's calculation of the amount of space available on your hard drive for video capture. If you choose a higher quality recording, you will have less space available.

Step: 4. On the bottom center of the window (Figure 2.3), under "Digital video camera controls," is a set of VCR-style buttons for controlling your camera (Play, Pause, Stop, Slow rewind, Slow forward, Fast rewind and Fast forward. Above and to the right is the "Record" button (which reads as "Stop" when the computer is recording your footage). To the right of this is an image of a 35mm camera, allowing you to take a still snapshot of your footage as an image file. Press "Play" and your footage appears in the window. At the point where you want it to start recording, press "Record." When you have finished recording your clip, press "Stop." (See Figure 2.4.)

Step: 5. The computer prompts you with a standard Windows "Name File" prompt. Type in the name of your clip and where you want to record it on your hard drive. Your footage has now been transferred to the computer. Repeat these steps until you have imported all the footage you want to use in editing your movie.

EDITING YOUR MOVIE

The next procedure explains how to edit your footage using Windows Movie Maker. Alternatively, you can import the file into a higher-end editing system, such as Vegas Video or Adobe Premiere.

Step: 1. After your clips have been recorded onto the hard drive, they appear in the Collections area of Window Movie Maker's main screen (see Figure 2.1). The clips that appear in the central Collections area can be dragged and dropped into the workspace along the horizontal bar on the bottom of the screen, which includes the storyboard (the visual, linear layout of each clip file you have dragged into the workspace) and timeline (the linear layout of your movie according to time, and the place where you can trim your clips). Drag the clips you have captured into the storyboard window in the order you want them to appear in your movie.

Step: 2. The small fim strip button located on the upper left side of the storyboard window allows you to switch from storyboard mode to the timeline (see Figure 2.5). Click the button. The two magnifying glass symbols below the button you just clicked (marked with the " + " and "—" signs inside) allow you to increase or decrease the units of time per inch on the timeline. We press the icon with the " + " sign a few times so that 1 inch on the timeline equals about 20 seconds. Below the magnifying glasses is a microphone symbol, indicating the timeline of any audio recording you might want to place in your movie (such as music from a CD). The slider button below the microphone symbol allows you to adjust the audio level of your video and audio tracks so that you can make the audio track louder or quieter than the sound on the video track (the audio footage recorded on your movie).

Step: 3. You can select any clip in the timeline by clicking it once with your mouse (see Figure 2.5). After one of the clips is selected, the ruler above the timeline turns yellow and two small triangles appear in its corners. Drag these triangles to set the start and

Figure 2.5 A close-up of the time line for Windows Movie Maker.

end points of your clip, trimming any footage you don't want. The yellow bar turns gray where the discarded footage is trimmed away. The clip automatically adjusts itself to the new size. Note that once you adjust the clip, it is permanently set.

Step: 4 Once you have trimmed all of your clips to the desired size, you can view your entire movie from beginning to end. On the menu bar located at the top of the screen, click "Play" (see Figure 2.1) and then select "Play Entire Storyboard/Timeline." You also may want to overlap transitions by dragging the beginning of one on top of the end of another for a cross-fade. You can also create special fades and effects on your DV camera, recording them on tape and then transferring them from your camera to your computer as clips in your Collections area. You can drag and drop these transitions into the timeline.

ADDING MUSIC AND SOUND

Step: 1. You may want to import music or other audio files into the Collections area so you can drag them to the audio timeline (below the movie's timeline, beside the microphone symbol). To bring in an existing sound file, go to the top menu bar and click on "File." Drag the mouse to "Import." Browse your hard drive to find the audio file you want. Double-click the file; it will be brought in as a clip in the Collections area. (You can also do the same thing for existing video files you may have on your hard drive.) If you want to record music from your CD player, click the "Record" button located at the far right of the menu bar (the same one you used to bring in your video footage from your DV camera), as shown in Figure 2.1. Click "Change Device" (Figure 2.3) and choose either "Line-In" or "CD Player," depending on whether you have your CD player connected to the line-in on your sound card or if you are using your CD-ROM drive (see Figure 2.6).

Uncheck "Create clips" and click "Record" when you are ready to record

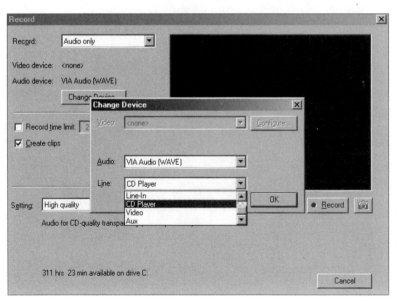

Figure 2.6 Windows Movie Maker allows you to input audio files in order to complement your movie. Screen shot reprinted by permission from Microsoft Corporation. Trademark owned by Microsoft.

your music from your CD player. When you have finished recording the selection you want, click "Stop." Windows Movie Maker prompts you to name the file before saving it. An audio icon appears in the Collections area, with the name of your selection below the icon. Drag-and-drop the file into the audio timeline. There, you can trim the file or move it to any point along the timeline.

FINAL STEPS

Step: 1. Select "Save Movie" on the top menu bar (see Figure 2.1). Fill in the title of the movie, your name, and a short description of your movie (see Figure 2.7). (For the selected scenes from the play Kurt directed, "A Doll's House: Between Heaven and Hell," we type in this title, list Kurt as the author, and provide a description: "Musing on the failed relationships of love, Dante leads us down into hell.") You can also set the rating of your movie, such as PG-13.

Step: 2. Click "OK." A "Creating Movie" window pops up stating, "Please wait while your movie is being created" along with a status bar (see Figure 2.8). You can click the "Cancel" button if you decide you are not ready to render the movie.

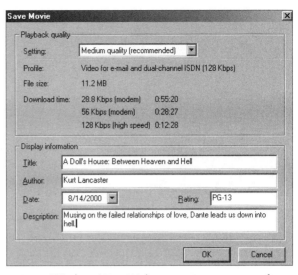

Figure 2.7 Windows Movie Maker gives you a summary of your movie to be saved as a Windows Media Player movie file. Screen shot reprinted by permission from Microsoft Corporation. Trademark owned by Microsoft.

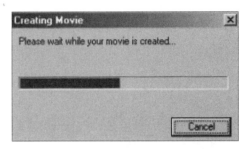

Figure 2.8 The status bar for Windows Movie Maker shows the process of your movie being converted into a Windows Media Player file. Screen shot reprinted by permission from Microsoft Corporation. Trademark owned by Microsoft.

At this point your movie is complete. It has been converted into a Windows Media Player file and can be viewed with your Windows Media Player. The movie is located on your hard drive and will play on your Windows Media Player if you double-click it. Go to Section III (p. 124) to learn how to put your movie up onto the Web.

USING APPLE'S iMOVIE

Apple's iMovie is included with iMacs and Power Mac G4s. If your Macintosh has a built-in FireWire card, then you are ready to capture and edit your movies. Films you create with iMovie will play on Apple's QuickTime video streaming player.

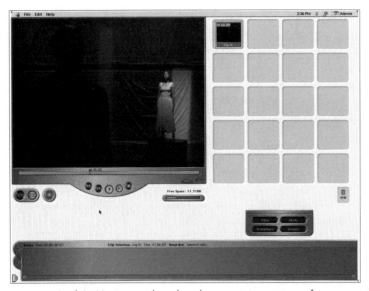

Figure 2.9 Apple's iMovie provides a bare-bones movie creation software. This screen shows the movie clip files, a video screen, and a timeline. Screen shot of software used by permission from Apple Computer, Inc. Image of movie used by permission of Kurt Lancaster. Laura Lapointe as Beatrice. Anand Sarwate as Dante.

Like Windows Movie Maker, iMovie (see Figure 2.9) has a "Monitor" or video window (on the left side of the screen), with a set of VCR-style control buttons on the bottom of the video screen. Each clip you import is loaded in one of the little windows within the right side of the screen. At the bottom of the main window is the timeline. Just below the video monitor window and to the left are three buttons: a video camera icon (for recording footage from your DV camera), a film strip icon (for viewing the main screen, as shown in Figure 2.9), and a computer monitor icon (for viewing your movie in full-screen mode). To the right of these buttons is a bar showing how much "Free Space" you have on your hard drive. Directly below the clips window is a small window showing four buttons: "Titles," "Music," "Transitions," and "Sounds." Clicking any of these buttons will open a small pop-up window, listing various options for typing in the title of your movie, importing music and sounds, and creating transitions (such as fade-outs). Along the bottom of the screen is a timeline, where you can switch between video and audio modes. This is the place you bring your clips to edit your movie.

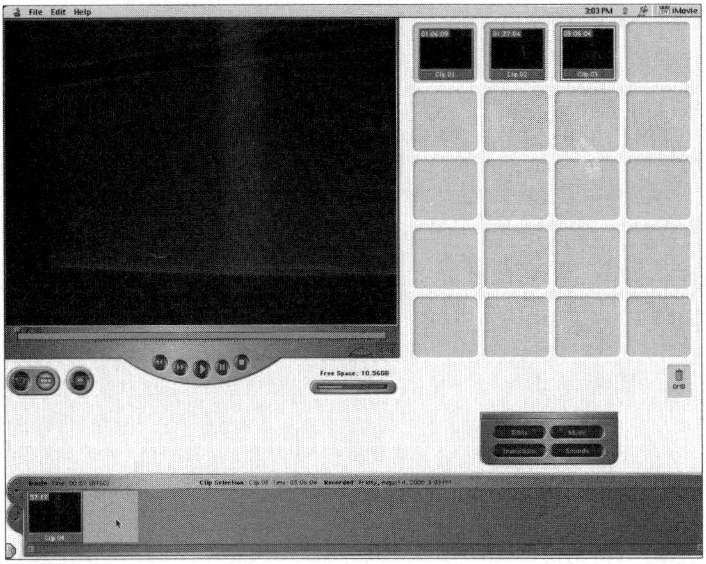

RECORDING

Step: 1. Load the program. Click the camera icon to record your movie. You can access your DV camera through the VCR-style buttons (Rewind, Fast-forward, Play, Pause, and Stop) located on the bottom of

Figure 2.10 Apple's iMovie allows you to drag and drop your movie clips into the timeline on the bottom of the screen. Screen shot of software used by permission from Apple Computer, Inc. Image of movie used by permission of Kurt Lancaster. Laura Lapointe as Beatrice.

the screen window. The volume control is on the bottom right corner of this window. Above the camera control buttons there is an "Import" button (appearing only when you click the camera icon; it's not visible in Figure 2.9, which shows movie clip mode). As soon as you press the import button, your footage will record onto the hard drive and the clip will appear in the clips window area. Press stop when you have finished recording the clip. Repeat this step until you have recorded all of the footage you want to edit.

Step: 2. Drag-and-drop your clips into the timeline (see Figure 2.10). Click on one of your clips, then click the mouse button and keep it depressed as you drag the image into the timeline on the bottom of the screen. Let go of the mouse button. The clip appears in the timeline. Do this for your other clips. You can move the various clips along the timeline and even delete them. (The original clip in the clips window will not be deleted.)

ADDING FEATURES

Step: 3. Select transitions to place between your scenes by clicking the "Transitions" button below the clips window. A menu of various transitions and a mini-viewscreen open (see Figure 2.11). Menu choices include such standard film features as "Cross Dissolve" (where one image from the previous clip will fade out and dissolve into the image in the next clip on the timeline), as well as "Fade In" and "Fade Out" (where the image will fade to black then fade in from black). You can preview each feature by pressing the "Preview" button in this menu window. The preview will appear in the small window, which also lists the duration of the transition.

Once you have decided which transition you want, drag it with the mouse from the mini-viewscreen window and drop it in the timeline between the two clips where you want your transition to appear. An icon of the transition choice you made appears between the two clips, with anchor points on the icon (Figure 2.11).

Figure 2.11 The transition screen for Apple's iMovie allows you to preview the transitions in the mini movie screen on the right. You can drag and drop the transitions between clips on the timeline. Screen shot of software used by permission from Apple Computer, Inc. Image of movie used by permission of Kurt Lancaster. Laura Lapointe as Beatrice. Anand Sarwate as Dante.

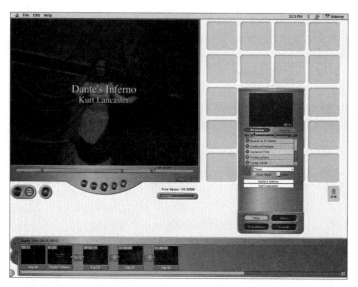

Figure 2.12 Apple's iMovie also allows you to place titles onto your movie clip. Screen shot of software used by permission from Apple Computer, Inc. Image of movie used by permission of Kurt Lancaster. Laura Lapointe as Beatrice.

Step: 4. Add titles and credits to your movie. Go to the same menu window that contains "Transitions" and choose the "Titles" option (see Figure 2.12).

The menu window provides space for you to write in the title and director of the movie (or any other credit you want to include, such as actors). You can also choose the font type, its color, and the duration of the title onscreen before it fades out. The menu allows you to choose such additional title effects as "Bounce to Center," "Centered Multiple," "Centered Title," "Flying Letters," "Flying Words," and so forth (which can be previewed by clicking the "Preview" button in the small window). (We chose the standard "Centered Title.") Just as with the fade effects, you can "Preview" the title, then drag-and-drop the title from the small viewscreen window to the place in the timeline where you want the title to appear. (You can even place it on one of your clips and the title will be composited into the movie image, as can be seen in our example in the video window in Figure 2.12.)

Step: 5. Use the same method for adding music and sound to your movie. Select "Music" or "Sounds" in the menu window located below the clips area window (see Figure 2.13). You can record music from a CD or record a voice-over through a microphone. You can also import existing sound clips. After you import or record the sounds you want, they will appear in the clips area window. Press the eighth-note symbol (right below the eye symbol) on the timeline. Drag and drop the audio files into the audio timeline as you see fit. You can trim their length as well as move them around the timeline. To the right of the audio timeline is a "Fade In" and "Fade Out" button, allowing you to fade the audio level of your sounds in and out.

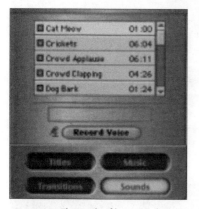

Figure 2.13 The audio file in Apple's iMovie menu allows you to input audio files from a list, or you can record your own audio files from a microphone or CD-player. Screen shot of software used by permission from Apple Computer, Inc.

FINAL STEP

Step: 1. Save the movie. Click "File" on the top menu bar (shown in the upper left corner of Figure 2.12) and scroll down to "Save." You have successfully imported, edited, and added transitions and titles to your movie. Your project is now saved as an iMovie file. To learn how to render the movie into QuickTime format, go to Section II (p. 115).

SECTION II—CONVERTING YOUR FILM TO VIDEO STREAMING FORMAT

In this section, we show you how to convert your movie, now stored on the computer, into a format that allows others to see it over the Internet using video streaming technology. Once your film has been edited and any music or sound added, you need to take it through another interpreter—the video streaming software that converts your movie file on the computer to a movie that can be placed on the Internet as a video streaming file. We show you how to convert your movie into formats for Windows Media Player, Apple QuickTime, and RealNetworks RealPlayer using Windows Movie Maker, iMovie, and RealNetworks' RealProducer, respectively.

USING WINDOWS MOVIE MAKER TO CONVERT YOUR FILM TO WINDOWS MEDIA PLAYER

Movie Maker converts your movie into Media Player format when you save your movie. Go to Final Steps (1 and 2) of Windows Movie Maker in Part I (as shown in Figures 2.7 and 2.8, page 111). The file you created in those steps is on your hard drive, so skip ahead to Section III (page 124) and learn how to send your movie to the web.

USING APPLE'S iMOVIE TO CONVERT YOUR FILM TO APPLE QUICKTIME

ESTABLISHING YOUR VIDEO SETTINGS

Step: 1. Click the "File" button on the top menu bar and scroll down to "Export Movie" (see Figure 2.14 for a picture of the main screen with the menu bar on top). You are prompted to choose "Camera," or "QuickTime." If you want to save your movie onto a

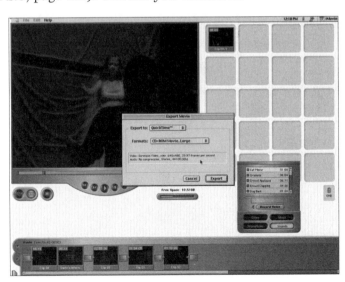

Figure 2.14 Before converting your footage into a complete QuickTime movie in Apple's iMovie, you can set the audio and video quality of the movie. Screen shot of software used by permission from Apple Computer, Inc. Image of movie used by permission of Kurt Lancaster. Laura Lapointe as Beatrice. Anand Sarwate as Dante.

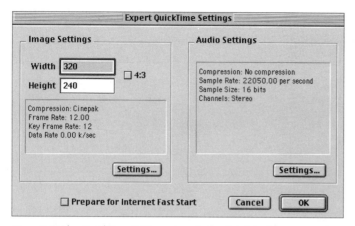

Figure 2.15 The QuickTime Settings menu in Apple's iMovie. Screen shot of software used by permission from Apple Computer, Inc.

DV tape, choose "Camera" and your movie will be sent to your DV camera for recording (be sure to first insert a blank tape). If you want to export it to "QuickTime" format, then you will be asked to choose among several preselected formats for recording the movie: "Email Movie, Small"; "Web Movie, Small"; "CD-ROM Movie, Medium"; "CD-ROM Movie, Large"; and "Expert" (see Figure 2.14). Each determines the quality of your movie image and the size of the file: "Web Movie, Small" provides the lowest quality and the smallest file size, while "CD-ROM Movie, Large" gives you the best quality image, but with a large file size. We chose "Expert" so we can change how the video file and audio portion of the file will be compressed see Figure 2.15.

In the "Expert" settings window you are given a summary of the current settings, as well as buttons to click should you want to change the "Image Settings" and "Audio Settings."

Step: 2. Under "Image Settings" (Figure 2.15), you can set the screen ratio of your movie, which will be set in the standard 4:3 (the dimensions of standard computer and television screens). The size of the image is 320X240 pixels. Below this is a window displaying a summary of the image setting you chose in the "Settings" window. Click the "Settings" button.

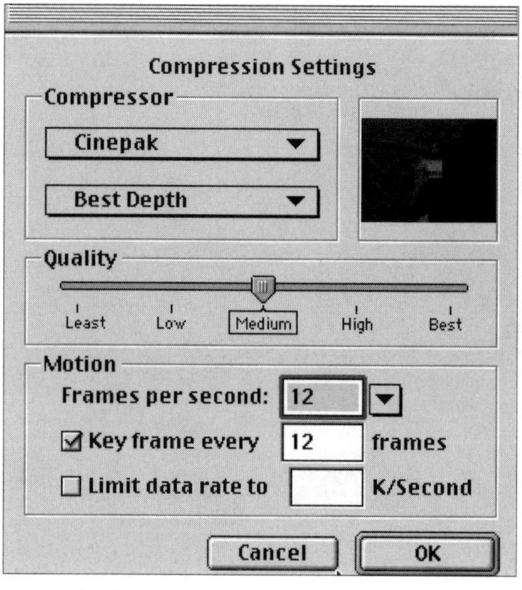

Step: 3. The "Settings" window allows you to select how your movie will be compressed on your hard drive (see Figure 2.16).

Choose the "Compressor" you want to use (such as "Cinepak," "Sorenson" or one of the others)—each one is a computer program that uses a different algorithm to determine how your movie gets compressed. Experiment with them to see which one works best for you. (We chose "Cinepak.")

In the expert settings, the "Quality" slider allows you to choose the image quality of your movie (from "Least" to "Best"). The "Motion" section of the window allows you to set the

Figure 2.16 The Compression Settings for converting your file into a QuickTime movie in Apple's iMovie. Screen shot of software used by permission from Apple Computer, Inc.

frame rate ("frames per second"), which will be adjusted automatically as you adjust the "Quality" slider. "Medium" gives you 12 frames per second—an acceptable image rate, but not the high-quality image of full-motion video (which is close to 30 frames per second). You can also set your "Key frame every X of frames." The key frame is the video image with the best quality of the video you shot. The other frames use less data and contain just enough information to calculate the image based on the quality of the data contained in the key frame. Furthermore, you can set the data rate of your movie for video streaming purposes with the "Limit data rate to X K/Second" option, such as 56K/Second, for 56K modems. Click "OK."

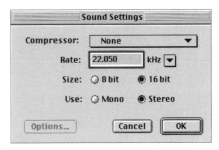

Figure 2.17 The Sound Settings for converting your file into a QuickTime movie in Apple's iMovie. Screen shot of software used by permission from Apple Computer, Inc.

ESTABLISHING YOUR AUDIO SETTINGS

Step: 1. After completing your video settings, press the "Settings" button in the "Audio Settings" window of the "Expert QuickTime Settings" section (Figure 2.15). You are taken to the "Sound Settings" window (Figure 2.17).

In this window, choose how you want your audio compressed and how you want to set the quality of the sound. (We chose "None" under "Compressor," since we don't want the audio to be compressed—this choice means we will use more hard drive space, however.) You can set the audio rate, which will also be adjusted depending on what you select under "Size" and "Use." (We chose "16-bit" "Stereo," providing an audio sampling rate of 22.050kHz— high-quality sound, but not the same as the higher quality 44kHz.) Press "OK" when you are done. The "Expert Quick-Time Settings" window displays a summary of your audio settings (see Figure 2.15).

FINAL STEP

Step: 1. Press "OK" in the "Expert QuickTime Settings" window. Your movie will be converted to a QuickTime Player file and saved on your hard drive

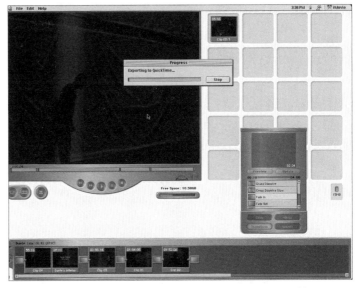

Figure 2.18 Apple's iMovie shows a status bar as it converts your file into a QuickTime movie [Screen shot of software used by permission from Apple Computer, Inc.]

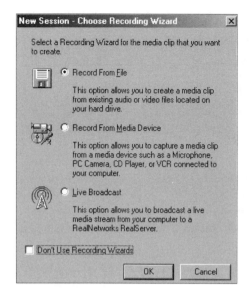

Figure 2.19 RealNetworks' RealProducer Recording Wizard Screen allows you to choose the type of movie you want convert to RealPlayer format. Screenshot used by permission from RealNetworks.

(see Figure 2.18). Name the file and tell the computer where to record it. After the movie is recorded, you can send it over the Internet or record it to a disk. When you double-click your movie file, the movie will play on your QuickTime player. If you want to learn how to send your movie to the Internet go to Section III (p. 124).

USING REALPRODUCER TO CONVERT YOUR FILM TO REALPLAYER

Below, we take you through the process of converting your movie file on your hard drive into a RealPlayer format using RealProducer Plus. However, the steps detailed are the same if you are instead using RealProducer Basic. In this example, we examine Kurt's first monologue, "To Touch a Rose," from his Web narrative Letters from Orion (located at www.lettersfromorion.com).

START UP

Start the program. The "New Session—Choose Recording Wizard" will prompt you at each step as you prepare your movie (Figure 2.19).

The Recording Wizard asks you to select the kind of Recording Wizard you want to activate. If you do not see an image similar to Figure 2.19, the Wizard is off and you will see the main start screen of the program instead (Figure 2.20); go to the "File" menu in the upper left-hand corner of the screen, click on "Recording Wizards" in the drop-down menu, and select one of the three options: "Record From File," "Record From Media Device," or "Live Broadcast." We select "Record From File," since we have already captured our movie onto the hard drive. If you need to capture your movie

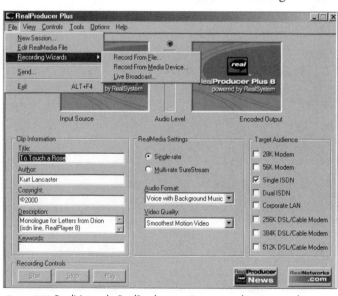

Figure 2.20 RealNetworks RealProducer main screen, showing you how to locate the "Recording Wizards" menu. The layout of the screen presents all the information you can select for converting your movie into the RealPlayer format. Screenshot used by permission from RealNetworks.

footage from your DV camera or VCR, select "Record From Media Device." Live Broadcast is a feature that allows you to import a file directly into RealProducer as you are recording it (such as live music through a microphone or video through a DV camera).

INPUTTING THE DATA FOR REALPRODUCER WIZARD

This is an eight-step process that allows you to tell the program how you want your movie compressed for RealPlayer playback.

1. Locate your movie file

Input the location on your hard drive of the movie file you wish to convert. Click the "Browse" button until you locate your film. It will appear in the "File Name" window (Figure 2.21). Click the "Next" button.

2. Fill in your movie info

Type in the requested information on the "RealMedia Clip Information" page (see Figure 2.22). Include the movie clip's title, author, copyright information, a brief description, and any keywords you want to associate (for possible searches on the Internet). The title of your movie will appear on the top bar of RealPlayer when it is viewed. Click on "Next."

3. Choose your server type

In RealProducer, you can choose to have your movie converted into one of two different RealPlayer types: "Multi-rate SureStream" or "Single-rate."

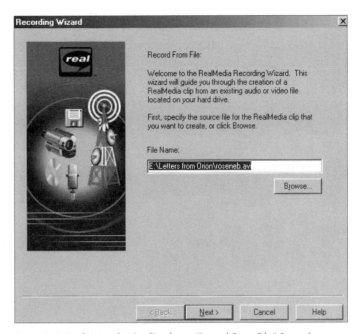

Figure 2.21 RealNetworks' RealProducer "Record From File" Recording Wizard. Here, you type in the location of the movie file you want to convert to RealPlayer. Screenshot used by permission from RealNetworks.

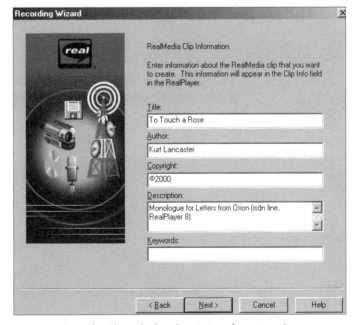

Figure 2.22 Input the title and other descriptive information about your movie in RealNetworks' RealProducer. Screenshot used by permission from RealNetworks.

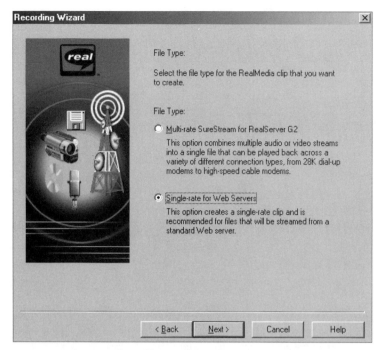

Figure 2.23 Select one of two file types for RealNetworks' RealProducer.
Screenshot used by permission from RealNetworks.

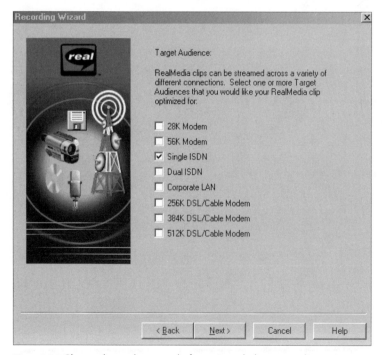

Figure 2.24 Choose the modem speed of your intended target audience in RealNetworks. Screenshot used by permission from RealNetworks.

SureStream, a format for Web servers that host the RealServer G2 or later server, allows viewers to stream your movie as a single file at any modem rate (from 28K to cable modems). Unless you will be uploading your movie onto a Web site that hosts a RealServer G2 server, do not choose this option. Instead, choose "Single-rate for Web Servers," which allows you to create one movie file rated for only one speed (see Figure 2.23). Press "Next."

4. Choose your Modem speed

Check off the modem speed of your intended target audience (see Figure 2.24). If you want as many people as possible to access your film, choose "56K Modem"; you will lose picture and sound quality, but most people with modems will be able to access your film. People with high-speed connectons (such as DSL or cable modems) will be able access the slower speed file, of course. (In order to increase image quality, we choose "Single ISDN.") Press the "Next" button.

5. Choose your audio format

You are taken to the "Audio Format" window (Figure 2.25). Here, you can select the kind of audio compression you want for you movie: "Voice Only," "Voice with Background Music," "Music," or "Stereo Music" (for sound recorded in stereo). The higher the quality chosen (such as stereo), the greater the bandwidth required, resulting in less bandwidth for the video image; increasing audio quality will sacrifice video quality. RealProducer optimize the balance between audio and video bandwidth depending on what you choose. (We choose "Voice with Background Music.") Press "Next."

6. Choose your video replay quality

In the "Video Quality" window (Figure 2.26) you can choose from several options, each one balancing the bandwidth of video and audio differently: "Normal Motion Video" (for use with normal-looking movies), "Smoothest Motion Video" (for movies with little motion, such as interviews), "Sharpest Image Video" (providing increased image clarity in movies with a lot of motion), and "Slide Show" (providing the best image quality in still-image shots). Since our movie is a monologue (a single actor speaking into the camera), we choose "Smoothest Motion Video." Click on "Next."

7. Name your movie file

In the "Output File" window (Figure 2.27), enter the location and name of your RealMedia movie file. (We

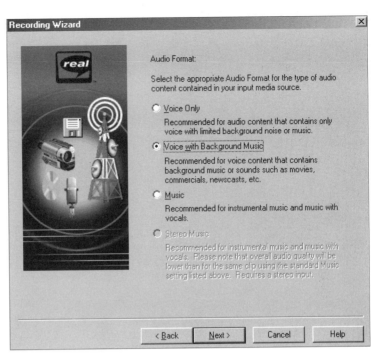

Figure 2.25 Several audio formats are available when compressing your movie into RealPlayer format in RealNetworks' RealProducer. Screenshot used by permission from RealNetworks.

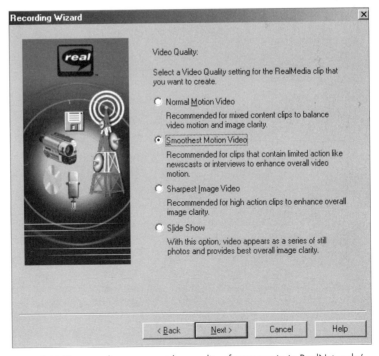

Figure 2.26 You can choose your video quality of your movie in RealNetworks' RealProducer. Screenshot used by permission from RealNetworks.

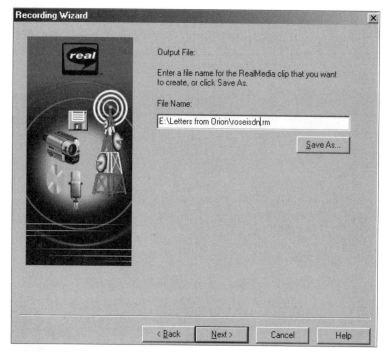

Figure 2.27 Name your movie file in RealNetworks' RealProducer. Screenshot used by permission from RealNetworks.

place this clip on the computer's "E" drive [an external hard drive we use for video storage] and name it "roseisdn.rm"). Click "Next."

8. Review the data

Review the information provided by Real-Producer in the "Prepare to Record" screen, a summary of the data you have chosen in the previous steps (see Figure 2.28). If you want to change anything, press the "Back" button. If everything looks good, complete the wizard by clicking "Finish." The "Recording Wizard" closes and you are taken to the main screen.

COMPRESS YOUR MOVIE

On the main screen (Figure 2.29) you can see all of the information you inputted in the "Recording Wizard." You can even open the various windows and drop-down menus and change any data before the movie conversion starts. Once you have reviewed all of your settings, click "Start." As RealProducer compresses your movie, you can choose to click "Stop" in the "Recording Controls" menu on the bottom left of the screen (see Figure 2.30). When the recording is complete, you can click "Play" to review the compressed RealPlayer movie. The Real-

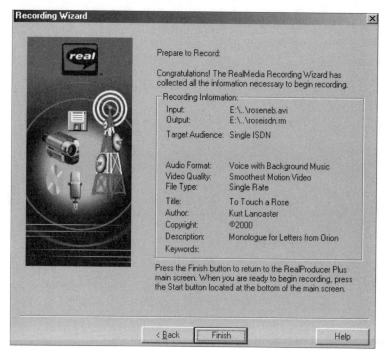

Figure 2.28 Review your movie data in RealNetworks' RealProducer before it is compressed into RealPlayer format. Screenshot used by permission from RealNetworks.

Player movie is now on your hard drive. You can play it any time by opening it with RealPlayer. The movie can also be uploaded to a Web site (see Part III).

You can see the extent of the movie's compression by comparing the original file size of the movie to the file size of the RealPlayer version. Our original "To Touch a Rose" example starts at 161MB. A compressed 56K modem version is 1.6MB (bringing its size down nearly 99 percent), while a high-speed modem version of this same clip measures at almost 11.5MB, still significantly smaller than the original version.

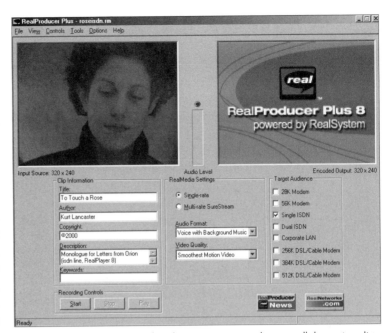

Figure 2.29 RealNetworks' RealProducer main screen showing all the various lists that you can choose when converting your movie into RealPlayer format. Screenshot used by permission from RealNetworks. Movie image from *Letters from Orion: To Touch a Rose* courtesy of Kurt Lancaster. Jessica performed by Rachel Werkman. Web site located at: www.lettersfromorion.com

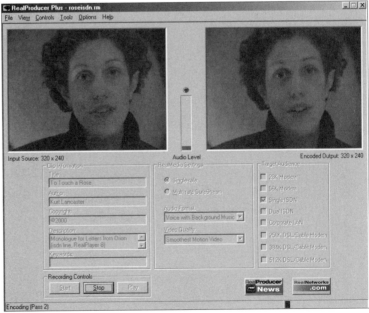

Figure 2.30 RealNetworks' RealProducer compresses your movie into a RealPlayer format. Screenshot used by permission from RealNetworks. Movie image from *Letters from Orion: To Touch a Rose* courtesy of Kurt Lancaster. Jessica performed by Rachel Werkman. Web site located at: www.ettersfromorion.com

Section III—GETTING YOUR FILM ON THE WEB

A Web site for your films is essentially a virtual movie theater. In this section, we walk you through the steps it takes to place a film on an AOL Web site. (You can find Internet Service Providers [ISP] that provide various amounts of free storage space for your Web pages and movies. Just do a Web search using such key words as "free Web space.") First, using Movie Maker and iMovie, we show you how to put your movie onto the Web site you created. Then we show you how to build a Web site using Microsoft FrontPage and how to post it to the Web using AOL. Also, we include the steps it takes to link your Web site to a bulletin board discussion list so you can receive audience feedback.

UPLOADING YOUR FILM USING WINDOWS MOVIE MAKER

To send your Windows Media Player movie file, you will need to get an ISP and a personal Web site (see "Building a Web Site Using FrontPage," page 126).

Step: 1. In Windows Movie Maker, click the "Send" button near the top menu bar (see Figure 2.1). You are given two options: "E-mail" and "Web Server." If you want to send the movie as an email attachment, choose "E-mail." If you want to send it to your existing Web site, choose "Web Server." You will then be given the "Send Movie to a Web Server" window (Figure 2.31). Here, you can select among the various options for the playback quality of your movie, including "Setting" ("Low quality," "Medium quality," "High quality," and "Other"), "Profile" (a description of the modem speed associated with the "Setting" for streaming or downloading a film), "File size" (the size of the movie file in megabytes), and "Download time" (the amount of time it takes for viewers to download your film, depending on their modem's speed of access). The window also provides information about the movie (the "Title," "Author," "Date," "Rating," and "Description"). After you choose and fill in the information you want, click "OK."

The movie will now be compressed according to the compression options you have selected. Name the movie file when prompted.

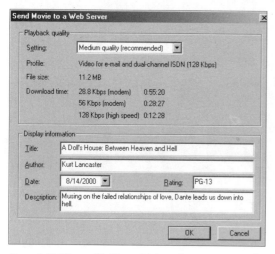

Figure 2.31 Microsoft's Movie Maker allows you to send your movie directly to a web server. This screen summarizes your movie information. Screen shot reprinted by permission from Microsoft Corporation. Trademark owned by Microsoft.

Step: 2. When the movie is compressed, the "Send to Web" window pops up (Figure 2.32). You are given the option to "Place this media file" you have just created "In my home page directory" or "In this folder in my site" (you enter the name of the folder on your Web site where you want to send your movie file). You must also enter the information for "Web site host settings," including the name of your ISP, or "host name," (which for us is AOL).

Step: 3. If your ISP is not on the list given, you have to choose "user added provider," which will take you to "Create Web Host Settings" (Figure 2.33). In this window you enter the name of your ISP, the address of the site, the address to which you want to send your movie, and the name

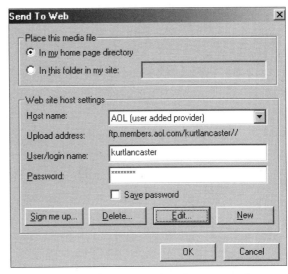

Figure 2.32 Microsoft's Movie Maker allows you to choose the location to send your movie to the web. Screen shot reprinted by permission from Microsoft Corporation. Trademark owned by Microsoft.

of the home page for your Web site. In the "Advanced settings" section, you can choose either "Use passive FTP semantics" or "This Web site host requires anonymous login" (required for AOL). (FTP stands for *File Transfer Protocol*, and it is yet another interpreter allowing the Web page stored on the computer to be sent to an ISP like AOL.) After you fill in this information, click "OK," and in the "Send to Web" window (Figure 2.32), enter in the additional information (the "User/login name" and "Password").

Step: 4. Make sure you are online, then press "OK" in the "Send to Web" window (Figure 2.32). If you entered all your information properly, the movie will be sent to the Web.

Step: 5. Your movie can now be played from the Web. Open your Web browser, type in the Web address of your movie, and view your film. (The web address is the same one you typed in Fig. 2.33.)

UPLOAD YOUR FILM USING iMOVIE

Apple's iMovie does not enable you to upload your film directly to the Web. After you have converted it into a QuickTime

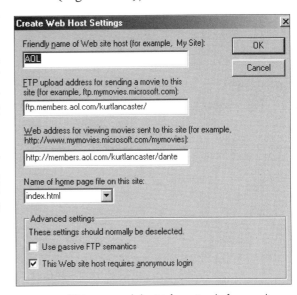

Figure 2.33 Fill in your web host information before sending your movie to the web in Microsoft's Movie Maker. Screen shot reprinted by permission from Microsoft Corporation. Trademark owned by Microsoft.

file (see p. 115), it can be uploaded to any Web site using any FTP software. Additionally, examine the steps in "Building Your Own Web Site Using FrontPage" (p. 126), or you may want to submit to an Internet Cineplex (see Chapter 4, p. 149). These will give you a good place to start in deciding where and how you want to upload your QuickTime movie to the Web. We use a RealPlayer example, but the process is the same for QuickTime or Media Player movie files. Just substitute your movie's name and follow the steps.

UPLOAD YOUR FILM USING REALPRODUCER

RealProducer has a simple Web editor that allows you to create a Web site within its program. It also includes features that allow you to upload this Web page to your ISP. Rather than showing you the details involved in creating and uploading a Web site with RealProducer, we prefer to show you the steps outlined below, "Building a Web Site Using FrontPage." In this way we won't repeat ourselves, given that the principles applied below can also be used in the RealProducer Web editor. In addition, the steps we prove below also include the process by which you can create a bulletin board discussion link for audience feedback.

BUILDING A WEB SITE USING FRONTPAGE

We use the FrontPage 98 Web Editor to explain the steps you need to take to create a Web site to contain your movie. Having your own Web site allows you to market your own films, as others can visit and view your films. Although we use FrontPage 98 in our example, other Web page creators such as Macromedia's Dreamweaver® or Adobe GoLive® can also be used. Even though these steps are specific to FrontPage, similar steps apply to these other software packages. Once you're familiar with this process, you'll be able to adapt it to other Web creation software since the principles are generic enough for use in any of them. Again, the Web addresses are used as an example and are not active. The actual location of this site can be found on www.dawn-joy.com/orion/kurt/intruder.htm.

In "Stage I: Setting up the Page," we outline the steps necessary for creating a Web site containing the short film, "Intruder" written by Kurt and directed by Scott Lancaster. Then we show you how to use an existing Web

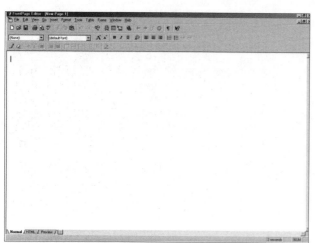

Figure 2.34 The opening screen for Microsoft's FrontPage. Screen shot reprinted by permission from Microsoft Corporation. Trademark owned by Microsoft.

site to create a free discussion list so you can receive audience feedback on your film ("Stage II: Providing Audience Feedback"). In "Stage III: Uploading the Web Page," we quickly show you how to send your movie file to the Web site you have created.

STAGE I: SETTING UP THE PAGE

Step: 1. Open your Web page editor (Figure 2.34). (We open FrontPage 98.)

Step: 2. Go to the File menu in the upper left-hand corner and drag the cursor down to "Page Properties." Click on the "Background" menu tab (Figure 2.35). You will be given the option to change the background color

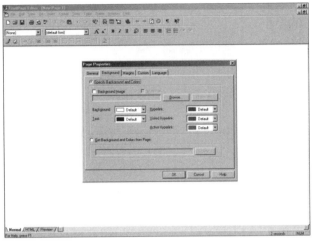

Figure 2.35 Choose your background and text colors in Microsoft's FrontPage. Screen shot reprinted by permission from Microsoft Corporation. Trademark owned by Microsoft.

as well as the color of the text. On the righthand side of the screen is a set of colors to choose from for names of hyperlinked files, such as the name of your movie file on your Web site. When someone clicks on the file name, the color will change to the "Visited Hyperlink" color. When you move the mouse cursor over a hyperlinked file name and click on it, the name will change color to the "Active Hyperlink" color. If you want to create a background image, then check the "Background Image" box in the upper left-hand side of the window.

Step: 3. After choosing the background colors and image, enter the title of your movie or Web site. You can list several movies. Figure 2.36 shows our page, with a black background and light blue text for the title of the film "Intruder."

If you want to add a background image, follow these steps. After clicking the "Background Image" box on the upper left-hand side of the window (Fig. 2.35), click on the "Browse" menu button to the right of the long, blank rectangle window, below the small "Background Image" button you checked. The "Browse" button allows you to browse your hard drive files so you can find the image you want to use (see Figure 2.37). Double-click the desired image file. (We double-click "intruder.jpg.") The computer

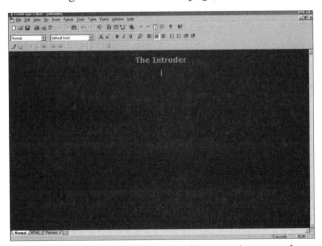

Figure 2.36 Start typing in your text, just like a wordprocessor, for your web site in Microsoft's FrontPage. Screen shot reprinted by permission from Microsoft Corporation. Trademark owned by Microsoft.

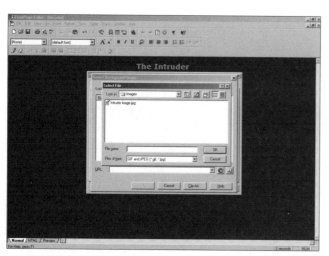

Figure 2.37 Select an image file on your hard drive to place on your web site in Microsoft's FrontPage. Screen shot reprinted by permission from Microsoft Corporation. Trademark owned by Microsoft.

takes you back to the "Page Properties Background" menu and lists the path of the image file in the file-name field below the "Background Image" field. Click "OK." Your Web page background should now show a set of wallpaper-style images of the image file you chose (Figure 2.38).

Figure 2.38 shows the page with a background image from the movie.

Step: 4. We prefer to use a black background for this page and insert one picture that best represents the film. We go back to FrontPage, drag down the "File" menu, click on "Page Properties," then the "Background" tab. Unclick "Background Image," and click "OK."

Step: 5. With the screen background now black, choose the center justification button on the menu bar. Then go to the menu bar and drag down the mouse cursor to "Image" (Figure 2.39). Search your hard drive for the image you want (Figure 2.40). Double-clicking the file automatically inserts the image into the Web site (Figure 2.41).

You now need to create the link to the movie file you created using either Windows Movie Maker, iMovie, or RealProducer; follow the steps from Section I if you don't have a movie file rendered. In any case, you want to work with a compressed file that can be read by either RealPlayer, QuickTime, or Media Player.

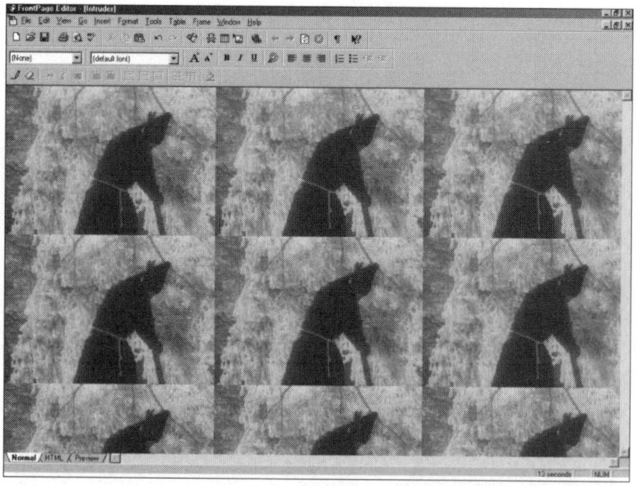

Figure 2.38 Background image in "tile" mode in Microsoft's FrontPage. Screen shot reprinted by permission from Microsoft Corporation. Trademark owned by Microsoft. Image from Intruder directed by Scott Lancaster. Used with permission. Dwarf played by Brian Johnson.

Step: 6. Click once on the image that you have imported. You will create a hyperlink from this picture, meaning that when someone clicks on this image the film will play. You can do the same thing by using a text menu, listing several different versions of your movie. (When you render a movie, you typically render it for a certain speed, be it for a 56K modem or a cable modem). Click the link icon (the image of Earth with a chain link below it). You will see the

Edit Hyperlink window (Figure 2.42). This window allows you to create a link to another web page from the image or text you just selected—or, in our case to the movie file—that will play when a user clicks on the image. In the URL file window (the one that has "http://" listed) enter the location of your movie file. We enter the URL of the movie on our AOL site along with the screen name, "lancasterdigital"; the folder name, "intruder"; and the Real Media file, "Intruder.rm." The URL reads http://members.aol.com/lancasterdigital/intruder/intruder.rm".

On the Edit Hyperlink page (Fig. 2.42), there are four buttons to the right of the URL address. The first two buttons allow you to create a hyperlink to a page on the Web or to a file on your hard drive. The third button allows you to create a hyperlink that sends email. The fourth creates a new Web page on the FrontPage editor, allowing you to provide an automatic link to this page from a menu of existing pages you have created. For our purposes, we don't need to use these other hyperlink options right now. After you have entered the Web address of your movie file, press "OK." In the event the user does not have RealPlayer, we provide a text link to the Real.com home site where the RealPlayer product can be downloaded for free.

Step: 7. Write a short blurb describing what your movie is about. We put ours below the image file from the movie. We have also created text links on the bottom of the screen that can take the user to other Web pages providing film credits, comments from the director, and audience feedback (see Figure 2.43). Also notice the border that has been placed around the picture; this shows that the image has a hyperlink, which, when clicked, takes visitors to the movie. If the border isn't there, highlight the picture, click on the

Figure 2.39 Select an image file on your hard drive to place on your web site in Microsoft's FrontPage. Screen shot reprinted by permission from Microsoft Corporation. Trademark owned by Microsoft.

Figure 2.40 Select the image file you want to place your web site in Microsoft's FrontPage. Screen shot reprinted by permission from Microsoft Corporation. Trademark owned by Microsoft.

Figure 2.41 This time, you will have a single image centered on your web site. Screen shot reprinted by permission from Microsoft Corporation. Trademark owned by Microsoft. Image from Intruder directed by Scott Lancaster. Used with permission. Dwarf played by Brian Johnson.

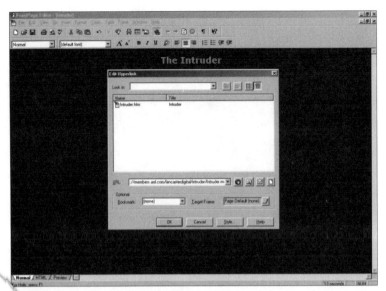

Figure 2.42 Clicking the image file presents a hypertext link page where you can select the file you want to be linked to your image in Microsoft's FrontPage.

HTML tab, and place a "1" where the HTML code says: "< p > < img border = "0"."

In producing each link, we highlight the phrase that we want to link and create the Web page that will include this information. For example, we highlight "Credits," then click on the "Hyperlink" icon (as explained in step 6). Instead of typing in the URL address, click on the fourth button to the right of the URL address bar (see Figure 2.44). This allows you to create another web page which will insert the URL of the page in the address bar when the page is created. We take similar steps when creating the "Director's Notes" page (see Figure 2.45); write the text you want and import the image again. As a shortcut, you could select (highlight) the contents of the previous page by pressing the Control A keys (copy all) on the keyboard and then import them into the new page by pressing Control V (paste). For the "Audience Feedback" page, we want to use an existing Web site providing free bulletin board access, which takes us to the next stage.

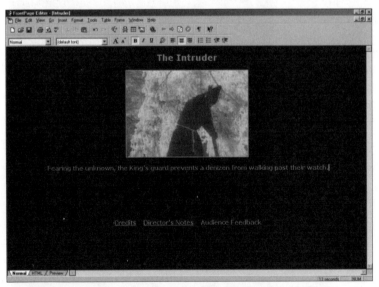

Figure 2.43 Write a short description below the image file in Microsoft's FrontPage. Note the border around the image. This indicates that there is a file linked to this image. When a user clicks on the image, the movie will play. On the bottom of the screen are links to other pages for this movie site. Screen shot reprinted by permission from Microsoft Corporation. Trademark owned by Microsoft. Image from Intruder directed by Scott Lancaster. Used with permission. Dwarf played by Brian Johnson.

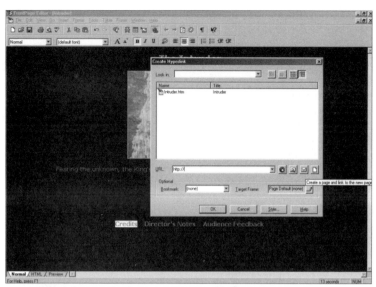

Figure 2.44 Clicking on the "New Page" icon in the Hypertext window allows you to link text or image to a new web page in Microsoft's FrontPage. Screen shot reprinted by permission from Microsoft Corporation. Trademark owned by Microsoft.

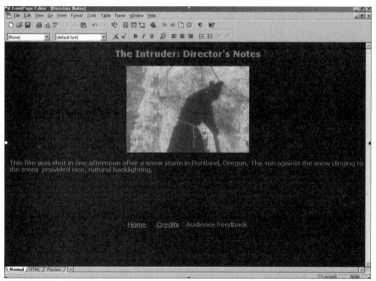

Figure 2.45 We fill out information on the "Director's Notes" page in Microsoft's FontPage. Screen shot reprinted by permission from Microsoft Corporation. Trademark owned by Microsoft. Image from Intruder directed by Scott Lancaster. Used with permission. Dwarf played by Brian Johnson.

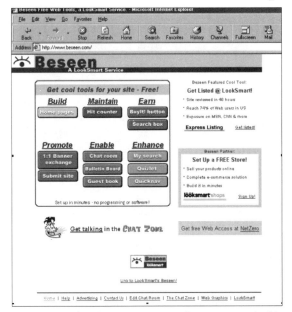

Figure 2.46 LookSmart's Beseen page allowing you to build a free web site, chat rooms, bulletin boards, and guest books (www.beseen.com). Select the Bulletin Board icon. Screen shot reprinted by permission of LookSmart.

STAGE II: PROVIDING AUDIENCE FEEDBACK

Step: 1. For audience feedback, we use a free public-access bulletin board on a Web site at www.beseen.com. If you're interested in using their service for creating a bulletin board discussion list go to their site (see Figure 2.46).

This site allows you to use Beseen's own tools to build web sites, set up a store, maintain a hit counter (so you can see how many people have entered your site), and set up a chat room, bulletin board, and guest book. All of these tools are free.

Step: 2. Click on "Bulletin Board" under the "Enable" menu, which takes you to the site that introduces you to the bulletin board service (Figure 2.47).

Step: 3. Click on "Start" at the bottom of the page. This takes you to the bulletin board registration page. Fill out your name and email address, and click on one of the categories that best classifies your web site. (We chose the "Movies" category.) Type "Yes" if you agree with Beseen's terms of service, then press the "Submit" button on the bottom of the screen (see Figure 2.48).

Step: 4. After registering for the bulletin board site, you will receive an email from beseen.com that includes a temporary password, your bulletin board's address, and directions on how to link your Web site to your newly created bulletin board. Your email will resemble the one below:

```
Hello,

Welcome to Beseen - a Looksmart
service, the leading category-based
Web directory. Your Beseen Bulletin
board has been set up and is readyto
use.

The address of your Bulletin board
is:

http://pluto.beseen.com/boardroom/
o/48314/
```

Figure 2.47 LookSmart's Beseen bulletin board page. Select "Add a Bulletin Board!" text. Screen shot reprinted by permission of LookSmart.

Please make a note of the following important information about your account:

Account Number: o48314
Temporary Password: 42Gate
Your Planet: pluto

You will need to remember your account number, password, and planet in order to customize your Bulletin board. When you are ready to make some changes, visit your Administration Page:

http://pluto.beseen.com/boardroom/o/48314/Admin

Here you will find utilities to change the colors of your Bulletin board, add graphics, change some of the features, clear old messages, and change your password to something more easily remembered. Be sure to book-mark your Administration Page so you can always get to it easily when you need to.

Figure 2.48 LookSmart's Beseen bulletin board registration page. Fill in the appropriate information and press "Submit." Screen shot reprinted by permission of LookSmart.

The key piece of information here is the address (or URL) of the new bulletin board we want to use for "The Intruder" audience discussion list: http://pluto.beseen.com/boardroom/o/48314/.

Step: 5. Before going to our bulletin board, we want to change our password as well as to add important information to our site. Enter the Administration Page address as they list it (for us, this is http://pluto.beseen.com/boardroom/o/48314/Admin). You will be taken to a page that looks like Figure 2.49.

Figure 2.49 After receiving an URL and password for your bulletin board from LookSmart, you can enter the bulletin board administration site. Type in your password. Screen shot reprinted by permission of LookSmart.

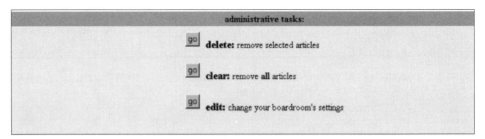

administrative tasks:

go **delete:** remove selected articles

go **clear:** remove **all** articles

go **edit:** change your boardroom's settings

Figure 2.50 LookSmart's Beseen bulletin board administrative task window allows you to delete, clear, and edit your bulletin board. Screen shot reprinted by permission of LookSmart.

Step: 6. Enter the password they gave you. (For us this is "42Gate.") This takes you to the administrative tasks page, where you have the option of deleting selected comments from your bulletin board, removing all of the comments, and changing your settings (Figure 2.50).

Step: 7. Select the third task, "edit." You are now at the administration page, where you can change your password, change the colors of the background and text, set up rules on how people will use the site (such as requiring visitors to include their names and email addresses). You can also enter the name for your bulletin board site as well as provide a link to your own site (see Figures 2.51 and 2.53).

The various menu options that allow you to change the color of your background, text, link (hyperlink), visited link, table, and table background (of the bulletin board list) all use standard HTML color code. If you want to know what that code is, you must go into FrontPage 98 or another editor, change various colors, and examine the HTML code in the HTML page section (see the highlighted line in Figure 2.52, which shows the color codes for background color, text color, and link color). After experimenting with the various colors, you can then enter that informa-

edit your boardroom settings

appearance

8080FF	**text color:** the color of plain (non-linked) text, like this
000000	**background color:** the background color of the page
FF8000	**link color:** the color of hyperlinks
FFFF00	**visited link color:** the color of visited hyperlinks
000000	**table background color:** the background color of the message list, for example
FF8000	**table heading color:** the color of the table title bars, for example

room title:

The Intruder audience discussion

enter the title of your BoardRoom discussion area

title graphic:

http://members.aol.com/lancasterdigital/intruder/intruder.jpg

enter the URL (address) of a graphic on your server you would like to place at the top of all of your boardroom pages (including the "http://" part), or simply leave it blank if you do not wish to use a title graphic

background image:

enter the URL (address) of a graphic on your server you would like to use as a background image (include the "http://" part), or simply leave blank if you do not wish to use a background image

behavior

Figure 2.51 You can edit your settings in "edit your boardroom settings" page in LookSmart's Beseen bulletin board. You can even change the color of the background screen and the text. Screen shot reprinted by permission of LookSmart.

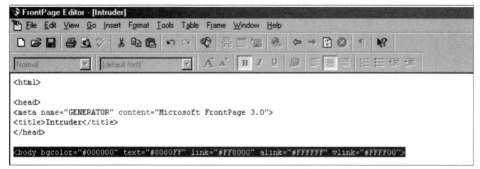

Figure 2.52 Microsoft's FrontPage allows you to view the HTML computer code of your web site. Here you can see the code for background and text images. With this information, we can change the background color and text color of the bulletin board so it matches the color of the web site containing our movie. Screen shot reprinted by permission from Microsoft Corporation. Trademark owned by Microsoft.

tion in the "Appearance" section of "Edit Your Boardroom Settings" (Figure 2.51). (We want to design the colors of the bulletin board to match the colors of our site, so we change them accordingly.) Enter the title of the page and the location of the image from your movie to be placed on your Web site. (We use the room title "The Intruder Audience Discussion." We want to continue using *The Intruder* image for our Web site. The name of the image is "intruder.jpg," loaded to our Web site on AOL.)

The beseen.com site also allows you to set the "behavior" or rules for those who visit your site (See Figures 2.51 and 2.53). Answer the various questions by clicking on "Yes" or "No." Under the "Miscellaneous" menu, you are asked for an "Escape link" address and the text for this escape link; this allows the user, who is on the bulletin board, to return to your homepage containing your movie. Also, enter your email address so people can email you directly if they have any questions about the site. (You can put in another person's email address, if someone else is administering your site.) The menu also gives you the option of changing the password, which we have done.

With all the information in place, you

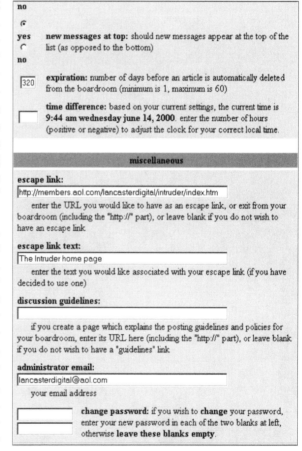

Figure 2.53 You can edit your settings in "edit your boardroom settings" page in LookSmart's Beseen bulletin board. Here, you can provide a link to your website so users can return to your movie page after visiting the bulletin board page. You can also change your password here. Screen shot reprinted by permission of LookSmart.

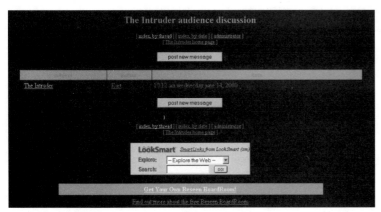

Figure 2.54 Our LookSmart's Beseen bulletin board after we have changed the background and text colors. Screen shot reprinted by permission of LookSmart.

can now take a look at your bulletin board (Figure 2.54). The page can be seen by browsing to the site address provided by beseen.com. Visitors to your site can click on the "Post new message" button to post a message about your film or films.

Step: 8. You need to create the link from your page to your bulletin board site. (In FrontPage 98, we highlight the "Audience Feedback" text on thebottom of The Intruder page, then select the hyperlink icon. We enter the bulletin board address in the URL window (see Figure 2.55), then press "OK."

Step: 9. As a courtesy to beseen.com, which is providing you with a free bulletin board discussion list, you should include their logo on your movie page. At the bottom of the email message they sent, they provided HTML code to be placed on your page:

```
<!--Begin Beseen.com Button-->
```

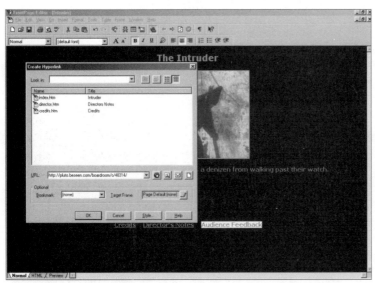

Figure 2.55 In Microsoft's FrontPage, enter the URL of the bulletin board address in the hyperlink page. This link will allow visitors to you web site to enter the bulletin board site. Screen shot reprinted by permission from Microsoft Corporation. Trademark owned by Microsoft. Intruder directed by Scott Lancaster. Movie image used by permission. Dwarf performed by Brian Johnson.

```
<img
src="http://www.be-
seen.com/images/beseen-
button1.gif"
   align=absmiddle
   height=31 width=88
alt=--"Beseen.com--">
   <!--End Beseen.com
Button-->
```

Go to FrontPage 98 and click on the HTML tab in the bottom left-hand corner of the screen. Cut-and-paste the beseen.com code in the location where you would like it to appear. (We placed it near the bottom of the screen, after our text list of Credits, Director's Notes, and Audience Feedback [Figure 2.56].)

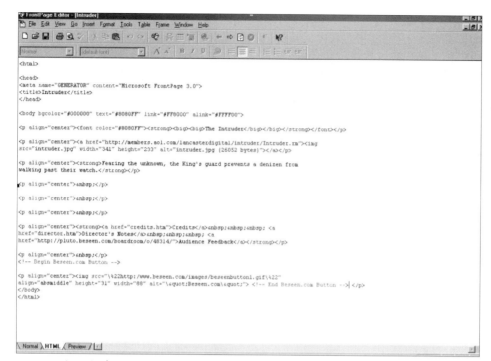

Figure 2.56 Input Looksmart's Beseen graphic icon by going to the HTML page and inserting it at the bottom of the screen. Screen shot reprinted by permission from Microsoft Corporation. Trademark owned by Microsoft.

You are now ready to upload your Web site! On to Stage III.

STAGE III: UPLOADING THE WEB PAGE

We now go through the steps for up-loading your Web site and movie to the Internet. We continue our example of using the pages we created with FrontPage for *The Intruder* movie, uploading the files to AOL.

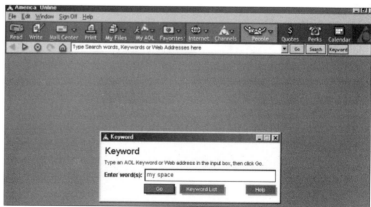

Step: 1. Enter AOL (under the screen name to which you wish to send the movie), click on "Keyword," enter "My space," and then hit "Go" (Figure 2.57).

Step: 2. AOL's "My FTP Space" page lists several options on the right side of the

Figure 2.57 We go to "my space" on AOL in order to upload our web site built using Microsoft FrontPage. AOL screen shot copyright 2000 American Online, Inc. Used with permission.

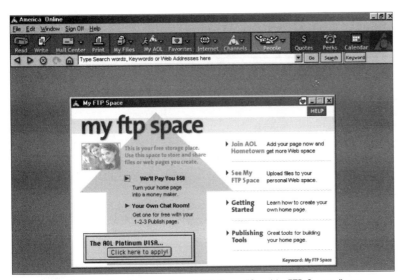

Figure 2.58 We go to "my ftp space" on AOL. Press "See My FTP Space." AOL screen shot copyright 2000 American Online, Inc. Used with permission.

window (Figure 2.58). The first choice is "Join AOL Hometown," which you may want to do if you require more storage space than the 2MB limit. If you join, you will receive 12MB of storage space. For now, click on the second choice, "See My FTP Space."

Step: 3. You will be taken to the FTP directory page, "Connected to members.aol.com" Figure 2.59, which lists two files: an AOL "Readme" file (providing directions on how to use this space) as well as a director named "Private" (for those using AOL's Web publisher creator). Neither of these items is needed, and they can be ignored. At this point, you can either upload the files directly to the FTP directory (such as members.aol.com/your screen name), or you can choose to have the Web page and movie sent to a subdirectory folder.

Step: 4. Click on "Create Directory" on the bottom of this window (Figure 2.59) and create a folder (in our case, "intruder" [Figure 2.60]). This is the "Remote Directory Name," a subdirectory of "lancasterdigital."

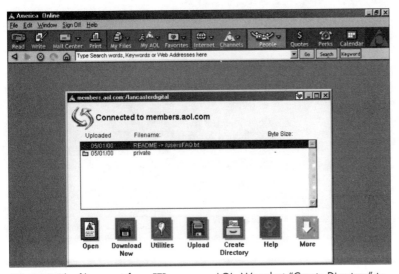

Figure 2.59 The file menu of our FTP space on AOL. We select "Create Directory" to place our movie files. AOL screen shot copyright 2000 American Online, Inc. Used with permission.

Step: 5. After creating the subdirectory, click on the "Upload" button, the middle icon on the bottom of the window. Type in "index.htm," the name of the first page (or home page) of your Web site. See Figure 2.61.

Step: 6. Click "Continue" and select the file from your hard drive (Figure 2.62). Double-click the file and then click on "Send." The file loads itself onto the AOL site. Select the other files for your Web site including images. One at a time, repeat this step until all of your pages and images are loaded. (In our example, we select and load the other two pages of our site, "credits.htm" and director.htm," as well as the movie image we used when creating the Web site, (intruder.jpg.)

You can now enter the address of your site in a Web browser, which will take you to your movie's web site. When entering a URL in the Web browser address window you can omit "index.htm"—the browser will automatically assume it and go to the first page of the site. Check all of your hyperlinks and the bulletin board discussion link to make sure that they are working properly. With that done, you are ready to send your movie onto your site.

Step: 7. Go to your ISP's site and upload the film as you would a normal file. (We go back to My Space in AOL, and just as in the previous steps, we go into our subdirectory file, intruder, and click on "Upload." We search our hard drive for the Real Media file we made for the film *The Intruder* [Intruder.rm] [Figure 2.63].)

With the film loaded, now you and anyone else around the world with an Internet connection can watch your film. You may want to provide separate versions of your film for several different modem speeds, in which case you must render each version (see pages 00-00) and then upload the different files to your site. Our final Web page appears as in Figure 2.64:

Congratulations! You have just created your own Internet cineplex.

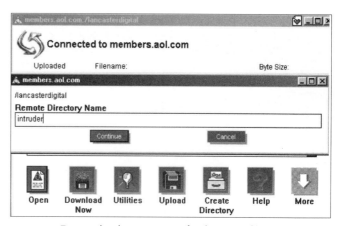

Figure 2.60 Type in the directory name for the movie file on AOL. AOL screen shot copyright 2000 American Online, Inc. Used with permission.

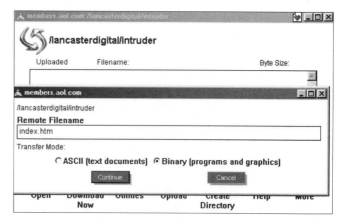

Figure 2.61 After selecting "Upload File," type in the name of your web page. Select "Binary" and press "Continue." AOL screen shot copyright 2000 American Online, Inc. Used with permission.

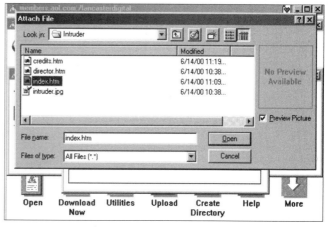

Figure 2.62 You can browse your hard drive to find your web page files. Press "Open." You will choose your files one at a time. AOL screen shot copyright 2000 American Online, Inc. Used with permission.

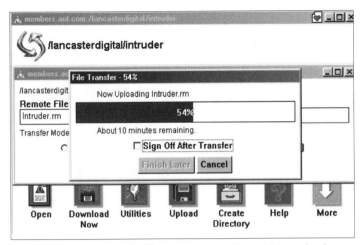

Figure 2.63 AOL uploads your files one at a time. Here, AOL is uploading the Intruder movie file. AOL screen shot copyright 2000 American Online, Inc. Used with permission.

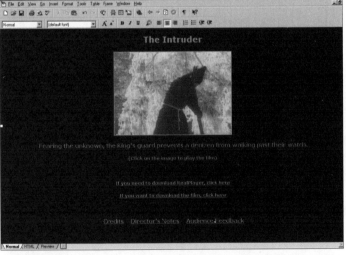

Figure 2.64 The final look of our web site for *The Intruder*. Directed by Scott Lancaster. Used with permission. Dwarf performed by Brian Johnson. Screen shot reprinted by permission from Microsoft Corporation. Trademark owned by Microsoft.

Now that you have completed your site, you may want to post your web pages to a site that gives you free web space. Go to http://100best-freewebspace.com, a resource listing different companies that offer free web space.

There are many ways to design a Web site. Choose a style unique to you and that best promotes the style of your film. Experiment with it. Have fun with it. In any case, some may ask, Can you make money on the web by charging "admission" fees to watch and/or download your films? Maybe. Like Stephen King, you need a lot of clout to demand money from your viewers. Beseen.com does give you the opportunity to set up a free store, and by using it you could easily sell your films online. Look at their site if you're interested: http://shops.looksmart.com. (If you want their company to build the e-store for you, they charge $90.) You should keep in mind that most sites allow free viewings of movies, but that may change in the future as Internet cineplexes become more established as cultural institutions.

Transferring Your Film onto a CD-ROM and DVD

As a filmmaker, you don't want to store your movie on your hard drive. You probably want to keep available space open for future film projects, and in case of a hard drive failure you want a back-up. You can record your movie on your camera or store your movies online, allowing others to access your film over the Internet (see Chapter 2). In addition, you may want to record your movies onto a recordable CD (CD-R) with a rewritable CD-ROM drive (CD-RW) so you can give away copies of your movies, thus enabling people to play your movie using their CD-ROM drives. You can also record your films so that people with DVD players can watch them on their television sets.

Sonic Solutions, a California-based software authoring company, has published DVDit!, a fairly inexpensive product (under $500) that allows you to create a DVD-formatted movie—including graphics, menus, and playback options found on traditional DVDs—which is recorded onto a CD-R disc and can be played on either a CD-ROM or DVD drive. Sonic Solutions provides a software DVD player so the DVD you make will play back on any PC. DVDit! converts your movie file into a DVD-formatted file, which can then be recorded onto a CD-R, a hard drive, or a DVD-R/RW drive.

This chapter will focus on how to convert your film into a DVD-formatted file that can be recorded to a CD-R, hard drive, or a DVD-R/RW. If you don't have DVDit!, you can still record your movie onto a CD-R disc. Go to "Recording Your Movie onto a CD-ROM with Direct CD" (page 144). There, we include instructions for recording your movie onto a CD-R disc as a regular file using Roxio's (formerly Adaptec's) popular DirectCD software (which comes as a standard feature of most CD-RW drives). In addition, with Windows XP you will be able to drag-and-drop files onto CD-R/RW discs without using any special software.

We show you the steps it takes to convert and record short films. One of the advantages of recording your shorts onto a CD-R disc is its large storage capacity (650MB, much more than the standard 1.44MB floppy disc and 4.7GB with a DVD-R disc), allowing you to record many shorts onto it. With DVDit! you can create a menu, just like on a regular DVD, that lets you select the movie you want to play.

Recording Your Movie Onto CD-ROM and DVD With DVDit!

INITIAL SETUP

Step: 1. Choose the "Start A New Project" button in the center of the screen (Figure 3.1).

The next screen will prompt you to choose a format for the movie (NTSC or PAL). Choose NTSC if you are in North America, Central America, or Japan; PAL is for locations in Europe, China, Australia, and South America. After completing the initial setting, you're ready to begin converting your movie into the DVD format.

COMPLETING THEMES

Step: 1. DVDit! comes with several palettes with different themes, allowing you to choose certain background types and buttons that express a certain style or theme. For this example, you'll use the default theme that comes with the software. (Figure 3.1 shows the phrase: "Theme: Default" in the upper right corner of the screen.) You can add your own images and video to it.

Step: 2. At the bottom of the palette window are five buttons: "Backgrounds," "Buttons," "Text," "Media," and "Play" (see the bottom right corner of Figure 3.1). Clicking on any of the first four buttons will show you different palettes of background images, button choices, fonts for text, and other media you import. (The "Play" button brings up a virtual remote control for your movie when it is completed.) Fonts for text are present in all the themes (including the default theme—these are the fonts available on your computer, such as those seen in your word processor). The buttons and backgrounds are artwork images provided by DVDit! Click on the "Media" button.

FIRST PLAY

The next step entails creating a "first play" window—the first image or clip that appears on-screen when the CD or DVD is placed into the CD-ROM drive or DVD player. (We are going to use the movie *Intruder* as our example for conversion to a DVD format. We want the viewer to see a still image from this movie to comprise the "first play" image.)

Figure 3.1 Opening page for Sonic Solutions' DVDit! ©2000 courtesy of Sonic Solutions—www.sonic.com.

Step: 1. First, you need to import the image into the "Palette window" on the right-hand side of the screen. In the Palette window you will place your various files and images, called "assets." Since our *Intruder* image is not on the asset list, we need to import it. Click on the "Media" button (the fourth icon from the left on the bottom of the Palette window).

Step: 2. Go to Windows Explorer and import your file. We look for the intruder.jpg image and drag-and-drop it into the Palette window (see Figure 3.2).

Figure 3.2 Import your files into the "Palette window" on the right. Sonic Solutions' DVDit! ©2000 courtesy of Sonic Solutions—www.sonic.com.

Step: 3. Click once on the image you imported to highlight it, and drag it to the placeholder menu to the immediate left of the palette (which displays a small black thumbnail-square labeled "First Play." The intruder.jpg image is now a thumbnail image in the First Play area and the same image appears in the large "video monitor" section of the screen (Figure 3.2). (This menu can be renamed by clicking on the name with your mouse. Simply type in the new name you want.)

Step: 4. This "first play" image will be the first thing that appears when the movie plays. If it is a still image, it is automatically set to stay on the screen for 5 seconds. (You can change the duration by right-clicking the thumbnail image in the placeholder section and entering a different number.) If the image is a short movie or animation clip, then it will play the length of the clip. You can also import different images or other files to replace it, if you choose not to use it. Just drag-and-drop a different file from the Media palette into the First Play thumbnail image, replacing the existing one. You may want to add different files to the Media palette to give you more options as you experiment with images or movie clips.

CREATING A MENU

By creating a menu, you allow viewers to select your movie, or to jump to other movies, if you have more than one. You can even add in the director's commentary as a menu item.

Step: 1. First, create the background. Click the "Backgrounds palette" button (the bottom far-left button on the palette screen). Click on the image that you want to use as your menu background image. You can import your own images if you do not want to use those DVDit! supplies. Drag your

Figure 3.3 Select the background image from a list in Sonic Solutions' DVDit! ©2000 courtesy of Sonic Solutions—www.sonic.com.

image over to the blank Menu 1 thumbnail in the menu list to the left of the palette (Figure 3.3).

Step: 2. If you would like a musical soundtrack to play while the menu is displayed, select an audio file (.wav) from your media folder. If you do not have a file in place, you need to import one from Windows Explorer. Then, drag-and-drop the file to the main window. An audio speaker icon will appear on the bottom of the screen. (We imported a file called "Menumusic.wav" from the media palette.)

Step: 3. Next, add buttons to the menu. Click on the button for the Buttons palette, select a button from the menu, and drag it into the video window. If you don't want to use any of these button selections, you can drag-and-drop your movie file into the main window, automatically creating a button linking it to the film. First, import your movies into the Media palette by going to Windows Explorer and dragging the movie files you want to put on the DVD into the Palette window. Next, open the Media palette and select the movie file for which you want to create a button. (We choose the intruder.mpg file.) Simply drag-and-drop it onto the menu background window, DVDit! automatically creates a button and links it to the movie. The software uses the first nonblack frame it finds from the movie to make the thumbnail button. (See Figure 3.4.)

Step: 4. You may want to include the title of your movie in your menu.

Figure 3.4 Create an image button for your movie in Sonic Solutions' DVDit! Three different short movies are shown, each with a button and a title. ©2000 courtesy of Sonic Solutions—www.sonic.com

If so, click on the text button on the bottom of the palette window (the one with a "T"). A list of the available fonts will appear in conjuction with their respective styles (Figure 3.4). After choosing your text, drag-and-drop it into the main window. (We placed the text beside each button image.) Click on the text, and type in the title of the movie or any other text you may want to include. Also, go to the Effects menu on the top menu bar of the window and click on "Text Properties" in the drop-down menu. This takes you to the screen shown in Figure 3.5, where you can change the font size and color as depicted at the right-hand side of the screen. In Figure 3.5, notice the dots around the text of The Intruder. These are the locations of the handles that let you drag and resize your image. It also indicates that the item has been selected and can be moved. Repeat this step for each movie or menu text you want to add to this menu screen. (Our final screen looks like that in Figure 3.6.)

You can also drag in buttons from the Button palette and place text on top of each button. This allows you to create a link to another menu, such as a list of cast and crew credits for each movie or directors' comments in text or audio. (Alternately, you can create the link on the text image itself without using buttons.) When you click on an image or text, you are given the option of showing the links from the image and text to the files. Figure 3.7 shows the final menu page with a textual description of the links to the movies.

DVDit! also allows you to manipulate the menu page by adjusting the background color and objects on the screen, affecting its hue, saturation, and brightness. You can even apply "drop-shadow" effects to the objects in the menu.

FINAL CONFIGURATION

Step: 1. The DVD project is now essentially complete. Before recording it to your DVD-R/RW, CD-R, or hard drive, click the Preview button on the far right of the bottom palette

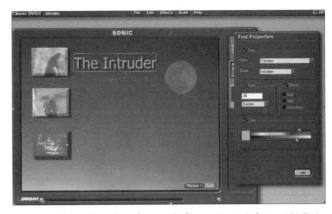

Figure 3.5 Select the color of your title font in Sonic Solutions' DVDit! ©2000 courtesy of Sonic Solutions—www.sonic.com.

Figure 3.6 Select the font type of your movie titles in Sonic Solutions' DVDit! Presented are three short movies. ©2000 courtesy of Sonic Solutions—www.sonic.com. The Intruder directed by Scott Lancaster. Used with permission. The Alien Within and A Dance of Death directed by Kurt Lancaster. Used with permission.

Figure 3.7 This page shows the link titles "behind" the movie buttons and titles in Sonic Solutions' DVDit! ©2000 courtesy of Sonic Solutions—www.sonic.com.

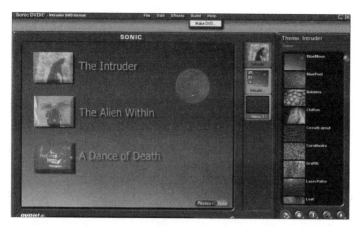

Figure 3.8 With the layout completed, you can now build your movie by selecting "Build: Make DVD" on the menu bar in Sonic Solutions' DVDit! ©2000 courtesy of Sonic Solutions—www.sonic.com. The Intruder directed by Scott Lancaster. Used with permission. The Alien Within and A Dance of Death directed by Kurt Lancaster. Used with permission.

menu. A virtual remote control appears, allowing you to preview your project before recording it. Just as with an actual remote, you can press play, jump to the next menu item (which in our case is the next movie on the list), and so forth.

Step: 2. The project can be recorded either to DVD-R/RW recorder—allowing people to play your DVD on a television DVD player—or on a computer DVD player. You can opt to record it to your hard drive for later recording to a DVD-R; however, a viewer would need DVD playback software to use it (which is included in the DVDit! product). Otherwise you can record it to a CD-R, which people can use to play your movie on a PC through a regular CD-ROM drive. Choose "Build" from the top menu bar (Figure 3.8). If you have a non .mpg file, it will convert the file to an .mpg file. (Your original file, however, remains untouched by this conversion.)

Step: 3. The next window shows the video quality settings (Figure 3.9). You can leave them at their default positions. However, if you want to increase the quality of the video, slide the blue ball image to the right, toward "Higher Quality." By doing so, the Bit-rate and File size increase. If you want a smaller file, slide the blue ball to the left. (The compression type is MPEG-2, the DVD standard). Click "OK."

Figure 3.9 Before processing, select the video quality settings for your movie files in Sonic Solutions' DVDit! ©2000 courtesy of Sonic Solutions—www.sonic.com. The Intruder directed by Scott Lancaster. Used with permission. The Alien Within and A Dance of Death directed by Kurt Lancaster. Used with permission.

Step: 4. The next window shows the various options for recording your DVD project (Figure 3.10). Choose either "Hard Disk," "DVD/CD Recorder," or "Tape Drive," depending on where you want to record your movie. If you select "Hard Disk," you can record the project to the hard drive in DVD format. Click "OK." Next, the program will ask you where you want the DVD file placed. Browse your hard drive and create a new folder called "DVD movies" after the program prompts you (Figure 3.11). Click "OK." Perform these steps for "DVD/CD Recorder" or "Tape Drive" options, as desired.

The DVD project is now on your hard drive. Whether stored on a hard drive, CD-ROM, or DVD disc, this format gives you the flexibility to store your movies in a menu-driven format.

You have successfully transferred your film in a DVD format.

Figure 3.10 Select either a DVD-R/RW or CD-RW drive to record your movie or place it on your hard drive. © 2000 courtesy of Sonic Solutions—www.sonic.com.

Recording Your Movie Onto CD-ROM With Direct CD

DirectCD software, which comes with most CD-RW drives, allows you to format a CD-R or CD-RW disc so you can record music, movie files, or other data. If you give the CD-R disc to someone, they will be able to read the movie file off the disc with their regular CD-ROM drive, allowing them to copy the movie to their hard drive. They double-click the file, and it plays on the QuickTime player or on another streaming media player, depending on the movie's file type. Windows XP allows for a simple drag and drop to your CD-RW drive, so you won't need to do the steps below.

Step: 1. Start Roxio (formerly Adaptec) DirectCD Wizard. The program automatically detects your CD-R when you insert a blank disc into your CD-RW drive. A window pops up asking you, "Please select the type of disc you wish to create," followed by four choices: a disc that can record data onto it like a floppy disk, a data disc for distribution (so other computers can read the data), an audio disc for playing in CD players, and back-up duplication of an existing disc. Choose the second one. This will enable others with regular CD-ROM drives to be able to read the movie file off the CD-R.

Step: 2. Next, you will be taken

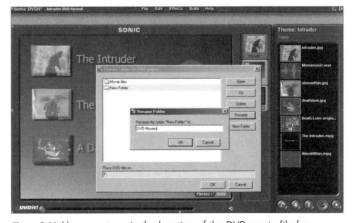

Figure 3.11 Here, we type in the location of the DVD movie file for recording to the hard drive in Sonic Solutions' DVDit! ©2000 courtesy of Sonic Solutions—www.sonic.com.

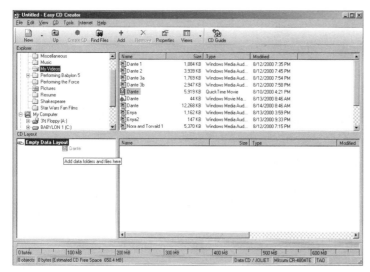

Figure 3.12 The "Data CD Layout" in Roxio's Easy CD Creator. This presents your files you can record onto a CD-R disc using a CD-RW drive. Screen shot portions reprinted with the permission of Roxio, Inc. ©2000 Rox10, Inc. All Rights Reserved.

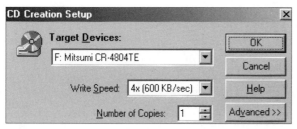

Figure 3.13 The "CD Creation Setup" screen allows you to choose your CD-RW drive, the playback speed of the recording, and single or multiple copies of the CD. Screen shot portions reprinted with the permission of Roxio, Inc. ©2000 Roxio, Inc. All Rights Reserved.

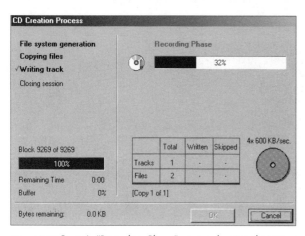

Figure 3.14 Roxio's "Recording Phase" screen showing the status of the CD recording. Screen shot portions reprinted with the permission of Roxio, Inc. ©2000 Roxio, Inc. All Rights Reserved.

to the "Data CD Layout" window (see Figure 3.12).

This window shows you a list of the files on your hard drive. Choose the files you want to record to the CD-R disc, then drag-and-drop each to the bottom window. (We choose the "Dante" QuickTime movie made in Chapter 2.)

Step: 3. The computer prompts you to select the "Target Device," "Write Speed," and "Number of Copies" (see Figure 3.13). The "Target Device" is your CD-RW drive, while the write speed determines how fast the data will record onto your drive. If you choose more than "1" for "Number of Copies," you can create a set of multiple discs. (When one disc is completed, you can insert another to record the same files.) Click "OK."

The computer tells you that it is "Checking the data transfer rate from drive C" (or another drive designation). When this is completed, the "CD Creation Process" window appears (see Figure 3.14), displaying the status of the recording.

When complete, the CD-R disc will be ready to play in any CD-ROM drive, allowing others to access your movie file from your disc. Remember, this procedure does not create a movie file that can be played in the same manner as a DVD. You have recorded a file that can be accessed by anyone with a CD-ROM drive; they can view the movie if they have the correct video streaming software on their computer.

Whether you record your movies in a DVD format or as a file on a CD-R disc you can now give away disc versions of your movies, sell them, or even use them as calling cards for showing your film talent to others.

Submitting Your Film to Internet Cineplexes: A Case Study for Lowell Northrop's *Organ Donor*

There are some important differences between Internet cineplexes and conventional cineplexes. Instead of a physical movie house that plays a few to a couple of dozen films, Internet cineplexes are found online and can potentially hold thousands of movies. In addition, most films in conventional cineplexes run from 90 minutes to 3 hours in length; Internet cineplexes present shorts (films running from a few minutes up to an hour), with longer films often presented in 10-minute units. This is not to say that *feature films* (approximately 80–120 minutes in length) are not found on the Web; in fact, some Internet cineplexes, like alwaysI, make a point of exhibiting feature films, and it is safe to assume that new fiber-optic technology will eventually allow for full-length features to be played with ease. For now, the majority of sites look for shorts because of their relatively small file size and because they hold the attention of online viewers. Furthermore, at this point in time, most Internet cineplexes do not charge you money to view their films. All you need is a computer, an Internet connection, and video streaming software, and you are ready to watch films on such popular sites as AtomFilms (atomfilms.com), IFILM (ifilm.com), MediaTrip (mediatrip.com), and alwaysI (alwaysi.com), to name just a few. (We provide a description of many of these sites in the Appendix.)

Figure 4.1 Lowell Northrop's experimental sf short, Organ Donor. Courtesy of Lowell Northrop. Used with permission.

Until recently, with the development of the Web, shorts have seldom been recognized commercially, but they have always had an important place in filmmaking. At the very beginning of cinema, during the late nineteenth and early twentieth centuries, nearly all of the films made were shorts. Although the feature-length film eventually became more popular commercially, shorts played in theaters and preceded many of the longer films through the 1960s.

For economic reasons, shorts are easier for independent filmmakers to produce, but they have not been shown in commercial movie theaters for the last 30 years. This situation has been problematic for producers of short films. If commercial theaters do not exhibit short films, how does an independent filmmaker showcase work to an audience? Before the Internet, film festivals (such as Cannes, Sundance, SXSW, and so on) were the primary venue for the public screenings of shorts. However, such events often involve tough competition and costly submission fees. In addition, a film will most likely have only one screening at a festival. If a viewer misses the screening, odds are there will not be another opportunity to see the film. All of these issues make it very difficult for the independent filmmaker to reach a large audience.

Today, however, with the rise of Internet cineplexes, viewers from all over the world can look at thousands of films whenever they want. In order to provide a variety of subject matter for a diverse audience, Internet cineplexes constantly look for new, exciting content, and they use different ways to find new films. For example, representatives from alwaysI and AtomFilms discover films by attending conventional film festivals as well as by seeking out films made by film school students. Most Internet cineplexes also find material through calls-for-submissions advertised on their respective sites.

In this chapter, we take you through all the steps involved in the submission process—from selecting a site to accepting a contract. Anyone with a film can submit it to an Internet cineplex, usually for free. To this end, we also show you how to select the right site for you; each Internet cineplex is distinct in its objectives, style, and collection. We explain what to look for so you can choose the one that best suits you and your film. In order to show the process of how you can submit your film to one of these sites, we trace the submission experience of independent filmmaker Lowell Northrop who had his film, *Organ Donor*, accepted by one of the largest Internet cineplexes. Although the particulars of your experience may differ from Northrop's, what he learned may prove helpful to you.

For about 5 years, Northrop worked as a production assistant on feature films, music videos, and commercials, but it was not long before he decided to leave this job and pursue his dream to direct. One day, after visiting the Los Angeles Zoo, he came up with the idea of making a musical short about gorillas that give up their organs for humans. This idea turned into *Organ*

Donor—a 3-minute science-fiction film, set to the techno-organ music of DJ Shadow's "Organ Donor." To shoot *Organ Donor,* Northrop used a Nikon SuperZoom 8 and a Beaulieu 7008 Pro II for Pro-8 film, which he describes as "a special 8mm film . . . that is basically professional-quality 35mm film, cut down to fit in a Super 8 camera." He edited with Adobe Premiere and used the special-effects software Adobe After Effects to create cuts and sweeps. (Both of these products are described in Chapter 1.)

Once the film was completed, Northrop, like most filmmakers, wanted to find a large audience for it. A friend of his had recently placed a film on the Internet cineplex IFILM and suggested that Northrop look into doing the same thing. Northrop took his friend's advice and began the submission process to get *Organ Donor* put on IFILM. The following steps explain the process for submitting a film to an Internet cineplex. They describe a process similar to that Northrop used when submitting his film, *Organ Donor.*

Selecting A Site

Before sending your film to one or several Internet cineplexes, you should find those that best fit your film and your aspirations for it. Here, we provide an overview of what you should look for when choosing an Internet cineplex for your film.

Start by making a list of the Internet cineplexes you have seen or heard about. At first, Northrop was interested in IFILM, AtomFilms, and ShortBuzz. Like Northrop, you won't initially know if any of these sites will accept your film, or even if you will want to submit to them, but at least they are good places for you to begin your research.

Take the time to research your list of sites. If possible, talk to your friends and colleagues and find out what they think about the sites to which you want to submit your films. (Northrop spoke with a friend who was one of the first filmmakers on IFILM to discover why he liked the site.) Next, look to see what the news media is saying about the sites. You can search for articles in magazines and newspapers. For example, after reading an article in *Entertainment Weekly* that gave IFILM and AtomFilms high ratings, Northrop decided to pursue these sites. You can also do an Internet search with the help of a search engine like Lycos (lycos.com) or Google (google.com), which may turn up many online articles and reviews. Easiest of all, you can turn to the last section of this book and check out our Appendix, which provides detailed descriptions of 25 Internet cineplexes. (Note that while doing your research, you will probably come across descriptions of other Internet cineplexes that interest you. Be sure to follow-up on any site that sounds promising because it might be just what you're looking for.)

Once you have done some research and have a better sense of the Internet cineplexes on your list, you should investigate the actual sites.

Examine each site closely. Be a detective, and search for clues that let you know if this is the right Internet cineplex for you. To help you begin, we have highlighted five areas for your investigation. Of course you are not limited to them, but if you look closely at these five features for each site on your list, you will be prepared to make your selection. (For an example of an Internet cineplex dossier, turn to any Internet cineplex description in the Appendix.)

TYPES OF FILMS

What reveals most about an Internet cineplex is the type of films it exhibits on its site. The film collection shows who the audience is, how the site is trying to position itself in the market, and, most importantly, what the site is looking for in its submissions. For example, the extreme and sometimes vulgar nature of many of AtomFilms' shorts reflects that the site is defining itself as "cutting edge," and that it probably attracts a less conservative, wilder crowd. By examining the films on a site, you can tell whether you want your film to be a part of the site. You also can get a sense of whether your film might interest the site. When checking out IFILM, Northrop noticed that its films widely ranged in style and content. For him, the collection's diversity was a good sign; *Organ Donor,* which in his opinion is "a very different film," requires an open mind from an audience.

Here are some specifics to note when looking at an Internet cineplex's film collection:

- the level of professionalism of their films and filmmakers (depending on whether you are looking for something more professional or more amateur)

- the special audience groups they address (see Appendix for sites that exhibit films only by *Star Wars* fans, or about homosexual issues, or by African-Americans, for example)

- the range of genres or categories (some sites stick to the standard genres, while others are more offbeat and inventive)

- the general length of most films (some sites have length requirements and will not accept features or shorts that run long)

- the most popular films on the site (a good way to narrow down what the audience is looking at and likes to see)

PRESENTATION OF FILMS

When checking out its collection of films, you should pay close attention to the way an Internet cineplex presents a film. Although many don't, there are some sites that generously provide each film with its own page, on which video streaming takes place. If there is enough space on the page, some sites allow you to post important facts like your biography, filmography, crew list, production notes, and a film synopsis. With IFILM, Northrop has a page for *Organ Donor* that lists facts about the film as well as his own "Filmmaker's Profile" page that offers information about him, including a link to his email address. Most Internet cineplexes do not provide enough space for you to list all of these facts, so you must decide which information is most valuable to you. Essentially, presentation is a matter of personal discretion and preference, but we advise you to find a site that allows you, at the very least, to list a synopsis—since a good description inspires people to watch your film—and some interesting facts about yourself (so viewers can attach a creative personality to the work).

PROMOTION OF FILMS

You also want to be aware of how an Internet cineplex promotes its films. Because many sites hold large collections of films, it is not likely that your film will get a lot of company-generated publicity, either on or off these sites. When conducting your investigation, you will notice that many sites promote their films through the "Top Rated" section that appears on their home page. Here, the Internet cineplex calls attention to the top-rated films of the week or of the site's life-span. Many Internet cineplexes also highlight a "Pick of the Week," sometimes a newcomer and others an old favorite. *Organ Donor* had the fortune of being in this position on IFILM one week, but "after that, little was done to publicize [the film] on the site," Northrop says, regretfully.

Word of mouth is another valid form of promotion. Most sites provide links enabling viewers to e-mail friends about the films they have just seen. Naturally, these links generate a lot of discussion about the site's films (so much so that alwaysI cites word-of-mouth as its "best form of advertising"). When you look at it this way, films on the majority of Internet cineplexes have a good chance at being well publicized. Ultimately, it is up to you to judge the importance of each type of promotion.

RIGHTS

Often upon submitting your film, and certainly by the time your film has been accepted to an Internet cineplex, you are required to sign an agreement with the site in order for your film to be hosted. Within each agreement, there is a section that discusses the rights an Internet cineplex expects to be granted from you, the filmmaker. Before choosing any Internet cineplex, you should be aware of all the rights they require, so be sure to read each agreement thoroughly.

To begin, rights can be broken into two categories: exclusive and non-exclusive. If you agree to hand over exclusive rights, then you relinquish authority and give the site complete control over your film for the term of the agreement. (Note that only one Internet cineplex can hold exclusive rights at a time, so if you submit to a site requiring an exclusive license, you should not submit to any others.) With nonexclusive rights, you sign over rights to your film for the term of the agreement, but you also maintain rights to do what you want with your film. For Northrop, a nonexclusive deal was the right choice. Even though he wanted his film on IFILM, he also wanted to continue to hold rights to *Organ Donor* so he could show it on other Internet cineplexes as well as at offline film festivals. For this reason, he looked for a site that required a nonexclusive license.

When examining agreements, you also need to ascertain whether the exclusive or nonexclusive license is just for exhibition (showing your film) or whether it includes distribution (selling your film—see below). Also, notice which areas of media—exhibition/distribution, television broadcasts, home video/DVD—are included in the agreement. (See Appendix for a further discussion of rights.)

DISTRIBUTION AND ROYALTIES

Some Internet cineplexes not only show your film but sell it as well. Currently, the majority of sites do not distribute their films, but always remember to check if the site you are pursuing is one of the few that does. If you agree to sign over rights for distribution to an Internet cineplex, you are usually entitled to royalties—a percentage of the profit for each copy of your film that is sold. Be aware that not all Internet cineplexes provide their filmmakers with royalties (such as icebox.com, an animation site with an agreement that is "royalty-free," yet requires rights for distribution). With nonroyalty sites, it is up to you to decide whether exposure alone is enough compensation for your work. For the sites that do offer royalties, you should note the royalty rate, which is the actual percentage you receive per copy. Royalty rates vary, but not by much. The typical range is 50 to 65 percent. And remember to look for any fine print listing distribution fees to be deducted from your profit.

Besides income from distribution, there is a chance you will earn money for exhibition, too. Though difficult to find, there are a couple of Internet cineplexes that pay you a small amount of money each time your film is completely (rather than partially) streamed or downloaded. (See Appendix for descriptions of royalty agreements.)

AUDIENCE FEEDBACK

Most Internet cineplexes cater to their audiences. One way they do this is by inviting viewers to share their thoughts about films and sometimes post them on the site. When checking out sites, Northrop was pleased to see that IFILM facilitated audience feedback. "The site was easy to access and I liked the idea of being able to have my film reviewed and ranked by anyone who watched it," he says. If this is something that is important to you, check whether your Internet cineplex of interest offers this feature. You may also want to note the other forms of audience participation a site offers, such as membership accounts and games.

After investigating the sites on your list, choose to submit to the one or few that are most appealing to you. Northrop advises, "It may be a good idea to send your film out to a bunch of sites in order to have a broader distribution." To make your selection, you should consider the six topics discussed—film collection, presentation, promotion, rights, distribution and royalties, and audience feedback—along with anything else that is important to you, such as the site's style, appearance, spirit, and so forth. Once you have made your choice, you have completed the presubmission process and are ready to move on to the next stage: the submission process.

Submitting Your Film

Now that you have chosen the Internet cineplexes to which you want to submit your film, you can begin the actual submission process. We will now walk you through each step.

The first step is filling out a submission form. Most Internet cineplexes require you to fill out and send in a submission form with a copy of your film. On submission forms you provide various facts about your film. Because each form is different, we cannot address each detail of every possible submission form. However, we will touch on the most common elements of submission forms so you know what to expect when filling them out.

You can find a particular site's submission form by looking for a link, usually in the "Submit" section. When you arrive at the page, the first thing to note is whether the Internet cineplex requests you to print out and mail in a hard copy of the form, or to fill it out and submit it online. After printing out or going to the online submission form, you can start to fill in the required information. For most forms, you begin by stating the title of the film, your name, and contact information. Along with your contact information, some (but not most) Internet cineplexes request your biography and filmography notes. Following this, you are asked to list information about your film, typically including its length, year, genre, budget, country of origin, aspect ratio, original format of production, submission format, and a brief synopsis. If you are in film school and are submitting a student film, you will probably be requested to note this fact. Other information may be required, including credits, previous screenings at festivals, and awards earned. Then, to complete just about every submission form, you must state that you hold the copyright to your film and all its parts (including music). Last but not least, you are required to sign the Submission Agreement (note that the title of the deal varies from site to site), sometimes embedded in the submission form and sometimes a separate sheet. This agreement discusses the exchange of rights from you, the filmmaker, to the Internet cineplex. Remember to carefully read this agreement before signing.

Once you finish filling out the submission form, you need to send the Internet cineplex a copy of your film. In the directions for submission, a site usually indicates the film formats that are acceptable to submit. As with the contents of the submission form, each Internet cineplex is unique in its format requirements. Some accept only videotapes sent through the mail, while others prefer digital files to be either sent through the mail on disc or CD-ROM, or uploaded to their site as an email attachment. As for the video formats typically requested, they are VHS (usually NTSC, but sometimes PAL), S-VHS, and DV, while RealMedia, MPEG, and Quicktime are examples of requested forms for digital files. Be sure the copy you are submitting meets the requirements of the Internet cineplex. Remember that the majority of sites do not return copies of films that are sent to them.

Before submitting your film, check for any submission fees. Although the submission process for most Internet cineplexes is free, a couple of sites require a fee with your entry. (They are primarily online festivals, which we will discuss later in this chapter.) If there are monies required, it is up to you and your checkbook to decide if submitting to the site is worth the cost.

Once you have filled out your submission form, signed the agreement, prepared a copy of your film, and checked for a submission fee, you are ready to pack everything up and send it to the Internet cineplex. (Note that if you have chosen a site with a submission process that is completed on-line, this step does not apply to you.) You will find the site's address in the directions for submission. If the address is not a post-office box, we advise that you send the package via a postal service that tracks its deliveries (such as UPS, FedEx, or DHL). You may pay more for this service, but knowing when and to whom your film was delivered is worth the cost.

DECIDING TO EXHIBIT

Just because you submit your film to an Internet cineplex does not guarantee it will be exhibited on the site. If your film is accepted, you will be contacted. With each site, the time between submission and acceptance varies. For Northrop, it took IFILM about a month to accept his film and put it online, and according to him, "that is considered fast."

Even if your film is accepted, a site may require that you agree to some other exhibition or distribution stipulations before hosting your film. In the excitement of your film's being accepted, you might be tempted to make a hasty decision about a deal; be sure to take the time to seriously consider it (especially if it involves an exclusive license). If in the end you decide that you don't feel comfortable with the deal, just remember there are always other sites.

ONLINE FILM FESTIVALS

Online Film Festivals are a subgroup of Internet cineplexes: all online film festivals are Internet cineplexes, but not all cineplexes host festivals. The submission process to online festivals is, for the most part, identical to the one described above, with the exception of time deadlines to which you must adhere as well as entry fees you must pay. (Note that deadlines and fees are customary for many but not all festivals.)

Within online festivals, there is a lot of competition between films both before and during the festival. Many festivals take only the highest- quality work, so getting accepted is sometimes a feat. After the preliminary acceptance stage, some festivals—like The Sync's Online Film Festival—judge your film by either committee or the audience. Depending on the festival, winners may receive cash prizes or, as in The Sync's case, a place on the site and in its archives. In addition to online exhibition, several online festivals, including D.FILM and Resfest, are traveling offline festivals. In other words, if the festival accepts your film, it will be shown in traditional venue settings all around the world, as well as on the Web. Because of such potential exposure, you may want to consider submitting your film to online festivals despite the fees.

TIME TO CELEBRATE?

Once your film is online a little celebration is in order, as thousands of people now have access to your film. (For example, through IFILM alone, 3200 people have seen *Organ Donor* as of September 2000.) This being said, it is important to remember that an Internet cineplex will not generate instant popularity for your film. As Northrop cautions, "You shouldn't assume that once your film is on an Internet site that you will be discovered by an agent and your career as a director will take off. Many sites seem to hint that this will happen." He recognizes that success stories like *George Lucas in Love* exist (see Chapter 6), but he says, "that's because the films were so exceptional."

We believe that your film's success will derive not only from its exceptional quality, but also from the site you choose to place it on. In Northrop's opinion, "the big sites are going to help your film the most." But we feel that a variety of sites offer different ways to market and present your films. We recommend that you study the Appendix and choose the best site for your film. Northrop believes that because the public is most familiar with the larger sites, such as IFILM or AtomFilms, people will be more likely to visit them rather than lesser-known sites. To a certain extent, this is true. But it is also possible that a really good film can make a site more popular. When selecting an Internet cineplex, it is important to consider all the issues we have discussed in this chapter. In doing so, we are certain that you will be in a good position to decide which Internet cineplex is right for you and your film.

PART II

THE NEW INDEPENDENT VOICE OF THE INTERNET INDIES

In the Introduction, we discussed the developments that the convergence of digital video, computers, and the Internet is bringing for independent filmmakers. As you saw in Chapter 1, you can own all the necessary tools for filmmaking for under $3000. You can build a web site to host your film, or you can exhibit a film of any style, genre, budget, and quality through an Internet cineplex. As these examples demonstrate, digital filmmaking and the Internet are breaking down industry boundaries that are long-standing and outdated. For this reason, it is difficult for anyone who works within the media industry to deny that the convergence of digital video and the Internet is a powerful event. Although most industry members agree that this technological merger is impacting the media industry, there are many disagreements as to the effect of the impact. Additionally, there are questions regarding how industry members should adapt to such convergence. Should they try working with digital video instead of film? Should they start treating the Internet as a respectable venue for all kinds of films? Should they see online cinema as a different medium rather than making it a subcategory of film? At this point, it is difficult to find any exact answers, but we have sought out the opinions of people who are in the process of responding to these questions.

In this section, we examine filmmakers and interactive web designers who are creating new kinds of work for the Internet, presenting overviews of their work and interviews with the creative teams. These people are at the center of this media convergence and produce work that start to address these issues. By discovering ways to combine digital video and/or film and the Internet, the media pioneers we profile here are in many ways helping to redefine the current entertainment industry. Some are even carving out something that looks like an entirely new medium altogether.

First, we look at Jason Wishnow, a filmmaker who created the Internet cineplex site New Venue, and explore the reasons why independent filmmakers need the Internet to help distribute their films. Next, we examine the film *George Lucas in Love,* produced by Joseph Levy and directed by Joe Nussbaum. We learn where they found inspiration for their film, why they made it, and how it came to be presented on the Internet. We discuss how the web is opening up new possibilities for experimental work by examining Anthony Cerniello's *Jaunt,* an example of a beautiful and disturbing film that incorporates digital special effects into a project shot on film. Next, we take a look at Jennifer Ringley's *The JenniShow* and her web page, JenniCam. We explore the reasons why she documents her everyday life through Internet cameras and an Internet broadcast show. Lastly, in Maya Churi's *Letters from Homeroom,* we see how a filmmaker incorporates film into the web medium as a way to tell her story.

CHAPTER 5

Jason Wishnow's New Venue: Taking Media Convergence to Another Level

Internet cineplexes are an integral part of the current digital film revolution. Simply put, they are the means by which independent filmmakers find a mass audience for their work. As is the case with traditional movie theaters, not all Internet cineplexes are the same. They differ in terms of size, types of films shown (such as "blockbuster" or "art house"), the audience they attract, and so forth. In the previous chapter, we took you through the steps involved in submitting a film to an Internet cineplex. In this chapter, we reveal the thought process behind the creation of an Internet cineplex by profiling Jason Wishnow, an independent filmmaker and web designer who created and runs New Venue (www.newvenue.com).

CREATING NEW VENUE

Wishnow founded New Venue at age 21 while attending Stanford University. The site grew out of Wishnow's combined interest in filmmaking and digital media, a curiosity he academically nurtured during his

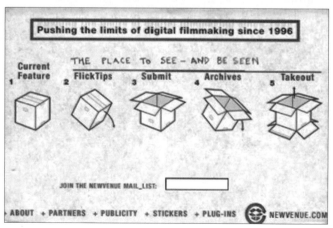

Figure 4.1 Intro screen to Jason Wishnow's internet Cineplex site, The New Venue. www.thenewvenue.com

undergraduate years through a self-designed major. In retrospect, Wishnow feels that Stanford was not an ideal place to study traditional filmmaking because of what he perceived as equipment limitations. However, the school's location offered him many opportunities. "I went to a school in the heart of Silicon Valley. Freshman year, every dorm on campus had a computer with a video input, and from what I've gathered, I think I'm the only one who noticed, let alone took advantage of it," he explains.

Before leaving Stanford in 1995, Wishnow wanted to create a "virtual theater" on the web—a site that would act somewhat like a movie theater by presenting short independent films to an audience on demand. During its conception phase, Wishnow was not sure what the site's design would look like, nor what the technology would allow him to do. At the time Wishnow was creating his site, web browser plug-ins for RealPlayer and QuickTime were not readily available. But from the very beginning, Wishnow was certain that he wanted to showcase only films that would "really push the medium in new directions, in terms of narrative, aesthetics, and technology."

In 1996, he encountered his first chance to create a "virtual theater." At the time, the Stanford Art and Technology Initiative was offering a series of small grants to new projects, and Wishnow applied. Intrigued by the idea, the Initiative provided Wishnow with the financial means to take a stab at creating his project. However, he waited until April of 1998 to launch his site to the public in order to give "both the technology and the scope of the site ample time to catch up." His decision to delay the launch allowed Wishnow to design an Internet cineplex that fit his vision, one that happened to strike a chord with many viewers. Once launched, it was not long before New Venue had a loyal audience of people interested in film, web design, and new media. Wishnow's site soon became the subject of several articles appearing in *Wired, Newsweek, The New York Times,* and *Le Monde.*

By the summer of 1998, the industry was buzzing with enthusiasm about New Venue. In addition to being one of the first Internet cineplexes, the site was showcasing some of the most exciting films on the web. Wishnow chose to host films that explored new technical and narrative ground; in other words, those that were specifically made for web exhibition and distribution and addressed qualities of the medium. According to Wishnow, many filmmakers shy away from online cinema because of certain features that they perceive to be limitations, such as smaller image sizes and lower frame rates. To this sentiment Wishnow responds, "Just because a movie is low resolution doesn't mean that it should be low quality." For him, such features are "constraints" to work within rather than "limitations" to work around, something he decided to address through New Venue. "From the start, I was really hoping that filmmakers and digital artists would see New Venue and start exploring how the generative constraints of technology could be integrated into storytelling," he says.

The following story illustrates Wishnow's point. During the second week of New Venue's online existence, Wishnow put up on the site a minute-and-a-half long short that he co-directed with Kristie Lu Stout. (In the credits posted on the site, Wishnow is not listed as a director of the film. "Originally, I didn't put my name on [*Persona*] at all," he explains, "because I didn't want anyone to know that I was involved in any of the first films to appear on New Venue. The site wasn't supposed to be an extension of my own web site.") Shot on Hi8mm, *Persona* is composed of one continuous close-up shot of a style-conscious girl telling a fast and biting story. In making the film, Wishnow and Stout decided to address the distinct aspects of the medium, including screen and file size, and produce an engaging narrative that complemented these elements. For example, in order for online viewers to receive a clear image of the film, Wishnow and Stout shot one fairly still scene depicting solely of a close-up of a woman telling a funny story in a commanding tone. Then, to keep the file size small, they made the film short and cut the frame rate from 15 fps (frames-per-second)—the rate at which they first edited the film in Adobe Premiere— to 7.5 fps by using Adobe AfterEffects with an image size of 160x120 pixels. Such planning resulted in a film that ended up becoming one of the favorites on New Venue and, more importantly, helped to define the aesthetics of online cinema.

For about thirteen months, New Venue remained one of the most popular Internet cineplexes by hosting the work of filmmakers who explored new approaches to making films and telling stories. Then, in July of 1999, Wishnow decided to take a six-month break from maintaining it in order to discover ways to further develop the site. During this time, he was invited by Apple to create a New Venue channel for QuickTime TV, which Wishnow describes as "Apple's portal to high quality QuickTime-based web content." For Wishnow, this opportunity was an "especially alluring prospect"—and one he decided to pursue. Of the 25 QuickTime TV channels, including those operated by such companies as MTV, Disney, and Warner Bros. Records, Wishnow particularly liked that his was "the only one being run from underneath a loft bed on Avenue C." To guarantee an expanded line-up of content for his audience on the New Venue channel, Wishnow partnered with D.FILM Digital Film Festival (www.dfilm.com), a traveling offline and online film festival that has access to some of the web's most daring films. With support from Apple, Wishnow re-launched New Venue in January of 2000 "with a more robust site, more movies," as well as "a stronger international presence." His brief hiatus had been a smart move for the site, leaving it with an even higher profile among Internet cineplexes. As Wishnow says, "This relationship with Apple definitely solidified New Venue's credibility as a viable online film alternative to newer, bigger sites like AtomFilms and IFILM."

A FILMMAKER AT HEART

Before creating New Venue, Wishnow was a filmmaker. In fact, Wishnow admits that many of his goals for New Venue, as well as much of the site's design, stem from the mind of a director. He says, "At the heart of the site is the question, How would I want my own work to be presented to the general public?" For this reason, New Venue contains features that rarely exist on most Internet cineplexes (for a further discussion of Internet cineplexes see Chapter 4 and the Appendix). For example, New Venue highlights only one film a week, whereas most Internet cineplexes showcase anywhere from five to twenty films on a weekly basis. Through this unique approach, Wishnow provides filmmakers the attention he feels they deserve. "By focusing on a single filmmaker at a time, New Venue draws attention to new movies with a 'Hey, check this out!' approach." Wishnow's decision to showcase only one film a week inevitably makes for a small archive of films in relation to most Internet cineplexes. However, he sees New Venue's small collection as an asset, and believes most filmmakers do also. He says, "Certain filmmakers have approached me after their movies ran on both New Venue and some of the bigger sites. [Following their film's debut], they [felt] as if their work [got] relegated to the basement of those other sites, whereas on New Venue they continued to get e-mail feedback on their films months after they [were] featured." Besides offering filmmakers a greater amount of sustainable attention, getting a film accepted by New Venue also carries a sense of prestige. Since Wishnow needs to fill only one weekly slot, he is in a position to be selective when it comes to New Venue's content.

Wishnow is committed to providing his filmmakers with a place to effectively exhibit their films because he knows what it's like to need such a place. Wishnow began his career when he was twelve years old, acting as a guinea pig for a new art program founded by his mother. Wishnow recalls, "My first filmmaking experience was participating in a childrens' workshop at the Long Beach Museum of Art Video Annex. My mom worked with the museum and established this program for middle school and high school kids to gain a hands-on approach to video art and documentary filmmaking." At the time, Wishnow "hated every minute of it," thinking "[filmmaking] was even more slow and tedious than baseball, which I also hated." Although it began with a rocky start, Wishnow's relationship with filmmaking gradually improved. He says, "Unlike baseball, I guess I learned to really enjoy it because I keep coming back to it."

In 1997, Wishnow made his most well-known work to date, *Tatooine or Bust,* a thirteen-minute documentary about *Star Wars* fans who camp out to see the re-release of George Lucas's *Star Wars Episode IV: A New Hope* on its opening night, January 31, 1997, nearly twenty years after its original release. *Tatooine or Bust* was shot simultaneously at five movie theaters around the United States—Mann's Chinese in Hollywood, United Artists Coronet in San Francisco, the Cineplex Odeon Ziegfeld in New York, the Sony Magic Johnson in the Crenshaw district of inner city Los Angeles, and a shopping mall theater in Danvers, Massachusetts. To accomplish this feat, Wishnow assembled five crews (with the help of some friends) and coordinated the shoots by way of the Internet. "I built a web site with detailed instructions [for each crew] covering everything from acceptable camera angles to interview questions," he explains.

Wishnow decided to shoot *Tatooine or Bust* on MiniDV. When selecting the type of camera his crews would use, he took a risk and chose one that he had never seen before—the Sony VX-1000. "I honestly hadn't seen what [the cameras] could do up until the day of shooting," Wishnow admits. "I had heard excellent things about them second-hand from a documentary filmmaker who hadn't actually used them herself. I went in blind. I was simply looking for inexpensive tools that could provide me with the highest quality end product." Fortunately, the VX-1000 proved to be an excellent camera. For the shoots, Wishnow required that his crews also use top-notch microphones in order to get clear recordings of the interviews with *Star Wars* fans. Once the evening's footage was shot, Wishnow collected the tapes from his crews and began the activities of post-production. "I couldn't afford a DV deck, so for logging and capturing footage I purchased a lesser digital camera," he says. He edited the film with a Media 100 system and used Adobe AfterEffects to put on finishing touches.

Like any filmmaker, after completing *Tatooine or Bust,* Wishnow searched for exhibition venues. Although he built a site for the film immediately after completing shooting, he did not consider putting *Tatooine or Bust* on the web until two years later when *Star Wars Episode I: The Phantom Menace* was released. He explains, "I had put so much effort into building New Venue as a web site dedicated to movies made specifically for the net that I didn't even think about putting up any of my movies that I had made for other venues." Instead of web exhibition, Wishnow began looking for traditional film festivals that would suit his film, the first step in what turned out to be an arduous search. "I actually have a difficult time placing *Tatooine or Bust* in festivals," he says, "because it has a very underground feel (which means it doesn't quite fit in big mainstream festivals), but it's about mainstream pop iconography (which means it doesn't quite fit into the underground festivals)." After surveying the possibilities, Wishnow approached D.FILM, "because I couldn't think of a better showcase for a film shot on DV, edited on a Mac, and about *Star Wars* fans." Along with positive responses from D.FILM and several other festivals, Wishnow received an offer to show *Tatooine or Bust* to the crew at Industrial Lights and Magic (Lucas's special effects company) that was working on *Episode I.* Needless to say, he "jumped at the chance."

In addition to George Lucas's crew, other members of the industry paid close attention to Wishnow's work, including Channel 4 in London. After seeing *Tatooine or Bust,* the station hired Wishnow to make a sequel to the film for British television, entitled *Star Wars or Bust* (1999), a documentary about *Star Wars* fans camping out for tickets to Episode I. Wishnow had reservations about the project. "Originally, I had no intention of making any kind of sequel because I thought [it] would be derivative, not only in terms of style and content, but in terms of the people who would be camping out." He ultimately agreed to do it mainly out of respect for *Star Wars* fans. In the end, Wishnow was pleased with how the documentary turned out, although the final cut does not resemble his original conception of *Star Wars or Bust.* "I initially intended to follow only one group of fans at the Ziegfeld in New York for an extended period of time," he explains, "as a sort of anthropological study of the evolution of a particular microcosm over the course of a month." Because a coherent narrative never developed from this approach, he had to create a "sort-of *Tatooine or Bust* 2.0" by sending crews to two other cities to collect additional footage at the last minute.

As it turned out, *Star Wars or Bust* was a hit on British television, and Channel 4 offered Wishnow the opportunity to work on another project. More importantly, the station inquired about his ideas for programs. "Since Channel Four and producer Sian Edwards were already developing a film review program called *Flicks,* and a documentary series about women dating in New York called *Chicks,* I suggested a documentary series about misogynist investment bankers dating in New York called *Dicks,*" he says. Channel 4 liked the idea, but not the name. For nine months Wishnow worked on developing the dating series, *In Bed with Manhattan,* which is being pitched around by Edwards, but has not yet been picked up (as of February 2001).

FUTURE OF NEW VENUE

In the near future New Venue will be expanding. Wishnow plans to broaden the site's scope by showcasing more international films, and is working toward developing a New Venue production studio. Even with these advancements, Wishnow is certain that New Venue will never become a corporate enterprise, since he believes that larger sites are not as interested in exploring unique aspects of the medium. He remembers the time when he met with venture capitalists. "When I arrived, one of them put his Rolex on the table and said, 'You have five minutes.'" Looking back on the meeting now, Wishnow says, "I should have picked up the watch [and pocketed it], said 'Thanks for the time,' and funded the site for the next six months with that."

At this moment, Wishnow is equally committed to filmmaking and running New Venue. However, he foresees a day when his passion for filmmaking will supercede his interest in the site. "Maintaining New Venue is incredibly time consuming, and, no matter how much I like it or how significant it is within the milieu of film on the web, it keeps me from making my own movies. The drive [for filmmaking] is what prompted me to start New Venue, and that is what will compel me to shut it down [some day]." Fortunately, this day has not come yet and probably won't for a while. According to Wishnow, New Venue still has a lot of life within it, as well as a great deal more to contribute to the development of online cinema. He says, "There is still so much that we can explore in terms of storytelling, and I am just hoping that sites like New Venue continue to prompt filmmakers to think about the prospects."

Although it will probably never become as large as some other sites, you can expect Wishnow's New Venue to keep showing some of the most exciting work to come out of the digital film revolution.

Joe Nussbaum & Joseph Levy's *George Lucas in Love:* Presenting Shorts Online and Finding Success

In the past, it was not very likely for an independent film to find a large audience. Most screenings would take place on the filmmaker's television set, surrounded by friends and family. Times are changing, and more and more the web is becoming a place where low-budget, independent films are finding success. Each filmmaker achieves success in a slightly different form. For some, success simply means presenting projects in a space that many people can access. For others, it is finding a fan base for the film. And for a select few, success is of a more commercial nature: earning royalties and finding a job in the film industry as a result of the movie's popularity. In this chapter, we look at a success story of this latter form, focusing on *George Lucas in Love* (1999), a short film that put its creators' names into the Palm Pilots of many Hollywood agents.

As the title suggests, the nine-minute long *George Lucas in Love* is a parody of the 1998 Oscar-winning *Shakespeare in Love,* with the character of present-day filmmaker George Lucas substituting for the part of Shakespeare. Set in 1967 at the University of Southern California, the film harkens back to the days when Lucas was in film school, struggling to write the script for what we now know as *Star Wars* (1977). All around him are people who act as prototypes for characters in his movies, though he cannot see the potential of his surroundings until the day he

Figure 4.1 Joe Nussbaum's and Joseph Levy's web hit, George Lucas in Love. Courtesy of Joseph Levy. Used with permission.

meets his muse. From this point on, Lucas begins to see every person and situation as a narrative opportunity, incorporating each one into his masterpiece. He finds his model for Darth Vader, for example, in his evil, competitive neighbor who wears black outfits and wheezes when he breathes (due to asthma). The film ends with Lucas finishing his script and, to his dismay, discovering that his muse is actually his long-lost sister (a reference to Luke Skywalker's hidden relation to Princess Leia).

The creators of *George Lucas in Love* could easily identify with their protagonist for a couple of reasons. Just like Lucas, both director Joe Nussbaum and producer Joseph Levy were students at the University of Southern California and were trained in film production: Nussbaum graduated from the School of Cinema-Television; and Levy, while earning a degree in music, took graduate-level classes in film production. Nussbaum and Levy also felt an affinity to Lucas because they understood the pressure involved in creating a film. They wanted to produce a high-quality short that would catch the eye of Hollywood agents and reflect their talents and skills as a filmmaker and as a producer. As Levy says, "Our only intention . . . was to do something that would get agents and producers to put the tapes into their VCRs instead of throwing them away." Nussbaum and Levy felt the time had come to make their film, and they started to search for worthy ideas. Like their future protagonist, they discovered that the best material surrounded them. As Nussbaum and Levy describe in a letter to viewers posted on MediaTrip (www.mediatrip.com), the entertainment site that hosts their film, they capitalized on the hottest entertainment news of the moment: "The hype for *Star Wars, Episode I* was all around us, and *Shakespeare in Love* was rapidly becoming a phenomenon of its own. A hybrid comedy that attempts to explain the origin of *Star Wars* was an idea ripe for the picking."

The original idea to parody *Shakespeare in Love* came from Nussbaum's friend Timothy Dowling. Nussbaum thought it would be funny to turn the Shakespeare character into Lucas, and in one evening he and Dowling came up with most of the narrative. Nussbaum and friend Daniel Shere wrote the film's script. It was completed in February 1999, just two months following Nussbaum and Levy's decision to make a movie.

MAKING A HIGH-QUALITY, LOW-BUDGET FILM

Not too long after completing the script, production on *George Lucas in Love* began. Much of the creation of the film must be credited to the connections that Nussbaum and Levy made at school. Being a graduate of USC film school and an employee at a post-production house allowed Nussbaum in particular, to meet many talented people who helped him during all stages of pre-production, production, and post-production.

Nussbaum and Levy went to school with the film's casting director, Jeremy Jones; director of photography, Eric Haase; and composer, Deborah Lurie. They also met actor Martin Hynes (who plays young George Lucas in the film) during their college years. USC also yielded settings for some of the most important scenes in the film. Using a 35mm camera donated by Panavision, Nussbaum and Levy shot for two days on the USC campus and also on a soundstage in the San Fernando Valley. Immediately following shooting, the film went into post-production at Nussbaum's place of employment, the movie trailer house 3-Oh!-5 Creative Advertising. Nussbaum and Levy took advantage of not only the equipment available to them such as an Avid editing system, but also the skills of several 3-Oh!-5 employees. Finally, the film was processed at Consolidated Film Industries (CFI).

On completion, Nussbaum and Levy realized that they had spent $25,000 making the film. Yet, the creators explain that this money did not come out only of their pockets. Everyone involved in the film's creation shared its cost, and Nussbaum and Levy post this point on MediaTrip's message board.

Through their dedication of time, money, and energy, everyone who worked on the film demonstrated they believed it was going to be worth it in the end. Nussbaum and Levy, however, never could have foreseen the tremendous success achieved by *George Lucas in Love*. As Levy describes, "it was the epitome of the type of project Joe Nussbaum and I were trying to create . . . [one] that would have the potential of catching on fire. But I never imagined it would do what it ended up doing."

FINDING AN AUDIENCE

As the producer, Levy had to do a lot of work to get *George Lucas in Love* seen by the right people. On May 24, 1999, less than a month after production, tapes of the film were ready to be sent out to as many industry contacts as he could find. According to Levy, the film's success was initiated with the playing of these tapes. In fact, he sees the "hundreds of televisions playing bootleg copies of the tape passed around through the Hollywood network system" as *George Lucas in Love's* "most crucial venue." "Had Hollywood not embraced the film, had assistants not passed the film to executives who passed the film to industry leaders, there would never have been a story for the press to run with. Because of the industry sensation," Levy continues, "the film seemed to have already achieved legendary status by the time the public would see it."

Soon after its Hollywood debut, the media picked up and propagated the buzz about *George Lucas in Love.* Entertainment magazines and news programs such as *Variety, Hollywood Reporter,* and CNN raced to be one of the first to report on the parody that everybody in Hollywood was watching. It appeared as though the film was becoming quite a success in the high-profile entertainment world, but for the creators, this buzz was not a signal to rest. Extending beyond Hollywood, Nussbaum and Levy submitted *George Lucas in Love* to several of the biggest film festivals, including the Toronto International Film Festival, the Mill Valley Film Festival, and the Texas Film Festival. Levy believes that traditional film festivals provide films and filmmakers with access to a unique experience and exposure that is not replicated anywhere. He says, "There are few things that rival the experience of sitting among an audience of roughly 900 *Star Wars* fans at midnight in Toronto enjoying your film so immensely that the soundtrack can barely be heard." In addition to the festival screenings, *George Lucas in Love* had a brief commercial run in a Landmark Theater in Los Angeles. Although it was for the purpose of qualifying for an Academy Award, this three-day run added to the impressive reputation that Nussbaum and Levy were earning. By going from Hollywood to festivals to commercial theaters, Nussbaum and Levy tried to promote their work in diverse areas in order to reach as many viewers as possible.

Through the various screenings at several different venues, Nussbaum and Levy found quite a large audience for *George Lucas in Love*. However, even with this success, they still did not come close to reaching the same number of viewers as a Hollywood blockbuster. To find such an audience, the film would need to go from projecting on a film screen to playing on a home computer monitor. In other words, Nussbaum and Levy would have to take advantage of the venue with the largest possible audience: the Web.

It was not long before entertainment web companies recognized the potential of *George Lucas in Love* and began to make Nussbaum and Levy offers for their film. Although they had not originally intended to show their film on the web, Nussbaum and Levy decided to seize the opportunity that lay before them. Once they decided to exhibit the film on the web, it was just a matter of choosing a site. "Joe and I were fortunate to have spoken with several sites, all of whom exhibited a great deal of passion for the content they exhibited," Levy says. He explains that they eventually decided on a new site with an exciting idea. "[The MediaTrip site] was a unique situation in that it had not yet gone online and they wanted to put *George Lucas in Love* at the very center of their launch." For Nussbaum and Levy, MediaTrip had everything they were looking for in a site: spirit in the exhibition of its content, passion for *George Lucas in Love*, and a good financial deal. Plus, there were some added benefits, as Levy describes, "In addition to realizing that we would be directly tied into the imminent press campaign associated with their launch, we were very impressed by the driving leadership and vision behind MediaTrip's management." In the end, Nussbaum and Levy granted the company an exclusive license to exhibit the film on the internet for a defined term. As part of the deal, MediaTrip was also granted exclusive rights for the film's home video and DVD distribution.

SELLING THE FILM

Although part of the deal, home video and DVD distribution was not Nussbaum and Levy's main concern with MediaTrip. Their priority was online viewership. They and MediaTrip watched to see how an online audience would respond to *George Lucas in Love*; just as the industry had predicted, the film was a hit.

It was not long before people were requesting to buy video tapes and DVD copies of the film. Nussbaum and Levy continuously received calls and found posted messages, all asking the same question, When is the video coming out? They quickly recognized the economic potential of *George Lucas in Love*. Levy explains, "In addition to the initial decision to make the film available online for free so anyone who wanted to see the film could do so, Joe and I also wanted to exploit the film in as many ways as possible to financially recoup our initial investment and perhaps make a little bit of profit above that. I must have received at least fifty calls from people who got my number just so they could ask me how to buy it. It did-n't take a marketing genius to take the next step." So on April 21, 2000, less than a year after the film's final cut was made and about six months after its debut on MediaTrip, video copies of *George Lucas in Love* became available for purchase exclusively on Amazon.com (www.amazon.com). According to the Amazon video sales charts, the film shot to the No. 1 position on its day of release, and stayed in the top 10 for months. For a period, it even outsold Lucas's summer 1999 blockbuster, *Star Wars, Episode 1: The Phantom Menace,* which to Levy was "astonishing."

As Levy has said, because of the sizeable requests for the video, the decision to sell copies of *George Lucas in Love* was not the move of a "marketing genius." However, even if Nussbaum and Levy are not brilliant marketers, they certainly understand the business of filmmaking. The evidence of their gift for cinematic storytelling is in the reception of the work. Before the film was a bestseller on Amazon, it was a favorite on MediaTrip, and before that in Hollywood circles. According to Levy, this occurred because online audiences and Hollywood have very similar tastes in movies. "I think the reason this ended up being such a valuable web commodity was that the elements that made *George Lucas in Love* so incredibly popular in Hollywood happened to be the same elements that appealed to the core online viewing audience," says Levy. "The love for and fascination with *Star Wars*, George Lucas, Academy Award winning films, parodies and comedies is a love shared by the industry as well as the online audience." Included in Levy's list of elements is *Star Wars*'s large and loyal fan base, a phenomenon that was established long before

George Lucas in Love. Nussbaum and Levy, who consider themselves to be *Star Wars* fans found that their most dedicated viewers already possessed an allegiance to Lucas and his *Star Wars* series.

LISTENING TO THE FANS

The fandom of the viewers becomes most evident when they express their opinions about the film. As it does for many films on its site, MediaTrip provides its viewers with a message board for sharing ideas about *George Lucas in Love.* From the film's page, a viewer can link to the message board and post comments about the film or questions for Nussbaum and Levy. Quite often, viewers will have something to say about prior comments and the message board becomes host to a discussion.

Besides acting as a place for fans to connect with other fans and parade their loyalty to *Star Wars*, the message board also enables viewers to write directly to Nussbaum and Levy. Not only does communicating with the filmmakers please the fans, but Levy says that receiving messages from viewers is also very helpful to him. "Feedback from an audience, whether immediate through laughing, cheers, and applause, or delayed through postings on a web site, is what feeds filmmakers." He continues, "It lets us know the work we do is appreciated, and it helps us learn how to do it better."

ELEMENTS OF SUCCESS

Although much of the success of *George Lucas in Love* comes from the story elements of *Star Wars* and *Shakespeare in Love,* George Lucas and parody, the short length of the film also contributes a great deal. "I believe taking all of these elements and immediately gratifying audiences by assembling them into a nine-minute package is what people refer to when they say *George Lucas in Love* caught lightning in a bottle," Levy explains. As the producer says, a lot happens in the film's nine minutes. The audience is provided with almost instant gratification since it does not have to wait long to experience comedy, romance, and drama, a unique advantage of the short form.

Besides offering an immediate experience, the short film is also conducive to web exhibition. As we mentioned in Chapter 4, web exhibition is bringing the short back into mainstream entertainment, and *George Lucas in Love* is a perfect example of this recent phenomenon. The film has made its way into the homes of hundreds of thousands of Americans. Most importantly, Nussbaum and Levy satisfied their original goal and found jobs in the entertainment industry: Nussbaum directs TV commercials and is attached to direct several features (none of which have been green lit as of February 2001), while Levy is a producer of new media content at Bandeira Production Company. It appears as though the USC graduates have stumbled upon a fairy tale ending to their own story. However, according to Levy, this outcome is more common than one might think. With the web providing a showcase for new talent, Levy predicts success stories similar to his will become "increasingly numerous." He says, "I absolutely feel the web is a completely legitimate and increasingly important source of new material and talent which is mined on a daily basis by Hollywood's eyes."

This is good news for independent filmmakers. Nussbaum and Levy's *George Lucas in Love* shows the power of a good story, talent, and lots of attentive eyes. Now all you need is the story and talent, and the Internet will supply you with the audience.

Anthony Cerniello's *Jaunt*: Non-Narrative Visual Films and the Use of Digital Special Effects

Since there are so many elements involved in the medium of film (story, visuals, music, dialogue, and so forth), it is difficult to say which is going to make your movie a success with audiences or the industry. As we saw in Chapter 5, Joe Nussbaum and Joseph Levy attribute the *George Lucas in Love's* popularity not only to its witty, humorous story, but also (and especially) to the fact that it is based on filmmaking legend, George Lucas. However, this does not mean you need to make a parody about your favorite filmmaker for your movie to become a hit. In fact, what one is struck by when exploring the "Top Rated" section of various Internet cineplexes is the diversity of the featured films. For example, the "Top Rated" list on IFILM one week consisted of *Scott's Play,* a comedy about a bad production of *Macbeth; More,* a melancholy stop-animation short about a secret invention that makes the world look better than it is; *Dildo Song,* a silly musical commercial for a sex toy; and *Urban Prisoner,* a true-to-life scene of one woman's serious encounter with sexual harassment. From looking at this selection, it can be gleaned that there is no such thing as a formula for a successful film produced for the web. Despite their differences in story, style, and mood, all these films have managed to draw a large online viewership. This list also demonstrates to us that Internet cineplexes look for diversity and invite filmmakers to experiment. On sites like IFILM, we find films that normally would not have much of a chance at expo-

Figure 4.1 Anthony Cerniello's experimental short film, Jaunt. Courtesy of Anthony Cerniello. Used with permission.

sure since they break various Hollywood conventions, including the film's length, subject matter, style, and narrative form.

In this chapter, we further examine the experimentation being conducted by web filmmakers by profiling Anthony Cerniello and his film, *Jaunt.* Cerniello originally conceived of *Jaunt* in the fall of 1997 while in film school at Manhattan's School of Visual Arts and submitted a rough cut of the film as his final project before graduating in May 1998. *Jaunt* was soon discovered by IFILM. The Internet cineplex was so enthusiastic about Cerniello's project that it requested to show the rough cut for the site's October 1998 launch, agreeing to replace it with the final cut once completed. However, after he finished the final cut of *Jaunt,* IFILM convinced Cerniello that "it would be a good experiment to keep up [both versions], and see how people react to both of them," he explains. For this reason, before watching *Jaunt* on the site, you must specify which version you want to see. Since the seven-and-a-half minute final cut is the version Cerniello prefers and we have decided to discuss this one (*Jaunt V2* that we will refer to as *Jaunt*) in this chapter.

In addition to being categorized as "action," "drama," and "sci-fi," ifilm lists *Jaunt* under the "experimental" genre. There are a couple daring aspects of Cerniello's film that have earned it an "experimental" label, the strongest by far being its lack of story. Cerniello describes *Jaunt* as a non-narrative film, it does not contain a story of any kind. "It doesn't really give the viewer much information to go on, which I think makes it a confusing experience for most people," he says. Automatically, this puts *Jaunt* at odds with most films and just about all Hollywood movies, a fact that does not bother Cerniello in the slightest. With *Jaunt,* he wanted to create a piece that "would be taken in on a visual level," he says, and evoke an emotional response from viewers through images rather than story. He knew the tool that would allow him to do so was high-quality special effects. He explains, "I made *Jaunt* to prove to myself that I could make special effects look good for not a lot of money." And although Cerniello recognizes that some filmmakers disapprove of this motivation behind making *Jaunt,* he realistically responds, "You need to make films [that are created for the purpose of testing your skills] in order to gain the experience." For Cerniello, *Jaunt* was a way to learn the craft of special effects production.

SPECIAL EFFECTS ON THE WEB

By choosing to learn special effects and by making *Jaunt*, Cerniello has become part of one of the most exciting online cinema movements. His film is one of a new breed found on the web featuring low-budget (yet visually astounding) special effects. Along with *Jaunt*, films like *405,* a comical short about an airplane driving on California's 405 freeway and tailgating a Jeep, are finding audiences of over a million viewers through Internet cineplexes. Using affordable software such as Adobe Photoshop and LightWave 3D, filmmakers Bruce Branit and Jeremy Hunt made *405* in three months on a tiny budget. Because of its popularity on IFILM and its professional look, Hollywood took notice. Shortly after the film's release, Branit and Hunt signed with the Creative Artists Agency.

Even though a success story like *405* is always impressive, Cerniello is not surprised that the film's triumph stems from special effects. Cerniello believes that "special effects have taken over for the most part." Whenever he sees a film that includes special effects, Cerniello observes that the effects are the "selling point of the movie." He feels that as time goes on and technology becomes more accessible, more and more filmmakers are going to experiment with special effects. Cerniello predicts, "Effects will only get more prevalent, to the point where using computer generated actors and computer generated backgrounds will be very common in the near future." In addition, Cerniello thinks it soon will be much easier and cheaper to produce effects for the screen because of the introduction of the High Definition format and digital projectors.

CREATING *JAUNT*

Creating stunning visuals involves more than simply knowing how to operate the appropriate hardware and software. Before generating any computer graphics within the post-production stage, Cerniello made good use of such pre-production duties as planning, sketching, and storyboarding.

It was during pre-production that he and his production designer, Nick Fisher, decided to give *Jaunt* the look of a science-fiction film, with some scenes resembling anime, a popular form of Japanese animation. Largely because of their planning, *Jaunt* achieves a distinct of style that immediately hits you at the film's beginning. *Jaunt* opens with a jarring pan across a city's horizon. This shot, which is seen repeatedly throughout the opening sequence, is characterized by its low-resolution. Although at first it simply appears to be a low-quality image, a few shots later you discover that it is actually a shot from the point of view of a mysterious man wearing hi-tech virtual reality goggles that make him look like a cyborg. What intercuts these shots (and eventually outnumbers them) are crisp, bluish-tinted images of a nervous woman coming into her spacious loft, pulling down the shades, sitting on her bed, biting her nails, and washing her face. At first, there appears to be no reason for her anxiety, but you soon discover its source when you see a close-up shot of a hand holding a tiny camera poke through the doorway of her apartment. On seeing this image, along with that of the man with the eyepiece seen earlier, you begin to recognize the threat of cameras and voyeurism. The film depicts a futuristic world defined by constant surveillance; individuals lacking political and social power do not have access to cameras, but instead are forced to be objects of a tyrannical gaze.

During the production of *Jaunt*, Cerniello saw this dynamic between power and technology not only in his film, but also in reality. Finding himself in a difficult financial situation and struggling to gain access to 35mm cameras, Cerniello engaged in some dubious behavior so he could shoot *Jaunt* 35mm film. To get his hands on an Arri 435 camera, he relied on his director of photography, who worked at a camera house in New York City. "We would sneak cameras out on the weekends. We had insurance, so if anything happened, we were all right. But that was one of the many laws I broke in order to get the thing made." In addition to saving on cameras, money was not needed for the cast and crew, who willingly worked for free in their spare time. "[The film] took so long to shoot because we shot on weekends to save on equipment rentals and because most people were available only on weekends," Cerniello says. For music and sound effects, he went to close friend Peter Kim and asked him to compose and create all the audio for *Jaunt*.

After all the footage was shot, Cerniello edited *Jaunt* on an Avid that he accessed through his employer, Edgeworx, a post-production facility. Besides the Avid, at Edgeworx Cerniello found someone who could assist him with creating scenes that involved more complicated visual effects. By using 3D StudioMax and After Effects, John Bair, a computer graphics expert at the company, helped Cerniello make a couple of crucial shots: One of the shots, found about halfway through the film, displays a ship that is barely visible navigating through the inside of a human body. Flying through a sea of bright red blood, the ship is surrounded by solid blood cells that are three times its size. Bair also played a role in making one of the most memorable shots part of the final sequence. At the end of the film, you revisit a shot seen at the beginning—the anxious woman washing her face. She looks up from the sink and sees a chilling sight: several tiny flying cameras buzz through the apartment and approach her. The scene abruptly ends at the first move of the woman's escape. In creating images of the blood and flycams, Bair worked with Cerniello through all the stages of effects productions, including plate and background photography, animation, compositing, rendering, and outputting. Cerniello adds, "Edgeworx was later instrumental in getting those shots bumped up and re-rendered at hi-definition resolution."

Despite Cerniello's attempts to keep the film's budget low by using cameras, actors, and an Avid that did not cost a penny, as well as finding friends who were willing to donate their talent, he still spent $20,000 to make *Jaunt*. Looking back, Cerniello says one way he could have conserved money was by planning better, and consequently, not shooting as many scenes as he did. "I spent a lot of money building a set that ultimately wasn't used very much. Also, I shot some stuff that ended up on the cutting room floor." Cerniello could have also saved money by shooting on digital video instead of 35mm film, but says he would never choose DV over film just because it's cheaper. In his opinion, you should choose the material based on the content needs of the project, and for this reason he allows working conditions to determine whether he uses film or DV.

PUTTING *JAUNT* ON THE WEB

Although *Jaunt* was shot on film, Cerniello could not afford to make a film print of the final cut. "Striking a print with all of the visual effects intact would have sent me into debt for the rest of my life," he says. Since he did not have a print, Cerniello decided not to submit his film to offline film festivals, which tend to prefer exhibiting film prints. After ruling out offline festivals, Cerniello began to think about exhibiting his film on the web, something he never considered while making *Jaunt*.

While at Edgeworx, Cerniello met Jonathan Wells, who at the time was involved with the soon-to-be-launched Internet cineplex IFILM and who continues to be festival director of the online film festival Resfest. Impressed by *Jaunt*, Wells decided to include the experimental film in the festival, and also asked if Cerniello wanted it to be part of IFILM's launch. Cerniello accepted Wells's offer and agreed to put *Jaunt* on IFILM because "I had nothing to lose by doing it and everything to gain." "Everything" was thousands of viewers for his work, as well as exposure on other Internet cineplexes such as PitchTV. In addition to these gains, IFILM did not require an exclusive license to host *Jaunt*. Although he would not make any money from the deal with IFILM, Cerniello maintained autonomy over his film. Cerniello says, "The deal itself was pretty simple. They sent me a non-exclusive agreement for the use of the film and I signed it."

For the most part, Cerniello has been pleased with IFILM as a venue for *Jaunt*; however, there are some aspects of the site that he is not entirely comfortable. Cerniello says, "Having your film in the company of other good films is important," and for a while, "[IFILM] will take practically anything," which makes for a large film collection and visits to the site a "little overwhelming." Cerniello also does not like the fact that viewers can rate the films on the site, a feature common not just to IFILM, but to most Internet cineplexes. He believes, "All sites should get rid of ratings. Films should be just shown on their own merit." This does not mean that Cerniello wants to banish all forms of audience participation from Internet cinplexes. On the contrary, he particularly enjoys reading viewer reviews of *Jaunt*, even if they are not always positive.

As we demonstrate in Chapters 5, 6, and 7, filmmakers learn a lot about their work and their audience by way of viewer messages and reviews. For Cerniello, viewer reviews continue to teach him that *Jaunt* does not touch many people in the way he had hoped. When conceiving of the film, he thought that the visual effects would inspire such a strong emotional response within viewers that a narrative was not necessary. Unfortunately,

Cerniello has found that many people are confused rather than moved by *Jaunt*. As one viewer, named "User 23," writes, "I'm lost on the attempt. What is this supposed to be about?" Cerniello thinks the film's brevity is one reason for the confusion. "I don't think you can achieve [a deep emotional response in viewers] in such a small time frame," he says. He also has discovered that many people dislike films without stories. "I learned that a lot of people don't appreciate non-narrative films."

However, not all reviews that *Jaunt* receives are critical. In fact, for every negative comment directed at the film, there is one that expresses support and enthusiasm for *Jaunt*. For example, one viewer writes, "This was phenomenal!!! Whatever one thinks of it stylistically, it is a very powerful journey." In fact, some responses even reflect a viewing experience that Cerniello had envisioned for his audience—one filled with emotion and an appreciation for the visual effects. Such is the case with "Tigerstyle," who writes, "I am not sure what [*Jaunt*] meant, but it did inspire thought. It is very beautiful piece . . . It pulls you in and moves you, but I can't really describe it . . . which is why I love it."

Never expecting the film to go very far, Cerniello made *Jaunt* mainly for the purpose of learning special effects production. Not only did he achieve his goal, but he also pushed through the boundaries of conventional film-making and created a wildly experimental film. Although never anticipated, it was through Internet cineplexes that *Jaunt* found an audience. And although viewers are not always accepting of Cerniello's short, their reviews demonstrate to us that online audiences are willing to watch experimental films. Because of the web, filmmakers no longer need to stifle their creativity in order to find a venue for their films. Just about every Internet cineplex highlights an experimental category which holds unusual films that in the past would only have been seen in underground festivals.

Jennifer Ringley's *JenniCam:* Live Images from Home

In the previous chapters, we discussed several creative individuals who have utilized the web to showcase their films to many viewers. In addition to the web being a venue for independent films, we also recognize that the Internet is a medium unto itself with unique characteristics that make for different kinds of storytelling. Frequently on the web, narratives are presented in a multimedia fashion by combining still images, streaming and downloadable video files, audio tracks, text, and audience feedback. In this chapter, we explore one of the new forms of web storytelling that we term "webcam cinema." As we discuss, webcam cinema is a relatively new type of non-fiction film in which average people turn cameras on themselves, push the record button, and document as well as exhibit their lives from within their own homes to anyone online. Not only are live images made available to an online audience, but the web sites that host the still or streaming footage also contain other types of media—such as journal entries—that help to further acquaint the audience with the site's subject. By blending web aesthetics with cinema, "webcammakers" define a new form of web documentary.

Such is the case for "JenniCam" (www.jennicam.org), a web site that presents an online documentary of the everyday life of a young woman. At the center of this site is a webcam that continuously snaps pictures of its creator, Jennifer Ringley, who started the JenniCam site in 1996, after observing "The Amazing Fish Cam" (www.netscape.com/fishcam), a web site that allows viewers to observe live pictures of fish swimming in a tank. For Ringley, this was a seminal moment that changed her life. Then a college student, she decided to become a fish in her fishbowl. She decided to document her life by setting up her own webcam. In her dorm room, Ringley hooked up a special tiny camera to her computer. The camera shot live pictures of Ringley behaving as she typically did: working on her computer, studying, watching television, and sleeping. Then, by way of webcam software, these images were immediately uploaded to Ringley's web site, making them available for anyone online.

Now, years after the founding of JenniCam, Ringley continues to broadcast her uncensored life every day and night of the year. After graduating from college, she moved to an apartment in Washington, D.C. and upgraded her version of the webcam system. Instead of snapping and uploading black-and-white images every three minutes, the new and improved JenniCam refreshed Ringley's site with color photos every minute, something that pleased viewers and proved reliable. While some "webcammakers" are experimenting with live video streaming, Ringley has stayed with a system that snaps still images, even in her new house in Sacramento, California for reasons of technical and financial stability. However, her decision to stick with the cheaper system does not mean running JenniCam is easily afford-able. Because of high site maintenance costs, Ringley must charge member-ship fees for the site. She invites guests to join JenniCam for fifteen dollars every 90 days. Membership yields access to webcam images every minute, as opposed to every fifteen minutes for guests, as well as those archived.

Over time JenniCam has expanded and now switches between the view-points of seven webcams (most are Axis Neteye cameras) that are dispersed throughout her home. The cameras are connected to a hub that is connect-ed to a DSL (digital subscriber line) modem. Connected to this modem is a server—a computer that Ringley uses to run her web site.

Pictures of Ringley in her bedroom, bathroom, office, living room, and kitchen are available to JenniCam viewers. Ringley thinks part of the popularity of JenniCam comes from people's desire to see spontaneous, uncensored moments in her life, such as when she is undressing or having sex. However, she attributes the majority of her success to the public's interest in seeing average lives represented in the media. Since the Hollywood cameras tend to privilege glamorous stars, and television pro-grams and movies often neglect to represent average people, Ringley feels compelled to provide realistic pictures of herself for the public to see. In other words, Ringley is committed to presenting pictures that are not glamorized and not manipulated when they come through JenniCam. She wants her viewers to see her as she actually exists within her home.

It is important to note that the webcam is only one piece of equipment that enables Ringley to document her life. The overall documentary narra-tive on the site is composed of journal entries, video cameras, still photographs, a webcast show, and poetry. The menu page allows people to access live screen shots, a gallery of past webcam shots, images of her pets (three cats, a ferret, and a hedgehog), a personal journal, and a webcast talk show. We examine three of the most dynamic sections of the site: Gallery, Journal, and *JenniShow*.

GALLERY

JenniCam takes innumerable pictures of Ringley. Through these pictures, viewers discover who she is, what her personality is like, what things are important to her, how she is feeling, and so forth. The "Gallery" is a space in which she selects certain images from a month's worth of JenniCam footage, and privileges them with her attention. She lays each month's selected images out in a matrix, and visitors can click on any picture to get a larger image. On many of the pictures, she has written a short comment to focus attention on one aspect of the picture. One photo, for example, shows Ringley eating an Oreo cookie as she is working on her computer. She has added the following text to the image: "Oreos before noon is never a good sign." Like other aspects of the site, these comments become part of her entire webcam documentary, one that she shapes and editorializes.

Along with it being a place where Ringley can personalize images of herself through written text, the Gallery offers an artistic presentation of JenniCam footage. For the most part, images from the webcams are not crisp, clear, or aesthetically pleasing. They have a tendency to look like spontaneous documentary footage: neither well-lit nor well-framed, and often lack engaging content. These features are typical of webcam images since their primary function is to document a subject, rather than present a work of art. However, through the Gallery, Ringley demonstrates that many of her JenniCam images contain beauty and artistic merit. In preparing images for the Gallery, Ringley digitally manipulates many of them with Adobe Photoshop to enhance their clarity and enliven them. Then, by re-presenting them in the Gallery, Ringley removes them from their original "JenniCam" context and reinvents the meaning of the images. They no longer serve as documentation of her ordinary existence, but rather are evidence of her creativity.

JOURNAL

Just about every five days, Ringley writes an entry for her "Journal" and posts it on her site. Her entries include a range of information, from the mundane (including detailed accounts of her daily experiences) to the very personal (such as her feelings about relationships, family, and politics). As with most of the text on her site, Ringley posts the Journal by using what she calls, "a plain old text editor" to write code for the site.

It might be said that visitors have access to Ringley on a deeper level through the Journal. On the pages of this section, she becomes a spokesperson for her generation by openly sharing her problems. Within her Journal, Ringley frequently discusses her parents, who are in a perpetual state of separating and reuniting, and her brother, who severed all contact with the Ringleys in 1994. Ringley also spends a lot of time indulging in gossip about her own love life, making every detail, including heartfelt confessions to her boyfriends, accessible to fans. (One such entry is an apology to a friend for making him feel "underappreciated" and "pulling away" when he wanted to get close to her.) By reading her intimate thoughts, viewers learn about another dimension of Ringley, one that most people keep private.

Besides adding to a viewer's understanding of her, the Journal also provides insight into the site's visual footage. Through JenniCam, you have access to images that provide a lot of visual details, but you are given hardly any textual explanation about what you see. Ringley's Journal entries serve to fill in many of the blanks that visuals alone cannot communicate. For example, you might see Ringley in bed all day but not know why, or you might catch her kissing a man who is unfamiliar to you. A couple days later, you are guaranteed to discover through a journal entry that she has been sick or learn the name of her new boyfriend.

JENNISHOW

JenniShow is Ringley's biweekly talk show that is produced and webcast through the Internet cineplex The Sync (www.thesync.com) (See the Appendix for a description of the site.) Unlike the live footage of JenniCam, *JenniShow* episodes are composed of pre-recorded footage that is shot with an SVHS Panasonic Supercam. Although not a high-end digital camera, this Supercam allows for a direct connection to a lavaliere microphone, which helps provide a clear audio recording (thus making it easy for viewers to follow the show, even with a 56k modem). After being shot, each episode is edited with Adobe Premiere and captured in .AVI format on a computer, which eventually converts the file into Real Video and Windows Media.

Ringley is both the host and, more often than not, the subject of *JenniShow*, which started in 1998 as a spin-off of the popular JenniCam. For Ringley's fans, JenniShow serves an important function by presenting a more personalized form of contact with her—one in which she talks to her fans through video. Initially, most of the content of *JenniShow* episodes came from fans. At the end of the very first episode, Ringley told her fans that she hoped they would provide the show's material and direction, requesting that they email her ideas for the show and questions she could answer on the show. Embedded in this call for feedback is an aspiration toward spontaneity. In other words, Ringley hopes to create a conversation with her fans that is unscripted (to a certain extent) and can be found only in real life.

After discovering what fans want to know about her and what they want to see on her show, Ringley makes an effort to cater to their requests. In many episodes, the majority of the show's time is dedicated to answering fans' questions, and most of the episodes' topics are carved out of her fans' curiosities. For example, some viewers had questions about Ringley's veganism, so in the episode, "Jenni Makes Hummus," she teaches fans how to make one of her favorite vegan dishes (containing no animal products).

Over the past couple of years, *Jennishow* has changed in several ways. Along with a more upbeat style and a faster pace, some of Jenni's episodes have taken place outside of her apartment, such as in an airplane or at the Blair Witch house in Maryland. However, one constant feature that has remained throughout the series is a question-and-answer session between Ringley and her fans. She makes time in every episode to respond to a new set of questions. This goes to show Ringley's fans have remained a priority for her; their curiosity has brought her fame, and she makes sure she keeps offering them what they find interesting.

Without any knowledge of filmmaking techniques, Jennifer Ringley is one of the first people to take advantage of web technology and use it as a way to present a new form of documentary. Through a firm grasp of the technology behind web design, webcams, and video streaming, she is able to present a compelling documentation of her life, becoming one of the leading pioneers in webcammaking.

CHAPTER

9

Maya Churi's *Letters from Homeroom:* An Interactive Narrative Style in an Age of Media Convergence

As we discussed in the Introduction, online cinema and traditional cinema are not the same media. Although they share some characteristics, online cinema is truly defined by its constant experimentation, both in terms of the production process and the final product. We saw an example of this in Anthony Cerniello's *Jaunt,* a non-narrative experimental short that presents ten minutes of beautiful but strange images (see Chapter 7). Cerniello's film would never be found in a commercial movie theater because of its unconventional content and style. However, as a result of the Internet indies movement, films like *Jaunt* have finally found a place of exhibition on the web and can indeed reach a large audience.

Filmmakers experiment with not only the content of online movies, but their form as well. Maya Churi's *Letters from Homeroom* (www.lettersfromhomeroom.com) is one such site that blends a fictional narrative with the interactivity of a web site. Of course, interactive movies have existed for some time on CD-ROM computer games; interactive movies were even found at the 1967 World's Fair in Toronto. But it is only fairly recently that web sites have become places of interactive storytelling.

Churi, a graduate of New York University's film school, decided to make her narrative into a web site because she felt it was the only way to fully tell her story. In this chapter, we trace the steps Churi took to do this.

Figure 9.1 Maya Churi's interactive web narrative, Letters from Homeroom.
Courtesy of Maya Churi. Used with permission.

Additionally, we pay close attention to the ways Churi capitalizes on the unique aspects of interactive web narratives, such as their nonlinear structure and their capacity to include various types of media.

Letters from Homeroom is a fictional web narrative about two sixteen-year-old girls who are in the midst of adolescence. Alix and Claire are best friends wrestling with issues familiar to many teenagers, such as popularity, relationships, alcohol, and sex. *Letters from Homeroom* details how Alix and Claire grow apart as they try to balance the pressures of school, boyfriends, and their friendship. Most of the narrative is presented through the voices of the two main characters in the form of notes that were written during class. The passing of notes is a quintessential part of the high school experience and something most people have done at some point during their youth. By making notes the primary source of information on the site, Churi feels that most people can relate to what they see onscreen.

In addition to viewers' familiarity with the act of passing notes, many people can also relate to the notes' contents. Within the notes, Churi's characters discuss events and feelings that are common to many teenagers, and a part of Churi's own adolescent years. She recalls, "At the high school I attended there was constantly something going on which merited a letter or a meeting in the girls bathroom—Friday night parties, watching movies in health class, having sex, experimenting with drugs, getting sick. [These stories] are forever imbedded in my mind," she says. They are now played out through Churi's characters. Churi thinks most viewers will also recognize the sense of excitement that is expressed in most of the notes. She attempted to capture this feeling through Alix and Claire's tone. She explains, "When one is a teenager, everything is exciting because it's new, it's never been experienced before. These girls' letters are a testament to that."

CONCEIVING THE STORY

Churi was reminded of the importance to teenagers of note passing after finding in her parents' attic a bag full of notes that she wrote and received in high school. She explains, "There were over 100 of them and I quickly sat down to read every one of them. They were so intimate and vulgar and dramatic and boring, all at the same time." The intensity and range of emotions within the notes convinced Churi to use them in a story. "I knew then I had to make a film about passing notes."

Although Churi originally intended to make a conventional film, she changed her plan for *Letters from Homeroom* after considering how she wanted to tell the story. She first decided the story should come from the teenage characters' perspectives, and should also be expressed through notes. Once certain about these two requirements, a web site appeared to be the best form for her project. She thought that if done right, a web site could respect the individual voices of Churi's characters and maintain the interactivity of note passing by allowing the audience to participate by writing to the characters.

Churi designed the *Letters from Homeroom* site to mirror a high school, with each section named a different room: Homeroom, Lockers, Bathroom, Auditorium, and Library. The purpose of each section loosely resembles the space after which it is named. Together, they recreate the high school experience for the audience. Each section has its individual function within the story.

HOMEROOM

After entering the site from the home page, you are sent to Homeroom. Similar to an actual high school homeroom, this space serves as an introduction. In the Homeroom page, Alix and Claire are presented for the first time. A still image of each character, with her name written directly above it, lies in the middle of the page. The close-up pictures reveal their faces and different hairstyles (Alix has long brown hair, while Claire has short bleached-blonde hair), and are arranged in such a way that Alix and Claire appear to be talking to each other.

Below the pictures are instructions about the tiny images, or "thumbnails," that are at the top of the page. The instructions state that you can gain access to a note by clicking on a thumbnail. Indeed, when you click on a thumbnail, the pictures of Alix and Claire become windows that display one of the notes; since there are two pictures (or windows) the origins of the note determines which window is active (that is, Alix's picture becomes a note from Alix or Claire's photo is replaced by one of her own notes). By having two windows instead of just one, Churi provides each character with her own space to express her own unique thoughts and feelings. In doing so, a window represents each character in the narrative, and the notes become their dialogue. By having two separate windows for Alix and Claire, "the audience can actually experience the dialogue that has gone on between them as if they were [to hear the two] talking to each other," Churi explains. This spatial design also reveals deeper pieces of Alix and Claire's friendship. For example, after going through the notes, you realize that most of the early ones come from Alix. Because the site continuously forces your eyes to the left side of the page, the situation of imbalance in the girls' friendship is driven home.

There are seventeen notes and three different ways in which to experience them. As the second instruction states, "Choose a format: video, audio only, or text." When a thumbnail is selected it fills one of the windows and three little icons appear beneath it: a filmstrip (video), a speaker (audio), and a bubble containing the letters, "ABC" (text).

To select a version of the note, you click on an icon. Your options are to watch a short video that is accompanied by either Alix or Claire reading the note aloud, to listen to the audio reading accompanied by a slideshow of images from the video, or to read the text on a page that appears to be handwritten and adorned with doodles. Although it first seems that the availability of three versions has to do with viewer's preference, the feature actually responds to issues of access. When designing the site, Churi kept in mind how her audience would receive the notes. She says, "I knew going into this project that a lot of [teens] at home weren't streaming video because their connections were just too slow. I've heard over and over how kids are streaming and watching video, but I've been to high schools and actually asked the kids [if they were]. The majority [of them] might start downloading a video, but rarely do they wait for it to complete." By providing versions that work well with all connections, there is more of a chance that viewers can easily see all the notes and receive a more complete picture of *Letters from Homeroom.*

Yet when it comes right down to it, the purpose of the three versions extends beyond issues of access. Even though the initial reason behind this feature was practicality, the three versions have gained narrative significance. Although many viewers have access to only the text version, there are some that receive and experience all three. Those who do get to see various dimensions of the material. As Churi describes, "Watching the video is great and the way it was made to be seen, but I love the text version as well. With the text, not only does one get to see the doodles on the page, but there are also hyperlinks to other sections of the site, so the audience can jump around. Not to mention, notes are meant to be read." From her research, Churi has found that most people who visit the site try out some of the notes in each version, which "gives people a full understanding of the story. I love that."

The sequencing of information has a lot to do with the way viewers come to understand *Letters from Homeroom.* Since a web site is a medium that demands non-linearity and interaction, viewers possess a great deal of autonomy, determining the order in which information will be received. They have the option of viewing note 16 before note 9, for example, or even skipping Homeroom altogether and going straight to another section. Churi believes that this freedom of narrative choice gives the interactive web filmmaker an advantage when telling a story over a conventional narrative approach. She says, "When one goes to a movie, they are presented with a road on which they must follow to get to the end. On the web, this is not necessarily true, and I don't think that enough video artists are taking advantage of what the web has to offer unless they are presenting the audience with a number of different paths on which to travel." This being said, Churi also makes sure to alert viewers to the benefits of choosing all of the notes in chronological order through the third instruction:

"Watch the letters in order to get the whole story." By "whole story," Churi means the linear story from beginning to end. Although moving through the notes in chronological order might not be the most innovative way to receive the story, for many people it is the most comprehensible pathway.

LOCKERS

In addition to Alix and Claire, there are five other characters in *Letters from Homeroom*. Even though Alix and Claire's points of view are exclusively represented on the Homeroom page, you hear about the other characters within their notes. Then, when the you reach the Lockers page, you are offered access to personal information about these five secondary characters: Andrew, Chris, Mike, Jenn, and Lisa. (You also receive some new low-down about Alix and Claire.)

Opening a locker is the only way to get a first-person account of a secondary character. Although the contents within each are short and not very descriptive, they offer enough information to help you understand the significance of the character to Alix and Claire. The impact of the locker is particularly evident when figuring out characters like Andrew, Alix's boyfriend, who cheats on her with Claire. In his locker, Andrew states, "I used to be a mamma's boy. . . . But then . . . I got myself to high school, felt myself some [breasts], and I forgot all about my mamma." After reading this, the viewer has more of an awareness of Andrew's present attitude about himself and toward women. In addition to giving dimension to a supporting character, the locker provides information that Andrew would never directly say to Alix and Claire, offering some explanation for his actions. As for the main characters, the lockers function similarly in that they offer little tidbits and anecdotes about Alix and Claire that add to their character development. And when considered with everything else, these facts that initially appear to be trivial end up adding a lot of personality to the characters.

Just like a high school student's locker that is hers to personalize, Churi's characters have their own private space on the Lockers page. In this virtual realm, the lockers are windows which pop-up when you click on a character's name. Assuming the style of a "Graduating Seniors" section in a high school yearbook, the lockers display black-and-white photos of the characters and list their two-sentence responses to topics that are typical for a yearbook. They hold such facts as a character's name, year in school, ambition, hobbies, most embarrassing moment, and "life-long" love.

There are a couple of notable differences between the lockers of the main and the secondary characters. First, the lockers of the secondary characters define their relationships to Alix and Claire (because of the inclusion of this information, you never forget the importance of the main characters). Second, only Alix and Claire have links to other pages from their lockers.

The links are to personal pages that hold first-person accounts of their lives. From Alix's locker, you can link to the home page of her own web site, while within Claire's locker there is a link to a long letter she has written to Alix. These pages continue the story of Alix and Claire.

At the home page of Alix's web site, there are links to Alix's report card, a digitally manipulated image of Claire's head, and her journal. This last section is the meatiest of the three. Alix's journal continues *Letters from Homeroom* from where the notes leave off, including stories of her and Claire's falling-out and the subsequent re-development of their friendship; Alix's new boyfriend; and her academic experiences in high school.

Claire continues her side of the story in "Claire's Apology Page." Though in the notes featured on the Homeroom page Claire never apologies to Alix for betraying her, here in a long letter she makes this point. In it, she gives reasons for her actions, "you were moving too fast and going places without me and you were going to ditch me for Andrew" and reassures Alix that she still cares for her, "I love you a lot, and I know you might never want to talk to me again . . . I hope that maybe one day you will . . . just call me or e-mail me or pass me a note."

BATHROOM

For Churi, the feature of the web that distinguishes it from other media is its capacity for interaction. She says, "Interaction is important. That's what makes the web so successful. Otherwise, it would be like watching television, but of really bad quality." For this reason, Churi has created two sections in *Letters from Homeroom* where you can make your thoughts part of the site. One of these is the Bathroom.

Like the walls of a high school lavatory, your responses to the story are written on the pages (or walls) of the Bathroom. At the main page of the section, there is a list of seventeen topics for you to choose from. The topics correspond to the titles of the notes on the Homeroom page, such as "Parents Stink," "Jealousy," and "Getting Caught." Once a topic is selected, you are taken to a message board that displays other viewers' comments about Alix or Claire. You can also post personal anecdotes regarding the topic here, such as posting to the message board, "The First Time," as one person did: "I'm a senior in high school and am still a virgin. I have very high standards for myself that I will live up to. I don't know how any of you can talk so casually about how you had sex at 13 and 14, and be proud of that!!" Or another person who wrote: "The first time I had sex I was 15 and it was my boyfriend's birthday. I did it kind of as a birthday present to him, it was pretty stupid of me, he was my best friend and my boyfriend, we had been going out for six months. It was very painful is all I can remember and I could barely walk afterwards. I guess I would have rather have waited until I was really in love and older to have done it."

These remarks and testimonies provide Churi with invaluable information about her audience. "They help me to gauge how effective the site is and if people are relating to the characters," she says. Churi believes message boards also benefit viewers by building a sense of community among themselves. "For the audience, I think it's a great way for teens to see what other teens are up to, get advice . . . and share their thoughts without all the negativity that can occur when talking face to face."

You can read the pages of Bathroom, as well as post messages there. The opportunity to express ideas comes directly after receiving the notes at Homeroom. On the page, the directions "Click to post a message" are just below the space in which notes are presented. If you have something to share, then you can click on the highlighted topic, which sends you to a space to write. This creates somewhat of a conversation between the character and the audience: a character says something, and without any delay you can reply to it. In a sense, you become one of the story's characters as you share your own anecdotes about high school life, which in turn becomes a part of the overall narrative of the site.

AUDITORIUM

Another way you can become a part of the narrative is by writing a note that is addressed directly to Alix or Claire. Dispersed throughout the site are links to Alix and Claire's mailboxes. After notes are submitted, they are posted on the Auditorium page. Although similar to Bathroom, Auditorium possesses a unique importance since it requires from viewers one of the most important acts of *Letters from Homeroom*: writing notes. Churi believes her audience should be allowed to participate in the act of note passing. "Since the site is about writing notes, it's only appropriate that there be a space for viewers to join in," she explains. "It gives people the sense that they are interacting with the characters. And they are."

Many of the posted letters in the Auditorium page reveal the connection that Churi's audience feels with her characters. Some people, based on their own past experiences, offer advice in the hope of helping out Alix and Claire. One viewer writes, "I had a best friend that I lost to drugs. She was the best friend that anyone could have. Whatever you do, don't let [Alix] go. Hold on with all of your might!!!" Because the characters appear so realistic and their experiences are so close to those of actual teenagers, not everyone realizes *Letters from Homeroom* is a fictional story. As Churi reveals, "Probably the most difficult thing about [the site] is that sometimes kids don't know that it is fiction, and they email the characters asking them to write back, opening up to them." Even though it is difficult not to reply, Churi feels that doing so would be deceptive. "I sympathize with the kids so much," she says, "but Alix cannot respond to them because there is no Alix. . . . Sometimes I wish there was an Alix just so she could write them back and tell them, 'It's all going to get better.'" On some occasions, when a reply is really required, Churi or one of the actresses respond. But they do clarify that the characters are fictional.

LIBRARY

Since one of the most standard features of the web is links, most web sites have a page that refers you to other sites of possible interest. On *Letters from Homeroom,* this page is called the Library. In addition to calling the audience's attention to other sites that may deserve a look, the Library plays a role in defining a site's identity. By highlighting certain sites, *Letters from Homeroom* associates itself with other things, including companies, toys, music, and ideas. Some of the listed sites include Planetgirl (www.planetgirl.com), which "features games, quizzes, advice, chat, bulletin boards, short stories and poems written by girls"; The Bit Screen (www.thebitscreen.com) which screens the video footage from *Letters from Homeroom* on its site; and Astralwerks (www.astralwerks.com), the band that did music for *Letters from Homeroom.*

For the most part, the listed sites do not play a role in developing the story; however, there is one exception. Included on the list is a link to the band Moxie (www.moxierock.com), "the all female pop/punk/folk band from New York" that is mentioned in Claire's letter of apology to Alix. When asking Alix to remember the fun they had together, Claire writes about a time when the two of them saw a Moxie concert: "It was like the best day ever when the two of us went to see Moxie play at the Den." In this instance, the real band is woven into the world of the fictional story, representing a bond that Alix and Claire share. The band is also used to reflect an aspect of the characters' personalities. The site implies that you can learn more about Alix and Claire through their taste in music, so you should go to Moxie's web site and listen to some of their songs for greater insight.

CREATING THE SITE

Being a trained filmmaker from NYU, Churi started creating *Letters from Homeroom* by working with what was familiar to her—film. "The process was much like that of making a traditional film," she begins. She wrote the script after she was named a Macdowell Fellow, allowing her to spend six weeks at the Macdowell colony—a place in Peterborough, New Hampshire where artists go to find seclusion and concentrate on their work. This creative period ended with a completed script for the project. "A month later," she continues, "I went and shot the film, again using a traditionally structured script." In shooting the video portions of her project, she used the Sony VX1000 miniDV camera (the predecessor to the VX2000). She then edited the footage using a high-end Avid system. (Churi makes sure to add, "Final Cut Pro would work just as well though.") "I edited the film as an entire twenty-minute linear piece, with sections of black in between each of the segments," she explains. In order to fully grasp the potential of the material, she followed her intuition and decided to put together the edited segments before separating them. "I needed it to work as a whole piece before I could put it out there for an audience."

Once she felt comfortable with the edits in a linear form, Churi designed the web site on paper, in a scripted flow-chart form. "This was the single most helpful document in creating the site," Churi says. "It shows everything about how the web site works." Churi adds that the flow chart was particularly useful for developing the site's structure, which "has to be in place; otherwise the audience could get lost."

Aside from planning the infrastructure, Churi spent a lot of time making the site visually appealing. "Designing the site was a gradual process," she says. She had help in this area from Fiona Brandon, one of the producers of the site. For the two women, one of the first steps in this process was brainstorming. Churi explains, "Fiona and I sat down one day and started drawing sketches of how we thought the site should look." In their sketches, they tried to answer questions like, What would make this page most interesting for the viewer? After going through many possibilities, Churi continues, "We eventually gave everything over to the designer, Ariel Churi (my brother), who took all the elements we liked and made them work together." Because designing the site involved three minds and a lot of conversation, Churi characterizes this stage as a "back and forth process." Without the contributions of Brandon and Ariel Churi, Maya would have had a difficult time achieving the final look of *Letters from Homeroom.*

Various software packages were used in the actual production of the site. For web authoring software, Churi selected Adobe Go Live. After using Avid to make the first round of final edits, Churi used Adobe Premiere for any necessary re-edits. To compress her edited footage, she worked with Media Cleaner, which Churi describes as "great software" because "it gives you a lot of choices and really lets you compare different compression rates so that you can get the best possible image." As for video streaming she decided to use QuickTime, but would advise others to offer three types of players: QuickTime, RealPlayer, and Windows Media Player. She explains, "We went with QuickTime for this project because it was the best for what we wanted to do and also because it was what we were familiar with." But she cautions, "It will limit the audience . . . to just use one program." Finally, the slide shows that accompany the audio version of the notes were created with Adobe Photoshop and Gif Builder, which Churi feels is "a really simple program."

After completing all of the production and building the site for *Letters from Homeroom,* Churi was still not ready to launch it. She wanted to test out the project with her main audience—teens—before making it available online. "When the web site design was complete," she recalls, "we recruited high school girls and some boys to test it out. We would put them in a room, without [them having] any prior knowledge of the site and [we] watched them as they went through [the site]." Through this exercise, Churi and her crew became aware of the parts of the site that the audience had difficulty with. It was important to be sure that the audience found the site accessible and enjoyable because, as Churi stated, "if they didn't get it, then no one would."

FUTURE OF NARRATIVE SITES

Maya Churi's *Letters from Homeroom* is a good example of the creative experimentation that many artists are currently exploring with web sites and storytelling. However, this form of experimentation is not necessarily new to the art world. Churi says that many artists have been experimenting with web sites as a way to create new narratives for years, "but only now is it really accessible to the general public." For this reason, right now there is a heightened interest in projects like *Letters from Homeroom*. This buzz can be found not only within the general public, but also throughout artistic circles. A testament to this is the artistic community's warm reception of Churi's project. In addition to her Macdowell Fellowship, Churi received a grant from the Creative Capital Foundation to fund *Letters from Homeroom*. She predicts that as more narrative sites are developed, the interest in such projects will increase and funding for them will become more available. And since "people are always interested in what is new," she anticipates that many filmmakers will keep experimenting with this form and pushing it to its limits.

25 Internet Cineplexes and Festivals

INTRODUCTION

This section is a guide to Internet cineplexes and online film festivals. Here, we provide descriptions of 25 sites to which you can submit your film. For each site, we state its niche (if one exists) and then provide a general description that includes the site's history, founders, and mission. We then discuss some of its most popular films. An explanation of the site's submission process is followed by a summary of any required legal agreements. (You should note that within each site description, we do not repeat those requirements that are found in all Internet cineplexes' agreements. They include your ownership of rights to the film and all its parts, and your indemnification of the site against any litigation that may come from streaming your movie on their site. You should also note that we do not include all details of the agreement; you should carefully read through each agreement before signing.) Next, we discuss the space a site allots for information about you and your film, and we detail how the Internet cineplex interacts with its audience.

Included are the following Internet cineplexes and online film festivals: ALWAYSi, AtomFilms, Bijou Café, Culture Jam, D.FILM Digital Film Festival, Exposure, Filmfilm, Force Flicks, Guerrilla Filmmakers, Hypnotic, Icebox, IFILM, LikeTelevision, MediaTrip, MovieFlix, New Venue, PopcornQ, ReelMind, Resfest, Screen47, TFN FanFilms, The BitScreen, The Sync, UndergroundFilm, and Urban Entertainment.

ALWAYSi

www.alwaysi.com
Hollywood Media Corp.
2255 Glades Road, Suite 237-W
Boca Raton, FL 33431

Part of Hollywood.com, ALWAYSi is one of the largest Internet cineplexes, with a collection of over 650 feature-length, shorts, and animated films, as well as television series. On its site, alwaysI posts two distinct mission statements, "consumer" and "business." Addressing the viewers, the company's goal is to offer diverse content to an international audience. At the same time, the company strives to serve independent filmmakers by creating a new means of distribution, as well as a place for showcasing their work to the industry. ALWAYSi is committed to catching Hollywood's attention and believes that the Internet's influence on the industry already is and will continue to be immeasurable. Says vice president of marketing Randy Greenberg, a former executive at Metro-Goldwyn-Mayer, "I am a 13-year veteran from the Hollywood studio world who has come to work for an on-line film site because of the way that this [Internet] world is changing the world of entertainment."

Viewers must subscribe to ALWAYSi in order to have access to the site's full collection. A subscription for three months costs $30, while one that lasts twelve months is $84.

MEDIA PLAYERS

Windows Media Player

FILMS EXHIBITED

ALWAYSi defines its collection by quality and quantity. There are five major categories that break down alwaysI's incredibly large and diverse film library: Independent, Classic, Foreign, Student, and Television. And within each category, there are two to six subcategories such as features, shorts, and documentaries. Many of ALWAYSi's films have already achieved some degree of recognition, mainly through exhibition at traditional film festivals or museums, or by winning awards. One example is *White Hotel* (1995). This 90-minute documentary about two female filmmakers who follow an American HIV-research team to Eritrea, Africa, has been screened at New York's Museum of Modern Art, Harvard Film Archive, Zanzibar International Film Festival, and Africa Long Beach Museum of Modern Art. One of the reasons behind the site's reputable content is that, like many of the larger sites, ALWAYSi's acquisitions department searches for new films and filmmakers at film festivals and film schools. When visiting alwaysI, you should take the time to check out its selection of foreign films (from Asia, Europe, and Latin America), classics (like Laurel and Hardy and The Three Stooges), and original webcast TV series, in addition to its enormous collection of independent features and shorts.

SUBMISSION PROCESS

ALWAYSi estimates a submitted film has a 70 percent chance of getting accepted onto its site. By becoming an ALWAYSi filmmaker, you are able to show and also sell your film to a mass audience. From the home page, click on "Submit a Film" and you can begin the submission process. You must either agree to a Non-exclusive Digital Distribution Agreement (if you want to submit your film to other internet cineplexes), or an Exclusive Digital Distribution Agreement (if you want ALWAYSi to be your film's sole internet exhibitor and distributor). These agreements differ not only in rights, but also in the amount of revenue you earn from the site. From the revenue ALWAYSi earns from subscription fees, they provide their filmmakers with a check each month—a figure based on the number of times their film is viewed, and the agreement they have chosen. While Non-exclusive Agreements earn 10% of this shared revenue, Exclusive Agreements receive 40%.

After choosing one of the agreements, fill out the online submission form, and send a VHS (NTSC) copy of your film and the $50 submission fee is treated as payment for a year-long subscription to the site.

LEGAL RIGHTS

For the Non-exclusive Digital Distribution Agreement, ALWAYSi requires non-exclusive rights to "encode, store, perform, display, copy, transmit, broadcast, and market" your film on the Internet, which includes other companies' and individuals' Internet sites, whereas the Exclusive Digital Distribution Agreement requires exclusive rights to do the same. Even after the agreements have expired, ALWAYSi has the right to keep a copy of your film for its archives.

FILM & FILMMAKER'S INFORMATION

ALWAYSi provides you with an entire page on which you can list information about your film, including film synopsis, crew, and cast. This page also includes production stills and will list any prior festival screenings or awards. In addition to the individual film pages, ALWAYSi offers a deeper look at its filmmakers by periodically profiling one in an article.

AUDIENCE PARTICIPATION

AlwaysI presents three fairly typical ways for audiences to interact with the site. If they see a film they like, they can recommend it to a friend by e-mail, post a review, or rate the film. Their comments could be posted along with others.

ATOMFILMS

www.atomfilms.com
Atom Shockwave
600 Townsend Street, Suite 125 W
San Francisco, CA 94103

One of the most well-known entertainment Web sites, AtomFilms is huge in terms of both its commercial success and its film collection. The company was founded in the fall of 1998 by Mika Salmi. Before starting AtomFilms, Salmi spent many years in the entertainment business doing media development at RealNetworks and at music companies such as Sony and EMI. Most notably, he is known for discovering Nine Inch Nails—a band that pushes the limits of mainstream music. Salmi's latest media venture repeats this performance. With AtomFilms, he has created a site that strongly maintains ties to the industry, yet also is a venue for Hollywood outcasts that are extreme in content and style. Containing an archive of hundreds of diverse short films, AtomFilms proves it is committed to its mission to bring "the best in short entertainment to every conceivable audience."

Media Player

RealPlayer, Windows Media Player

Films Exhibited

The most famous films on the site possess an edge and are found under the heading Extreme, one of the site's eight genre categories. Extreme films typically put humorous spins on sex and bodily functions; they also thematically support the company's catchy, punning logo that brandishes all of their advertisements as well as the opening flash animation on their home page: "Get into our shorts." Some of AtomFilms' most popular extremes are *Saving Ryan's Privates* (1999), a parody of the Oscar-winning Stephen Spielberg film that puts a soldier's genitalia in grave danger; and *Angry Kid* (1999), an animated, live-action series about a foul-mouthed child engaging in all sorts of nasty behavior.

Other genre categories include Comedy, Drama, Animation, Thriller, and World.

Submission Process

In order to submit a film to AtomFilms, you must be sure it meets two requirements. First, because AtomFilms specializes in short films, a film must be less than 40 minutes in length. In addition, since the company commerically distributes the films on its site, a film must have all clearances and rights for commercial distribution. After meeting these requirements, you can begin a very easy submission process. Go to the

"Submit Films" page by clicking on "working with us" and print out a submission form in PDF format. Fill out the form and send it with a VHS tape to AtomFilms in Seattle or to its London office.

LEGAL RIGHTS

If AtomFilms accepts your work, you must agree to the site's holding an exclusive license. Since AtomFilms intends to distribute your film to television networks, airlines, movie theaters, the home video and DVD market, the Internet, and broadband services, the site requires a complete commitment from its filmmakers. Following acceptance of the film, AtomFilms discusses royalty rates with its filmmakers. Each deal is unique, and for this reason, the site does not present standard royalty rates.

FILM & FILMMAKER'S INFORMATION

For each film, AtomFilms posts standard information including its running time, genre, country of origin, and key crewmembers, as well as a brief synopsis. Depending on the film, pages may include a longer synopsis, some background about the film, festival and awards history, and licensing information.

AUDIENCE PARTICIPATION

After watching one of Atom's films, you can either recommend it to a friend or rate it between 1 and 5. Along with others's reviews, average ratings appear on a film's page.

BIJOU CAFÉ

www.bijoucafe.com
5632 Van Nuys Blvd. #186
Van Nuys, CA 91401

Bijou Café sums up its commitment to promoting independent films and videos without charging filmmakers with its motto, "Independent and damn proud of it!" Decorated by bizarre yet fun images that define its style, the site's pages complement its eclectic and obscure collection of films.

To have access to the site's complete collection of films, viewers must sign up for a BijouPass Gold—a subscription that costs $3 a month. If this price is too steep, viewers can choose to register for BijouFlix On Demand and pay $.45 for each film they watch. Additionally, each week Bijou Cafe presents five films that can be downloaded for free.

MEDIA PLAYERS

RealPlayer

FILMS EXHIBITED

Bijou Café appeals to the film buff by showing both classic retro films and the newest artsy flicks. These include the British spy saga *Secret Agent* (1960) and the science fiction series *Radar Men from the Moon* (1952). Some feature length cult classics in the collection are Ed Wood's *Glen or Glenda* (1953), *White Zombie* (1932) with Bela Lugosi, and *Horror Express* (1972) with Telly Savalas. Unlike the features, most of Bijou Café's shorts are new, independent films brandishing a quirky edge; these add to the campy tone of the site. Two examples are *Diva* (1999), a narrative that explores three scenes of Hollywood divas from different decades, and *Images* (1997), an experimental film comprised of random images—of the filmmaker, his friend, abstract shapes, and feet—that are created by various techniques (such as pixelation and double exposure).

SUBMISSION PROCESS

Send in a copy of your film on VHS, VCD, or MiniDV. If you want to submit more than one film, then you must fill out a form for each one. However, to save space and money, you may put copies of all your films on one tape or CD. If your film is accepted, Bijou Café will contact you about sending higher quality copies for exhibition purposes.

LEGAL RIGHTS

If the site accepts your film, you agree to provide Bijou Café with a non-exclusive license to your film. This license, which may be terminated at your discretion at any time, includes the right to convert your film into a video streaming file, and the right to use your film for promotional purposes. The option to earn royalties is proposed only after a film is accepted.

FILM & FILMMAKER'S INFORMATION

Bijou Café does not have a template for its film pages, but rather posts any information about the film that seems suitable. Most film pages contain a synopsis, and sometimes a couple of facts about the filmmaker are woven into these descriptions. The Internet cineplex neglects to post a film's running time and year, but if you have your own site you can create a link to it from your film's page on Bijou Café.

AUDIENCE PARTICIPATION

Bijou Café provides a chat room for viewers to discuss with the barkeep (the person who runs the site) their thoughts about the Internet cineplex or independent films.

CULTURE JAM

www.culturejam.com
PO Box 73401
Davis, CA 95617-3401

The antithesis of just about all other Internet cineplexes, Culture Jam features an eclectic collection of films that "subvert mainstream mediaculture with intelligence, creativity, or meaning." This site showcases films that go against political institutions and dominant cultural beliefs and give voice to the marginalized. Unlike other sites, Culture Jam is more concerned with content than presentation, and for this reason its films are not broken down into genres but rather are compiled into one long list under the heading "Arkive." Culture Jam does not rate its films, nor does it offer its filmmakers any royalties. When you exhibit on this site, you do so for a higher cause, not for any potential financial profit.

NICHE

Counterculture activists

MEDIA PLAYERS

RealPlayer

FILMS EXHIBITED

Culture Jam does not organize its collection. When you choose a film, you simply select from a long list of titles that are presented without explanation. Because of the eccentricity of the site's films, you never truly know what you are in for until you press play. You could choose *On Nothing Days*, a poignant commentary on adolescence made in 1967 by a fifteen-year-old boy. Or you may select *Subway Map* (1992), which turns subway graffiti into a discussion on racism and religion. Another possibility is *Awakening* (1997), a short film narrated by techno music instead of words, about a teenage girl who looks inside someone else's briefcase and is never the same again.

SUBMISSION PROCESS

Every 3 weeks Culture Jam reviews the submissions it receives. When choosing films, the site does not look for a particular style or genre. What it wants are creative films with aspects of subversion (in form or narrative). The only requirement is that your film's running time be no more than 10 minutes. If you have a short that fits in terms of content and length and it is already online, fill out and submit the short submission form and include the film's URL. Otherwise, send a VHS or Hi-8mm copy to the site. Be sure to enclose with the tape an information sheet with your film's title, year, and running time, and the equipment used in its production.

LEGAL RIGHTS

Culture Jam does not make its filmmakers sign any agreements, nor does it offer any distribution deals. As directly stated by the site, "We showcase fliks we like. Basically, we provide a screening site and point traffic to the filmmaker."

FILM & FILMMAKER'S INFORMATION

On each film page, the site presents the film's synopsis, which sometimes includes a few details about the filmmaker.

AUDIENCE PARTICIPATION

None

D.FILM DIGITAL FILM FESTIVAL

www.dfilm.com
7095 Hollywood Blvd. Suite 1001
Los Angeles, CA 90028 USA

D.FILM Digital Film Festival is one of several online film festivals featured here. This festival is not only online, but also travels to various big cities such as New York, San Francisco, San Diego, London, and San Juan, Puerto Rico. According to D.FILM, its mission is to exhibit cutting-edge work done by "today's new breed of digital filmmakers." Since 1998, the site has provided its audience with downloadable festival movies, interviews with its filmmakers, a place to buy and sell equipment, and information on how to make digital films.

MEDIA PLAYERS

QuickTime

FILMS EXHIBITED

Since D.FILM is an annual festival, the standards for technical quality are very high. As a site, its collection is limited; however, it is worth looking at each film. At this time, D.FILM holds in its archive 25 films or excerpts from films, and accepts about 20 films for each year's event. Most of the films are defined by their surrealist tendency and many feature computer generated animation. One such film is *The Week Before* (1998), in which Dave McKean presents an interesting rendition of the biblical story of creation by way of stunning 3D animation. Although strange narratives are the norm at D.FILM, non-narrative shorts are also welcomed, like *Equiis* (1998), an animated sequence set to pumping techno music described as a "'digital homage' to the wildstyle graffitti of Brooklyn." D.FILM's collection also includes a few documentaries, but of course their topics have a twist. *Tatooine or Bust* (1997), a film by New Venue's founder Jason Wishnow (discussed in Chapter 5), depicts the passion of *Star Wars* fans by documenting in five different cities the premiere of the film's 1997 re-release.

SUBMISSION PROCESS

D.FILM's submission process follows the two most common rules: fill out the submission form and send it in with a tape of your film. The festival accepts mainly VHS (NTSC) tapes; however, if you have only a PAL or SEACAM version of your film, you should contact D.FILM. Unlike many film festivals, D.FILM does not charge any entry fees because, as it says on the site, "entry fees suck." D.FILM also does not have any deadlines since the festival is in a perpetual state of travel, continually going to different cities. Feel free to send in your film at any time.

LEGAL RIGHTS

One difference between online entertaiment Web sites and online festivals is that festivals tend to be less detailed with their filmmaker agreements. This is certainly true for D.FILM, which requires only that you give permission for your film to be used to promote the festival. In other words, you must agree to the posting of your images in the press and the festival program guide and on the site. Expect your film to be on D.FILM for an entire year. (To be sure that D.FILM does not host for a longer period, contact D.FILM, info@dfilm.com.)

FILM & FILMMAKER'S INFORMATION

You will not find any lengthy filmmaker's biographies on D.FILM's site. However, you will find a description of each film that is written by the filmmaker, and perhaps a brief filmography. D.FILM posts transcripts of interviews it has with its filmmakers in the place of the traditional filmmakers' bios. These interviews are at least a page long and provide a lot of details about the filmmaking process, in terms of both creativity and technical skills.

AUDIENCE PARTICIPATION

When it comes to festivals, most judging takes place before the film is accepted; the event represents an appreciation of the work. For this reason, the audience is not asked to review films for the festivals. D.FILM does provide spectators with digital video production tips and classifieds. Viewers can also click on "D.FILM Movie Maker" on the menu bar to make personal animation sequences that can be emailed to friends.

EXPOSURE

www.scifi.com/exposure/
SCIFI Channel
525 Washington Blvd
Jersey City, NJ 07310

Exposure, dubbed "The Future of Film," is the Sci-Fi Channel's Internet cineplex, presenting imaginative science fiction, fantasy, horror, and suspense films (live-action, animation, and stop-motion). The site promises that each of its filmmakers "obsesses over the impact of possibilities and celebrates the creation of fantastic worlds and ideas." In addition, the Sci-Fi Channel also presents a televised version of Exposure, an hour-long program of shorts shown every week (this material is also presented online). Furthermore, the site sponsors the "Exposure Future of Film Festival," held in New York City, in which full-length features as well as shorts are screened. The Sci-Fi Channel also allows people to apply for an Exposure Film Grant, through which filmmakers receive financial support to make a movie.

NICHE

Science-fiction

MEDIA PLAYERS

RealPlayer, ON2 broadband

FILMS EXHIBITED

On both the television program and the Internet cineplex, Exposure presents a wide variety of science fiction works by newcomers as well as seasoned professionals. Here, you can see the student works of George Lucas (*Freiheit* [1966] and *Electronic Labyrinth* [1967]) as well an experimental film by Alex Proyas (director of *The Crow* [1994]). In Proyas's early film, *Groping* (1980, Australia), he tells the story of a man watching a rape and murder through his apartment window. As the film was shot in a stop-motion style, the actors move in surreal jitters against the concrete backdrop of urban darkness. *Dust City* (1997, France), directed by Sebastien Drouin, is a computer-animated short about robots dueling in the wild west. *Searching for Carrie Fisher* (1998), directed by Stephen Dooher and produced by Daniel Loflin, is a 20-minute documentary about Dooher and Loflin's trip from Dallas, Texas, to Los Angeles, California, as they look for Carrie Fisher so Dooher can give her a recording of a love letter he made when he was 7 years old.

SUBMISSION PROCESS

You can submit science-fiction related shorts to Exposure for consideration for television or Internet broadcast. Exposure requests that you download a PDF release form, fill it out, sign it, and then submit it with a VHS copy of your film.

LEGAL RIGHTS

If your film is accepted for either the Exposure television series or the Web site, the company USA Cable will negotiate a License Agreement before showing your film.

FILM & FILMMAKER'S INFORMATION

Exposure posts a brief synopsis, of the film and a list of cast and crew, along with the filmmaker's biography. In addition, Exposure sometimes streams footage of interviews with filmmakers.

AUDIENCE PARTICIPATION

Viewers can send an "e-ticket" to friends as a way to advertise a film. In addition, they can review movies with written comments. Viewers can also choose to join Exposure's "Director's Guild," an online filmmaking community of people interested in filmmaking. Here, you can review and discuss films by posting to an online bulletin board or talk with others live in a chat room.

FILMFILM

www.filmfilm.com

Filmfilm, run by professional filmmakers, is billed as an "Internet based movie studio, complete from development to post-production to distribution." The site's founders include both independent and industry filmmakers. Three members of Filmfilm's creative team are Nora Ephron—writer/director/producer of *You've Got Mail* (1998) and writer/director of *Sleepless in Seattle* (1993); G. Mac Brown—executive producer of *You've Got Mail*, co-producer of *In & Out* (1997), and associate producer of *Scent of a Woman* (1992); and Ron Brown—writer/director/producer of *A Bedtime Story* (1997).

Serving as a place for exhibition, Filmfilm also helps filmmakers make films. And since the site's creators are so well-versed in the art of filmmaking, they know how to address every step of the process. For filmmakers, they offer specialized message boards that aid in casting your film as well as in finding a crew. Producers can post a story pitch or find a completed screenplay. For those still learning the art, each week the site provides access to a famous filmmaker, who shares insight and wisdom in the form of a video interview and an online chat room.

MEDIA PLAYERS

RealPlayer

FILMS EXHIBITED

Filmfilm is open to showing films of every genre and at any length. There are both short and feature-length films in the collection. Their genre list includes Action, Drama, Fantasy, Horror, Sci-fi and Western. From surveying its collection, one can gather that Filmfilm accepts thematically daring films of both average and high quality. Not surprisingly, the site's most popular films have a tendency to be quite technically polished, such as *A Bedtime Story* (a film by a member of Filmfilm's creative team, Ron Brown), a comedic look at one couple's troubles in the bedroom; and *Malicious Intent* (1999), the story of a 10-year-old boy who uses his supernatural powers for purposes of revenge. However, if you search through the archives you can also see films of a more amateur nature, like *Pizzalero* (1998), described as "a coming attraction for a sexy-Mexican-Science Fiction-Action-Comedy," which was edited on outdated video equipment.

SUBMISSION PROCESS

Submitting your film to Filmfilm involves signing the Registration Agreement, filling out the submission form, and sending it with a copy of your project to the Internet cineplex. Both the agreement and the form are available on the site. Filmfilm accepts DV, SVHS, and VHS tapes. If your film is accepted, Filmfilm will take care of formatting it for streaming video.

LEGAL RIGHTS

Filmfilm does not require an exclusive license to host your film. By signing the Registration Agreement, you agree that Filmfilm reserves the right to remove your film from its site without first notifying you. Also, it is important to keep in mind that the site does not commercially distribute films (the sole purpose of exhibiting on Filmfilm is exposure).

FILM & FILMMAKER'S INFORMATION

Unlike bios on most sites, Filmfilm's bios are not short paragraphs, nor are they edited to fit the typically small alloted space on a film's page. For the biography, Filmfilm provides each of its filmmakers with a full page, accessible through the film's exhibition page. This allows filmmakers to be as detailed as they want in the description of their life and career. On the exhibition page, Filmfilm provides a generous amount of space for a synopsis, the cast and crew credits, the director's comments to the audience, and festivals and awards history.

AUDIENCE PARTICIPATION

Since this site is committed to serving the filmmaking community, Filmfilm encourages its audience to use its features. On the Talent Search page, those interested in production can post a crew call or a casting notice, use a production guide, or find a screenplay. Screenwriters also can sell their screenplays, actors can post their resumes and photos, and crew members can read the crew calls. The audience can further interact with the site by posting a review and or rating a film.

FORCEFLICKS

forceflicks.com

Owned and operated by one woman, Julia Hoffa, Force Flicks is a nonprofit Internet cineplex for fans of *Star Wars*. After meticulously searching the web for all the fan films she could find, Hoffa found just one site devoted to *Star Wars* fan films. However, many of her own film discoveries were not listed there. It was then that she decided to "take a stab at helping my fellow *Star Wars* fanatics by creating this site."

NICHE

Stars Wars fans

MEDIA PLAYERS

QuickTime, RealPlayer, Windows Media Player

FILMS EXHIBITED

Force Flicks consists mainly of low-budget films written and directed by fans of *Star Wars*. Inspired by their passion for George Lucas's series, many fans have created their own films based on the *Star Wars* story. Force Flicks has links to all of the most well-known fan films, including Kevin Rubio's *Troops* (1997), a parody of the television show *Cops*; Evan Mather's various series, including *Quentin Tarantino's Star Wars* (1998); and *George Lucas in Love* (1999). In addition to these hits, you can find lesser-known films.

Although fan films comprise most of its collection, the site also offers a glimpse at the for-profit, professional productions of *Star Wars*. Trailers, *Star Wars* related commercials, and professional parodies (such as Weird Al Yankovic's *The Saga Begins* [1999]) are also available on Force Flicks.

SUBMISSION PROCESS

The submission process is quite casual: from the menu bar, click on "Add a Movie," and send the site a message about your film. Generally, Hoffa accepts any fan film that is brought to her attention. It sounds very simple, but there is a catch. Since Force Flicks is just Julia Hoffa and not a profit-generating Internet cineplex, the site is faced with limited resources, including bandwidth. For this reason, Hoffa is more likely to link to your site containing the film file than host your film on her site. However, there are exceptions to this rule, and you should not hesitate to ask her to consider hosting your film.

LEGAL RIGHTS

Since Force Flicks is a non-profit web site, there are no agreements made between filmmakers and the site. If you submit your film, you are free to remove it or disconnect the link at any time.

FILM & FILMMAKER'S INFORMATION

Force Flicks does not post any biographical information about its filmmakers, but it does offer links to filmmakers's e-mail addresses and to links to their web pages (which contain the films). Also, a brief synopsis is posted for some films.

AUDIENCE PARTICIPATION

None

GUERRILLA FILMMAKERS

www.guerillafilmmakers.com
Guerrilla Filmmakers.com
2304 9th Avenue
Los Angeles, CA 90018

Crediting the digital video revolution with the recent explosion of filmmaking talent, Guerrilla Filmmakers features some of the most raw, low-budget films on the Web. When not distracted by "partying, drinking, and lounging in our Jacuzzi," the Internet cineplex is committed to bringing exposure to the young talent of this medium.

MEDIA PLAYERS

QuickTime, RealPlayer, Windows Media Player

FILMS EXHIBITED

Because of its small collection, Guerrilla Filmmakers presents all of its featured films on one page for viewers to sort through. In addition to commonly seen genres such as Action, Drama, and Comedy, the site also shows films that fall under unusual categories like Films Your Mother Wouldn't Approve Of, Politically Incorrect, and Student Films with Attitude. Under such original genres are films like *Heaven 17* (2001), a cyberpunk short about teenage virgins who are impregnated by a supernatural force, and *The Brother From Another Borough* (1998), a short that explores homophobia in the inner city streets of South London. While the site has established genres, Guerrilla Filmmakers is open to accepting films that do not fit ones already listed on the site.

Submission Process

Fill out the online submission form, and send in a copy of your film as an AVI, Quicktime, MPEG, or MPEG4 file on a CD-ROM. While the site prefers receiving digital files, Guerrilla Filmmakers also accepts VHS (NTSC) copies of films and trailers. You should also enclose 3 production stills on a floppy disk or on the CD-ROM with your film file.

Legal Rights

Following your film's acceptance, Guerrilla Filmmakers discusses its rights agreement with you.

Film & Filmmaker's Information

Guerrilla Filmmakers provides each of its films with an individual page, on which it lists a synopsis, filmmaker, crew, cast, festivals and awards, date, and running time, as well as production stills.

Audience Participation

The link "Discussion" brings viewers to a message board where they can post comments about films on the site or questions about digital video production.

HYPNOTIC

www.hypnotic.com
80 South Street 3rd Floor
New York, NY 10038

Hypnotic is one of several Internet cineplexes we discuss that exclusively exhibits short films. The site was founded in February 1999 by CEO Jeremy Bernard, a former film and television producer who saw that the Internet "provided a powerful platform through which [independent] filmmakers could be discovered." In March 2000, Hypnotic extended itself into offline media by partnering with Universal Pictures, an alliance that works toward creating a connection between the independent film community and Hollywood. By securing this partnership, Hypnotic asserts that it is a source for budding industry talent, and for this reason it has very high standards for the films it hosts.

MEDIA PLAYERS

RealPlayer

FILMS EXHIBITED

You won't find any unique genres at Hypnotic—just your typical comedy, drama, action, documentary, and so forth. However, you will find high-quality shorts within every category. On its home page, Hypnotic spotlights its current Most Popular film, an Editor's Choice, and the highest rated. Some of the highest rated are *Girls on Boys* (2000), a documentary featuring four generations of American women, and their opinions of men; *Necrosis* (1998), a dark narrative about the attempt by two thugs to dump a dead prostitute's body; and *The Family Dog* (1999), portraying a family dinner that almost ends in disaster. These films represent Hypnotic's collection by way of their diversity and their technical and narrative qualities.

SUBMISSION PROCESS

Just about the only requirement for submissions to Hypnotic is that films be between 30 seconds and 40 minutes, no shorter or longer. After establishing that your film falls within this running time, go to the site's submission form and fill it out online. Before submitting it, print out a copy to send with a VHS (NTSC) copy of your film.

LEGAL RIGHTS

Hypnotic discusses licenses only after a film is accepted by the site. If Hypnotic is interested in exhibiting or distributing your film, chances are it will require an exclusive license.

FILM & FILMMAKER'S INFORMATION

Each film on Hypnotic is provided with two pages: an introductory page and a film details page. On the introductory page is listed a brief two-to-four-sentence synopsis, the filmmaker's name, the film's running time and genre, and the average rating by viewers. For many filmmakers and viewers, this is not enough information. To satisfy those who want to see more, Hypnotic also presents a details page that is comprised of the submitter's name, her relation to the film, and her e-mail address, as well as the filmmaker's name, the film's genre, original format, country, and year, and any awards the film has won.

AUDIENCE PARTICIPATION

For viewers interested in chatting with other film lovers, Hypnotic offers Hypnotic Forum, which can be accessed from a link on the home page. Here viewers can post reviews about any film (including Hollywood blockbusters), post questions about production, or share ideas or techniques with other filmmakers.

ICEBOX

www.icebox.com
3453 S. La Cienega Blvd.
Los Angeles, California 90016

Icebox produces various animated series for an audience between the ages of 15 and 40 that try to be cutting edge. Cofounder John Collier has had plenty of experience creating cartoons for mature audiences, working as producer on the Fox series *King of the Hill* and *The Simpsons*. Icebox's list of creators is also impressive, drawing talent from a wide range of successful television programs and movies like *South Park: Bigger, Longer, Uncut* (1999), *Seinfeld, Dawson's Creek, The X-Files, Ren and Stimpy, Futurama, Party of Five*, and *The Net* (1995).

MEDIA PLAYERS

Flash

NICHE

Animators and viewers interested in animation

FILMS EXHIBITED

The majority of Icebox's content is generated by the company. Under the title Icebox Originals, Icebox lists about a dozen original series conceived of and created by its own staff. Although there is nothing pornographic or X-rated in these programs, they have a tendency to include racy content. For example, *Hard Drinkin' Lincoln* is a cartoon featuring one of the United States' most famous presidents, Abraham Lincoln. Instead of presenting the humble, honorable man found in the history books, however, the Icebox program fantasizes about a hidden side of Lincoln and portrays him as a drunk who likes to sit in front of the television, guzzle beer, and yell insulting remarks at his wife. Icebox also offers a "private" look into the life of President Bill Clinton in an episode of *Hidden Celebrity Webcam*: sneaking down to the refrigerator for a midnight snack, Clinton finds the treat that gets him in the most trouble (you have to check out the program to see what it is). Along with these presidential spoofs, you can watch *Superhero Roommate*, a serial about two roommates—Neil, a superhero, and Russell, a regular guy—and the problems they encounter. There is also *The Elvis & Jack Nicklaus Mysteries*, in which these old time celebrities fight crime and solve mysteries.

Animated programs by others are listed on the Icebox Independents page. The focus of such programs tends to be the visuals more than the narrative, with all running just a few minutes long. A couple of samples from this group are *Deathwatch*, a mini-short about the Grim Reaper, who will take a watch in exchange for someone's life; and *The Scarecrow*, which cleverly reverses the traditional roles between bird and straw man, here portraying a crow that frightens away little scarecrows.

SUBMISSION PROCESS

If you have an animated short that is 1 to 3 minutes long, no larger than one megabyte in downloadable size, and contained in a Flash (.swf) file, then you should consider sharing it with Icebox. (Note that Icebox does not accept any "hate" material, pornography, or active links.) Submitting to Icebox is a completely digital process. Fill out and submit the submission form online, upload your file to the Icebox web site, and agree to the Submission Agreement by clicking on "Submit." Following this, you will receive an e-mail from Icebox that lists a confirmation password, which you need to hold on to for your show to be posted.

LEGAL RIGHTS

The Submission Agreement explains that Icebox requires a "royalty-free, perpetual, irrevocable, non-exclusive, worldwide license" from its animators. In other words, once you sign on with the company, you cannot terminate the agreement, nor will you ever receive any financial compensation for your work. Icebox has the right to "display, reproduce, edit, and distribute" your show on its own Web site and on other sites that contain Icebox areas or windows, and also to use it for promotional purposes.

FILM & FILMMAKER'S INFORMATION

Icebox does not provide its independent animators space to post synopses or biographical information. Only the most basic of facts—the animator's name, and the date and time of submission—are included.

AUDIENCE PARTICIPATION

"Icebox Labs" is a section of the site dedicated solely to animated games that can be played by the audience. These often star characters from Icebox shows. Viewers can also go the standard route and rate the independent Icebox programs, and recommend both independents and originals.

IFILM

www.ifilm.com
1024 N. Orange Drive
Hollywood, CA 90038

IFILM launched in October 1998, an event brought about by several media executives, including the site's CEO, Kevin Wendle—cofounder of the popular Web sites, CNET and E! Online. More than just one of the largest Internet cineplexes, IFILM is also a film portal and directory which, according to the site, contains "links to more than 10,000 Internet films from every major broadband content provider." Unlike most Internet cineplexes which do not automatically accept submission, for a fee IFILM hosts any film that is submitted to the site, excluding pornography and home videos. For this reason, IFILM contains thousands of films, a size that is not matched by many sites. Besides exhibiting films, IFILM links to other film sites, provides guides to film production, and lists recommended online film festivals.

Media Players

QuickTime, RealPlayer, Windows Media Player

Films Exhibited

The films that IFILM exhibits are separated into 12 genres, including Drama, Action, Gay and Lesbian, and Celebrity. One of the first films that IFILM exhibited was *Jaunt* (1998) (examined in Chapter 7), a non-narrative short that bombards you with repeated disconcerting, but beautiful imagery. Among its most popular films are *405* (2000), a comical short featuring special effects that create the illusion of an airplane driving on California's 405 freeway; and *More* (1999), a melancholy stop-animation short about a secret invention that makes the world appear better than it is. IFILM also categorizes films based on their appeal to special groups such as teenagers, gays and lesbians, and women. One such film targeted to female viewers is *Urban Prisoner* (2000) which depicts a true-to-life scene of one woman's serious encounter with sexual harassment.

Submission Process

You can complete the majority of IFILM's submission process online. Read through and agree to the IFILM Release by clicking on the "Agree" button underneath the form. By doing so, you are brought to the first page of the submission form, to be filled out online. When you complete the submission form, IFILM will provide you with a reference number. It is important to keep a record of this number. Write it, along with your name and the title, length, and format of your film, on the front and spine of the copy of your film that you send to the site. IFILM accepts just about every format available in videotapes (VHS, SVHS, BetaSP, DV, DigiBeta) and digital files (MPEG1, uncompressed QuickTime, Flash, or .AVI file on CD-ROM, ZIP, JAZ, or DVD media).

Unless your film is chosen for the complimentary Premium Benefits (in other words, accepted to be exhibited on the site for free), you have to pay a fee for exhibiting your film on IFILM. Based on the running time of your film, the amount of benefits you desire, and the length of your exhibition period, fees can range from $50 to $300. Be sure to read closely through the details of the different exhibition packages posted on the FAQ page when choosing which one is right for you.

LEGAL RIGHTS

IFILM requires a non-exclusive license, which is a "world-wide royalty free license to publicly display, publicly perform, distribute and reproduce your film on or via the Internet." The term of the agreement is undetermined. However, if you decide you want to terminate the agreement, you may send a Revocation Notice which takes effect 90 days after IFILM receives it. If on the other hand IFILM decides to terminate the agreement, it can do so immediately and without providing any notice.

FILM & FILMMAKER'S INFORMATION

IFILM provides each of its films with two pages, one for the film and one for the filmmaker. On the film page, basic facts are listed such as the genre, running time, subject, a brief synopsis, and a list of the cast and crew, along with information that is not-so-standard, like the average rating by IFILM viewers and the number of viewings a film has received while on the site. The filmmaker's page lists what IFILM refers to as the "stats"—including the filmmaker's gender, location, and filmography—and also posts a link to the filmmaker's e-mail address.

AUDIENCE PARTICIPATION

IFILM wants to hear the viewer's opinion, and it offers several forms the viewer can use to express it. After viewing a film, one can rate it, review it, or e-mail it to a friend. IFILM also allows its audience to contact filmmakers, either through e-mail or (if the filmmaker sets up a chat line) by chatting with the filmmaker online.

LIKETELEVISION

www.tesla.liketelevision.com
6128-A Brookshire Blvd.
Charlotte, NC 28216

LikeTelevision was founded in 1999, to provide an alternative medium to display artistic content. As the name reveals, LikeTelevision loosely resembles cable television. The site offers several different viewing channels, including Movies, Weather, Music, and Sports, and is optimized for broadband. Although it offers a video slideshow option for those without broadband access, LikeTelevision clearly caters to viewers who possess the best technology, attempting to move toward converting the computer monitor into a television screen.

MEDIA PLAYERS

RealPlayer

FILMS EXHIBITED

Like cable television, LikeTelevision is defined by its eclectic collection of entertainment. A site that does not want you to forget about its forerunners in audio/visual media, most of LikeTelevision's collection consists of classics such as episodes of *Betty Boop* (1933), *Bonanza* (1959), and *The Lone Ranger* (from the early 1940s). In addition, there is Alfred Hitchcock's *Murder* (1930), and John Huston's *Battle of San Pietro* (1945). Mixed in with these gems are more contemporary Hollywood films, independently-made music videos, webcam images of the company, and *Zim Zum*—a weekly webcast variety show packed with musical performances and sketch comedy.

SUBMISSION PROCESS

There are two different ways to submit your film to LikeTelevision. With either option, the first step is agreeing to the Limited License Agreement that is posted on the site. Then you can submit your tape either via mail or digitally. If you decide to send a copy of your film, LikeTelevision accepts BetaSP, VHS, SVHS, Hi8mm, 8mm, DVCAM, and DV tapes. If you instead choose to upload your video to the site, you need to sign up for either a Basic (free) or Deluxe ($300) Account. If you choose the Basic Account, LikeTelevision provides you with tentative space on which to create your own Web pages and upload your film files. Before you are guaranteed space with a Basic Account, however, your film needs to be approved by the company. If you instead go with the Deluxe, you are guaranteed space on LikeTelevision. With the Deluxe Account, LikeTelevision will also make a page for you, encode your film, and allow you access to your page to update information.

LEGAL RIGHTS

Before submitting to LikeTelevision, you must agree to the Limited License Agreement by clicking on the phrase, "I am ready! Sign me up!" By agreeing to the contract, you grant LikeTelevision a limited license to exhibit your film on the Web, webcast clips of it in the weekly show, and broadcast it on television, cable, satellite, and other networks that broadcast the weekly show. You can choose to end this agreement at any time and for whatever reason. Also, it is important to note that even if your film is broadcast on network television and LikeTelevision receives royalties for your film, you will not receive a percentage of these royalties.

FILM & FILMMAKER'S INFORMATION

Very little information about your film gets posted on LikeTelevision. In fact, with many of the new shows (as opposed to classic films), even the filmmaker's name is hard to find.

AUDIENCE PARTICIPATION

Viewers can post reviews and share their opinions about programs with other viewers. Through a poll viewers can vote on their favorite films on the site.

MEDIATRIP

www.mediatrip.com
11111 Santa Monica Blvd.
Suite 300
Los Angeles, CA 90025

MediaTrip debuted in October 1999, making a splash on the Internet cineplex scene by premiering the hit comedy *George Lucas in Love* (1999) as part of the launch (see Chapter 6 for a discussion of the production, exhibition, and distribution of *George Lucas in Love*). Not only a venue for exhibition, MediaTrip is also a center for a community of independent filmmakers and other artists. One of its primary goals is to build "an interactive artist community" by featuring a "Community" section that allows different types of artists to meet and possibly find work.

MEDIA PLAYERS

RealPlayer, Windows Media Player

FILMS EXHIBITED

Both shorts and features are showcased on MediaTrip, along with animated series that are produced by the site. Although the site's complete list of films is found under Movies on Demand, MediaTrip features its ten most popular films on its home page. In the number-one spot is *George Lucas in Love* (1999). Other parodies in MediaTrip's top ten are *Swing Blade*

(1997), a hybrid of *Sling Blade* (1996) and *Swingers* (1996), and *Film Club* (2000), which transposes the energy in *Fight Club* (1999) onto a group of film lovers. Most of MediaTrip's favorites are comedies, with the exception of a couple of animated films, like *Sentinelles* (2000), a love story about two metallic birds that are building ornaments which come to life because of their feelings for each other.

SUBMISSION PROCESS

MediaTrip accepts both shorts (anything 60 minutes or less) and features (anything over 60 minutes). Send either your film's URL or a VHS (NTSC), CD-ROM, or Mini-DV copy of your film. With the tape, enclose a sheet of paper containing your contact information and the film's genre, format, aspect ratio, running time, language, country of origin, and completion date. Also be sure to include information about the rights availability of your film (which rights have been sold, and which rights are available), as well as its festival and screening history.

LEGAL RIGHTS

MediaTrip does not discuss licensing agreements until it accepts a film. This being said, the site has been known to request an exclusive license from its filmmakers, and at times even to pay for such rights.

FILM & FILMMAKER'S INFORMATION

Each film on MediaTrip has its own page, which lists its genre, year, running time, and synopsis, any prior festival participation and awards received, as well as the director, producer, writer, and distributor (if the film already has one), with a link to the distributor's site.

AUDIENCE PARTICIPATION

In an effort to build a loyal community of viewers, Mediatrip features the Community section offering various ways in which viewers can interact with the site and each other. MediaTrip assumes many of its viewers are artists who are looking for work. For this reason, the site provides space for each viewer to create a personal artist page to showcase her talents, abilities, and interests. Viewers can also post comments or e-mail films to friends.

MOVIEFLIX

www.movieflix.com
Code 7 Entertainment, Inc.
P.O. Box 480764
Los Angeles, CA 90048

An Internet cineplex that has over 2000 titles in its library, MovieFlix is committed to raising the quality of online movie-viewing by presenting its films in broadband as well as the typically-seen narrowband. In addition to this option in streaming technology, MovieFlix viewers choose between paying a monthly fee of $4.95 to the site and having access to every film in the collection or visiting the site for free and watching only a limited number of films.

MEDIA PLAYERS

RealPlayer

FILMS EXHIBITED

Along with its large size, the collection of MovieFlix films is characterized by its diversity, with a wide variety of genres, including B-Western, Black Culture, Family, Martial Arts, and Religion, in addition to old standbys such as Action, Comedy, and Drama. MovieFlix presents famous classics like *The Big Trees* (1952) with Kirk Douglas and *Hi De Ho* (1948), one of Cab Calloway's famous musical reviews, as well as lesser-known independent films, such as the comedy *Sex, Lies, and Ravioli* (2000), a 5-minute film-noir spoof about a woman looking for sexual pleasure. The site also contains a fair amount of erotica and soft-pornography which is nonchalantly distributed throughout its collection, although not found in a category labeled as such. For example, in Drama, viewers find the *Cheeks* trilogy (1986, 1987, and 1988) listed on the same page as *Catherine the Great* (1934).

SUBMISSION PROCESS

After clicking on "Submit Your Movie," fill out and print the online entry form. Sign the form and send it to the site with a VHS (NTSC) copy of your film.

LEGAL RIGHTS

Once MovieFlix accepts your film into its collection, the site requires non-exclusive rights to your film, which includes the right to sublicense, reproduce, distribute, publish, and display.

FILM & FILMMAKER'S INFORMATION

For each film, MovieFlix posts a brief synopsis, filmmaker's name, cast list, length, and rating, as well as a link to a site where the film can be purchased.

AUDIENCE PARTICIPATION

In addition to rating films, MovieFlix viewers can chat with each other in the "Community" section of the site. It is there that viewers find message boards for each film genre listed on the site.

THE NEW VENUE

www.newvenue.com

New Venue is an Internet cineplex that differentiates itself from other sites through its collection and philosophy. Founded by Jason Wishnow in April 1998, and then relaunched with support from Apple 2 years later, New Venue showcases one film every 1 to 2 weeks. Wishnow chooses to present films that "really push the [Internet] medium in new directions, in terms of narrative, aesthetics, and technology." In addition to its main film program, New Venue occasionally holds festivals characterized by unique themes, such as the "Aggressively Boring Film Festival" which features movies made for the Palm O.S. (to be watched on a Palm Pilot's 1.5-inch screen at either 4 grays, 16 grays, or 256 colors, and without sound). As a service to filmmaking newcomers, New Venue also provides a complete guide to digital filmmaking.

MEDIA PLAYERS

QuickTime

FILMS EXHIBITED

Being a filmmaker himself, Wishnow knows the look of a daring, high-quality film. On the site, you find comedies like the animated *Buena Vista Fight Club* (2000), about angry Latin jazz musicians who run through a Scandinavian furniture catalog and knock off the heads of models. You also find films that are self-referential to the medium, such as *video : war : leverage* (1999), a short made from video, text, and audio found on the web, which comments on the marketing of video on the web. There are also vignettes that address social, political, and gender issues like the animated film *Cosmo Tells All* (1998), a brief look at the messages *Cosmopolitan* magazine sends to women about their role in American society.

SUBMISSION PROCESS

New Venue accepts films only as QuickTime or Flash digital files. If your film is under 5 MB or under 15 minutes (for streaming purposes), then you should proceed to the site's short submission form and fill it out. To complete the form, you must agree to its "Legal Part," and a method of submitting your film: upload it, present its URL, e-mail it, or FTP it.

LEGAL RIGHTS

By agreeing to New Venue's "Legal Part," you give permission to the site to use clips from your film for promotional purposes. The site requests nonexclusive rights, although it appreciates spoken (and not signed) exclusive agreements concerning exhibition on the Internet (which it has with many of its filmmakers).

Film & Filmmaker's Information

To complement each film, New Venue presents a lengthy interview with the filmmaker, which can be accessed by way of the individual film page or the collective film catalogue page. The interviews contain information about tools of production, the filmmakers' past work, and links to personal home pages. The site also provides e-mail links to the cast and crew of its films.

Audience Participation

As of right now, viewers can e-mail cast and crew members of films. New Venue is currently looking into other features for reviewing films and e-mailing them to friends.

PLANETOUT

www.planetout.com/popcornq
657 Harrison St.
San Francisco, CA 94107

PlanetOut is an Internet portal that caters to a queer audience. During spring 2000, the site founded the PlanetOut Short Movie Awards. This annual event is for filmmakers who are interested in screening their films to queer audiences. Although the winners are selected by a judging committee that is compiled by PopcornQ—the entertainment section of PlanetOut—the event allows viewers to vote for their favorite films. Winners are awarded cash prizes and offline screenings at Outfest: Los Angeles Gay and Lesbian Film Festival. Not strictly an Internet cineplex, PopcornQ also provides updates on the latest queer and straight entertainment news. In this section of the site viewers have access to an enormous online archive of film reviews, movie and television news, a list of current film festivals, and resources for film professionals. There are also movie trailers and webcasted interviews with stars.

Niche

Gay, Lesbian, Bisexual, Transgender

Media Players

QuickTime, RealPlayer

Films Exhibited

Although a relatively small event, the PlanetOut Short Movie Awards has the diversity of a large Internet cineplex, with films from past events ranging in style and subject. Examples of this range include *Family* (1999), in which the filmmaker documents the process of coming out to his loved ones, as well as to strangers; *How to Fake an Orgasm* (1998), an uninterrupted black-and-white monologue that comically walks viewers through the steps to achieving this tricky moment of intimacy; *Guileless Guile* (1999), an animated three-minute short about a love triangle between a woman, her suitor, and a naked cowboy; and *Jean* (2000), a sophisticated film about an older woman haunted by a mysterious young man.

SUBMISSION PROCESS

Before submitting your film to the PlanetOut Short Movie Awards, make sure it satisfies the event's two major requirements: the film must be under 20 minutes long, and it must be by, for, or about gay, lesbian, bisexual, or transgender people. PlanetOut accepts films of five different genres: Drama, Comedy, Animation, Documentary, and Experimental. Like most film festivals, the PlanetOut Short Movie Awards holds to its deadlines, and for this reason your first move should be to check the entry deadline on PlanetOut's web site. Print out the entry form, fill it out, and send it in with a VHS (NTSC) copy of your film. Be sure to include your entry fee. Note that by submitting an entry, you agree to the Movie Awards Official Rules.

LEGAL RIGHTS

If your film is accepted, PlanetOut requires an exclusive license even if you do not win an award. If your film is a non-winner, PlanetOut obtains exclusive rights for 90 days; if your film wins, the term is 1 year. If at the end of the term you decide you no longer want your film on the site, you may send PlanetOut a Revocation Notice—a letter requesting the removal of your film—and the site will remove your film and terminate the agreement. (If you do not request the removal of your film, PlanetOut's license will shift from exclusive to non-exclusive on the expiration date of the original agreement.) During the period of the license, PlanetOut has the right to exhibit your film in two different places: online, both on PlanetOut and IFILM (the other sponsor of the event), as well as any of the affiliate sites; and, if you are a winner, at Outfest: Los Angeles Gay and Lesbian Film Festival. PlanetOut and IFILM also have the right to use excerpts of your film for promotional purposes.

FILM & FILMMAKER'S INFORMATION

PlanetOut does not go beyond listing basic facts about a film, such as its genre, running time, original format, and country.

AUDIENCE PARTICIPATION

Nominees of the PlanetOut Short Movie Awards are judged by the audience as well as the official judging committee. During the event, viewers can look at the five nominees in each category and vote for their favorites. At the end of the event, the audience favorites are listed alongside the actual winners. The audience also can share with the site its comments about the films.

REELMIND

www.reelmind.com
PO Box 1957
Monterey, CA 93942-1957

Like a few other Internet cineplexes, ReelMind accepts any material submitted. Part of Bendal, Inc., ReelMind launched in January 2000 with the objective to offer exposure to as many independent filmmakers as possible. For this reason, it exhibits films regardless of their quality. Each filmmaker is provided with space to make a home page through which a film is screened, and an e-mail account for exchange with viewers. The site also aids filmmakers with links to film festivals, film schools, and equipment.

MEDIA PLAYERS

Windows Media Player

FILMS EXHIBITED

Because of its open-admissions policy, ReelMind showcases all genres of films, made with varying degrees of skill. You find the 2-minute documentary-like compilation *How to Sleep on Floors*, which profiles footage of eight independent rock bands; as well as *The Pedestrian*, a comedy about a salesman who hits a pedestrian with his car and spends the rest of the day desperately trying to hide the crime. Even Ben Reneker, founder and president of ReelMind, has a page on which he exhibits *Cut*, a short film about high altitude climbing.

SUBMISSION PROCESS

To put your film on ReelMind, you must first become a site member by clicking on Join! on the menu bar, filling out a form, and agreeing to the Terms of Service. Once a member, you are provided with space for your own personal page, which you can access through the Member's Area. Here you can also obtain the film submission form, to be filled out and submitted online. Send in a VHS, SVHS, Beta, MiniDV, DV, or Hi-8mm copy of your film for ReelMind to encode and serve from your personal page. The site allows you to post up to 18 minutes of film and does not censor content.

LEGAL RIGHTS

ReelMind does not require any rights to host your film. Upon your request it will immediately remove your film from the site. Likewise, the site reserves the right to remove your film at any time if it discovers you have not followed the Terms of Service. ReelMind is not a distributor; however, it does feature a store through which you can sell VHS or DVD copies of your film. (Note that in order to participate in the store you must supply ReelMind with ten copies of your film.) ReelMind takes 20 percent of your sales made through its store.

FILM & FILMMAKER'S INFORMATION

With the independence of a personal page comes the freedom to post all kinds of information, as well as photos, scripts, and graphics. Standard facts found on every page are the film's genre, running time and format, the filmmaker's location, the number of times the film has been watched, as well as a link to the filmmaker's e-mail address. There is also a Directors section that provides an alphabetical listing of its director-members and contact information for each.

AUDIENCE PARTICIPATION

Since the site provides each member with an e-mail account, viewers can send messages to any filmmaker exhibiting work on ReelMind. Anyone interested in participating in a discussion forum—on topics from animation to digital video to job possibilities—can check out the Discussion Forum.

RESFEST

www.resfest.com
601 W. 26th Street, 11th Floor
New York, NY 10001

The online and offline film festival RESFEST was established in 1997 so that digital filmmakers would have a place to exhibit their work and discuss their influence on the development of this medium. RESFEST is also committed to showcasing the "empowering new digital tools, and an emerging style of storytelling" of the digital film movement. The festival is the product of the RES Media Group—a company that promotes digital filmmaking and is a pioneer in the field. RMG has been organizing digital film festivals since its 1995 Low Res Festival, the first desktop digital film festival. Out of this early model evolved RESFEST, which is accessible both on the web and in traditional offline venues such as the Directors Guild of America in New York and Los Angeles, and the Palace of Fine Arts in San Francisco.

MEDIA PLAYERS

RealPlayer

FILMS EXHIBITED

Reflecting its line-up of innovative films, RESFEST groups films into categories that are not common to many Internet cineplexes. For example, Cinema Electronica is composed of videos for electronic music, including the year 2000 participant *Man With the Red Face*, filled with scenes from Bollywood (an industry word referring to the cinema scene in India, "Bollywood" being a contraction of "Bombay" and "Hollywood") and astounding dance numbers. Net Cinema Shorts is an annual program determined by each year's "new thing" in digital filmmaking. In 2000 the program featured Internet animation, and many of the films were made in Macromedia Flash, such as *Kozik's Inferno* (2000), which portrays an updated version of Dante's Hell, rife with hot-rod flames and she-devils. Along with these original categories, RESFEST also offers the more typical Shorts, Long Shorts, and Features. Although the groups are familiar, the films themselves are certainly new experiences: *Ferment* (1999), a 4-minute short depicting an instance in space (rather than time), begins with the death of an old man and ends with the birth of a baby; for 5 minutes *G* (1999) privileges you with the view of a camera dropped from a plane at 30,000 feet.

SUBMISSION PROCESS

As stated in its mission statement, RESFEST is looking for films that make use of new digital tools. So while you can submit a film that is shot on any format, your production process must have involved extensive use of computer editing software and/or effects software to be eligible. Begin the submission process to RESFEST by checking the upcoming tour's deadline. If your timing is right, print the online submission form and fill it out. Put the form and a check for your submission fee along in a package with a copy of your film on either VHS (NTSC), BetaSP, or Mini-DV. Be sure to mark the case of your tape with the film's title and running time, as well as your name and contact information. If RESFEST notifies you that your film has been selected, you will have to provide high-quality stills from your film, a photo, and a brief personal biography.

LEGAL RIGHTS

For most traditional festivals, the exhibition agreement covers the length of the event or tour (since RESFEST is a traveling festival), whereas exhibition agreements for online festivals tend to last a year. To be exactly certain about the length of the term, you should e-mail RESFEST at resfest@resfest.com. In addition, by sending stills, photos, and your biography, you automatically agree that they may be used for RESFEST's promotional and publicity purposes.

FILM AND FILMMAKER'S INFORMATION

Because RESFEST is a festival and not a typical Internet cineplex, your film is considered to be part of the event's program. For this reason, films are not provided with their own film page. Instead they are listed on a category page, with a brief amount of information posted about each one, including its country, running time, year, crew, cast, and synopsis.

AUDIENCE PARTICIPATION

None

SCREEN47

www.screen47.com
100 Park Avenue, Suite 1600
New York, NY 10017

Taking its name from the atomic number for silver—47 (as explained on the site, "So it's kind of a play on 'Silver Screen.' Get it?")—Screen47 promises plenty of individualized attention to its filmmakers. Going the minimalist route (unlike the large Internet cineplexes), this Internet cineplex has few links, and those that it does have take you to Screen47 content rather than outside the site. Along similar lines, Screen47 has a modest collection of about 60 films, making it possible for viewers to actually see most of them. As filmmaker Lowell Northrop, whose film *Organ Donor* (1999) is on Screen47, says, "It's a very straightforward film site that isn't out to make loads of money off of advertisers or the people who are submitting their films." (Northrop's process of finding Internet cineplexes for *Organ Donor* is discussed in Chapter 4.)

MEDIA PLAYERS

RealPlayer

FILMS EXHIBITED

Because of its manageable size, Screen47 does not need to organize its films by genre like most Internet cineplexes; they are instead organized in order of submission. On one page is the experimental film *Laundromat* (2000), a visual exploration of one woman doing her laundry and bathing in a pond in the middle of the woods; a documentary entitled *World War III* (1998), in which a group of people are questioned about the possibility of a future war; and *The Basement* (2000), a twisted narrative about a deranged dentist. Unlike most Internet cineplexes, Screen47 does not highlight its top-rated films; although a rating is posted next to each film, those with higher ratings are not prioritized.

SUBMISSION PROCESS

Screen47 looks for films that are less than 30 minutes long. If your film meets this criterion, fill out and submit a submission form online. Note that to complete the form, you must agree to the site's Terms and Conditions of Submission. Send Screen47 a copy of your film in the form of a VHS (NTSC), Betacam SP, DV, or 3/4" tape, or a MPEG or QuickTime digital file.

LEGAL RIGHTS

By agreeing to the Terms and Conditions of Submission, you allow Screen47 to hold a non-exclusive license for exhibition and distribution in the event that it hosts your film. Screen47 makes a commitment to aggressively market your film (a promise similar to one a traditional film distributor would make), and offers a 25 percent royalty rate for each sale (a rate similar to one a traditional film distributor would offer). Screen47 reserves the right to use your film for promotional purposes, and also to remove your film at any time without having to provide you with any notice. Likewise, you may request removal of your film from the site at any time.

FILM & FILMMAKER'S INFORMATION

On each film page, Screen47 provides a long list of information about the film. You find a two-to-three-sentence synopsis, the film's genre, running time, language, and production format, the filmmaker's school (if produced by a student), the film's year, crew and cast members, the music composer, and any awards the film has won.

AUDIENCE PARTICIPATION

Audience reviews and ratings are found on each film page.

TFN FANFILMS

www.theforce.net/theater
PO Box 65
Hummelstown, PA 17036

A subsection of the site for die-hard *Stars Wars* fans, TFN (The Force Net), TFN FanFilms is dedicated to showcasing the best in *Star Wars* fan films. Formerly known as TFN Theater, a recent merge with FanFilms.com has left the Internet cineplex with a new name, and a new commitment to hosting fan films of only the highest quality. (TFN FanFilms credits Kevin Rubio and the making of his 1997 *Troops*, which appears on the site with beginning the *Star Wars* fan film movement.) In addition to exhibiting fan films, TFN FanFilms provides future filmmakers with information on how to make their own fan films, including steps for specialized *Star Wars* production work, such as creating lightsaber effects and costumes.

NICHE

Star Wars fans

MEDIA PLAYERS

Flash, QuickTime, Real Player

FILMS EXHIBITED

TFN FanFilms accepts all kinds of fan films: shorts, animated films, trailers, music videos, and special-effects projects. Despite their differences in form, most films on the site are united in spirit, all paying homage to *Star Wars* creator George Lucas. In *Star Dudes*, an animated recreation of Lucas's *Episode IV: A New Hope* (1977) done in Flash, the characters' dialogue is minimal consisting mainly of the word "dude." Another popular animated short is *Star Wars Gangsta Rap* (2000), a music video in which the characters of Darth Vader, Luke Skywalker, and Yoda rap scenes from the series. Among the live-action shorts are *Dark Redemption*, a 30-minute story set 2 days before *Episode IV*; and *Fan Wars*, a 3 1/2-minute film about two groups of *Star Wars* fans fighting over the best seats in the theater to the premiere of *Episode I* (1999). Both films, like many other shorts, are packed with exciting lightsaber duels that look professionally made.

SUBMISSION PROCESS

The site does not enforce running-time or genre restrictions. However it will accept only high-quality work (in terms of production value and story) that is deemed clean (equal to a G or PG rating). If your film satisfies these requirements, fill out the submission form and send it to the site. Include on the form the URL where a still image or video of your film can be seen. (TFN FanFilms requests that you not send them an attachment of your film via e-mail.) If it likes what it sees, the site will contact you about hosting your film.

LEGAL RIGHTS

Though you do not have to sign an exhibition agreement, TFN FanFilms requests that it be the only Web site that hosts your film. In other words, the site requests (but does not require) exclusive Internet rights. TFN FanFilms simultaneously supports your right to exhibit and distribute your film through other venues such as conventions and traditional film festivals.

FILM & FILMMAKER'S INFORMATION

A film page contains useful information about both the film and the filmmaker. Each film details its running time, synopsis, and cast and crew. For each filmmaker, there is an address for a personal Web site and a "word from the director." When one clicks on the latter, a window opens up displaying remarks from the filmmaker, such as an anecdote or a personal statement.

AUDIENCE PARTICIPATION

TFN FanFilms provides viewers with two ways to connect with other *Star Wars* fans and fans of fan films: those mainly interested in posting a comment can go to the Theater Forum, a message board created for the purpose of fan film discussion; for those looking for more immediately interactive conversation, TFN FanFilms also provides a chat room. Occasionally, special chats are scheduled for with a featured filmmaker. During these online conversations, viewers have an opportunity to directly ask a filmmaker about her work.

THE BITSCREEN

www.thebitscreen.com
PO Box 343
Narberth, PA 19072

The BitScreen presents films that contribute to the development of the Internet medium. Nora Barry, an interactive media specialist and owner of Druid Media, started The BitScreen in July 1998. Since the beginning, Barry has been interested in showcasing films that explore a new form of storytelling, one that is encouraged by the hypertext structure of the Internet. It exhibits only a few films at a time, instead of the hundreds or even thousands more commonly found on other sites, and so the selection is limited. However, what does appear on The BitScreen is some of the most exciting work by both media industry professionals and non-professionals.

MEDIA PLAYERS

RealPlayer, Shockwave

FILMS EXHIBITED

"High quality" does not begin to describe the shorts on The BitScreen. Technically, the site's films are at the utmost professional level. The stories tend to be unconventional and are told in a daring way. One recent week included *Darwin Bug* (2000), an animated short (done in Flash) about the evolution of a bug species; *Amazon* (2000), a brief streaming flash documentary that discusses the history of rubber tapping in the rainforest; *Heart to Heart* (2000), a musical Russian film done in 3D animation in which a skeleton sings about death; and *The Magic Watering Can* (2000), an animated film about a woman with a watering can who cannot stop watering.

SUBMISSION PROCESS

Possessing one of the easiest submission processes, The BitScreen simply requests that you send a VHS tape or CD-ROM of your film. (The BitScreen requires its films be from 1 to 10 minutes long.) If your film is already online, send its URL. Although not required, be sure to enclose in the package a sheet with your contact information.

LEGAL RIGHTS

The BitScreen does not discuss the exchange of rights until after a film has been accepted.

FILM & FILMMAKER'S INFORMATION

From each film page, viewers can link to a page containing credits, a lengthy filmmaker's biography, and a statement from the filmmaker (which sometimes reveals more information about the film or addresses the personality of the filmmaker).

AUDIENCE PARTICIPATION

Viewers can click on the appropriate link to comment on a film or the site.

THE SYNC

www.thesync.com
312 Laurel Avenue
Laurel, MD 20707

Targeting what the company calls the "Internet Generation," ("the highly-online 16-34 demographic"). The Sync offers a mix of popular shorts and feature films, along with original webcast programs that make up a major portion of the site's content. Most of the site's films are part of its ongoing Online Film Festival, and are rated by a public audience. (A film's ratings determine if it stays on the site.) By allowing its audience authority over the site's content, as well as original programming, the Sync proves it is inventing a new form of entertainment for the freshest consumers of media.

Media Players

RealPlayer

Films Exhibited

The Sync exhibits its fair share of short independent films, both through the program Independent Exposure—a monthly screening event curated by the company Blackchair Productions—and through The Sync's Online Film Festival. Although the festival accepts films that are up to 30 minutes long, the audience seems to prefer extremely short works, such as *Silent Voices*, a three-minute video poem about the spontaneous graffiti tribute on the site of Yitzak Rabin's assassination. Besides its shorts, what sets the site apart from others are its original webcast programs, such as *Cyberlove*, an interactive talk show about love and relationships hosted by four young adults; */etc: geekTV*, one of three programs for "geeks" about computer technology; and *JenniShow*, a talk show starring one of the most famous webcam celebrities, Jennifer Ringley (see Chapter 8).

Submission Process

When you submit it to The Sync's ongoing Online Film Festival, you agree to have your film judged by an audience. To submit, fill out the short entry form, sign the release, and, for all but one of the categories, send a VHS (NTSC or PAL) or SVHS copy of your film. Note that if you are submitting to the "Made for the Net" category (for films that are exclusively intended for Internet screening), you must submit your film as a RealMedia file via FTP or Zip disk. The Sync requires that your film be shorter than 30 minutes and non-commercial. In a contest fashion, if your film has one of the highest scores after the voting period, it remains on the site.

Legal Rights

By signing the Release form, you agree to The Sync holding a non-exclusive license to show and distribute your film on its and its partners' sites. Films on The Sync do not earn any royalties, and the length of the agreement is indefinite—if you are a festival winner.

Film & Filmmaker's Information

The Sync does not provide filmmakers with space to share any facts about themselves besides their names and one-sentence synopses. Even if festival winners, they do not receive their own pages. Rather, winners share a page with other winners from the same month.

Audience Participation

The Sync allows its audience to determine which films stay on the site and which ones are booted off. By voting in its monthly festival, viewers can voice their opinions as to what the site should keep in its collection.

UNDERGROUNDFILM

www.undergroundfilm.com
Undergroundfilm.com
Box 461
70A Greenwich Avenue
New York, NY 10011

Unlike some Internet cineplexes, Undergroundfilm does not promise fame or wealth to its filmmakers. Instead, the site intends to create a network of colleagues and audiences for independent filmmakers, screenwriters, and musicians—a place of diverse, critical voices that aid in the development of films that are made outside of a corporate environment. At the same time, Undergroundfilm hopes to attract professionals interested in finding innovative work and creative people.

MEDIA PLAYERS

QuickTime

FILMS EXHIBITED

The majority of films on Undergroundfilm are under fifteen minutes (although the site does not have a running time restriction on its submission form). Genres range from Animation to Experimental to Music Video to Romance, and even in the most traditional genres, the shorts of Undergroundfilm tend to be offbeat. Cross-listed under Interview and Music Video is *Kronick* (1993), a montage of various rap artists. Unique to the site because it is 45 minutes long, Kronick combines music videos with interviews for an in-depth look at the world of rap. In a different vein, *Kung-fu Kitchen* (1999), listed under the genres Action, Children, Comedy, and Experimental, is an animated short about vegetables who practice martial arts.

SUBMISSION PROCESS

In order to submit your film to Undergroundfilm, you must fill out an online submission form, sign-off on the submission agreement, and send either a VHS (NTSC), Mini-DV, or Beta copy of your film to the site. Undergroundfilm also accepts your film as un uploaded Flash or QuickTime file if under 1 gigabyte.

LEGAL RIGHTS

Undergroundfilm's submission agreement requires that you provide the site with non-exclusive rights to perform, broadcast, display, copy, exhibit, and distribute your film. Either you or the site may terminate this agreement by notifying the other 30 days prior to the date of termination.

FILM & FILMMAKER'S INFORMATION

Undergroundfilm provides a generous amount of space to its filmmakers. On each film's page is posted a synopsis, crew list, festivals, filmmaker's bio, filmmaker's comments, running time, original format, genre, viewer's comments, and a link to the film's official Web site.

AUDIENCE PARTICIPATION

Viewers can rate and post their opinions about films. They can also email friends about a film directly from its page.

URBAN ENTERTAINMENT

www.urbanentertainment.com
9200 Sunset Blvd., Suite 321
Los Angeles, CA 90069

Michael Jenkinson, a former vice president of feature film production and acquisitions at 20th Century Fox, founded Urban Entertainment at the beginning of 1999. At this time one of the few Internet cineplexes to program for strictly an African-American audience, Urban Entertainment exhibits and distributes films by independent black filmmakers. In addition to the films by independent filmmakers, Urban Entertainment itself produces four animated series that present new episodes each week.

NICHE

African-Americans

MEDIA PLAYERS

RealPlayer

FILMS EXHIBITED

Urban Entertainment presents a range of material, including features, shorts, animated weekly series, interviews with famous filmmakers and celebrities, and cultural documentaries, most of which are the work of independent filmmakers. Several of the films promote social and cultural understanding, such as *Black Sheep* (1999), a narrative short about a young African-American man who, while teaching English in Japan, attempts to overcome discrimination as well as have a positive influence on his students; and *And Still I Rise* (1993), a documentary that tries to deconstruct the myths and stereotypes about black women. The site also presents thrillers such as *Cappuccino* (1998), a neo-noir feature about a married man who finds his mistress with her nasty husband; dramas like *The Appointment* (1999), the story of a desperate salesman who won't take no for an answer; along with comedies, romances, and science-fiction films.

SUBMISSION PROCESS

Urban Entertainment accepts both narrative and non-fiction films for an African-American market. If you have an appropriate film, go to the online submission form, and fill it out. Before clicking on "submit form," print it out; include this printed form in the package containing the VHS (NTSC) copy of your film.

LEGAL RIGHTS

If you want your film to be hosted by the site, you must sign over exclusive rights to Urban Entertainment for both the Internet exhibition and television broadcast. This is because Urban Entertainment both exhibits and distributes your film and wants to have complete control over its licensing. The site chooses not to address royalty rates (or even whether it provides its filmmakers with royalties) before your film is accepted. Following the site's acceptance of your film, expect Urban Entertainment to discuss the terms of its agreement in detail.

FILM & FILMMAKER'S INFORMATION

Each one of Urban Entertainment's films is provided with its own page on which is listed the filmmaker's name and the film's year, running time, cast, and a detailed synopsis. Underneath the synopsis, the film's past festival screenings and any awards won are also posted. Urban Entertainment does not allow for biographical information about the filmmaker.

AUDIENCE PARTICIPATION

Viewers are encouraged to pass the word on about a film on the site by reviewing it and e-mailing films to friends.